EXISTENTIALISM, FEMINISM AND
SIMONE DE BEAUVOIR

Also by Joseph Mahon

AN INTRODUCTION TO PRACTICAL ETHICS

Existentialism, Feminism and Simone de Beauvoir

Joseph Mahon
College Lecturer in Philosophy
University College Galway

Consultant Editor: Jo Campling

First published in Great Britain 1997 by
MACMILLAN PRESS LTD
Houndmills, Basingstoke, Hampshire RG21 6XS and London
Companies and representatives throughout the world

A catalogue record for this book is available from the British Library.

ISBN 0–333–65912–0

First published in the United States of America 1997 by
ST. MARTIN'S PRESS, INC.,
Scholarly and Reference Division,
175 Fifth Avenue, New York, N.Y. 10010

ISBN 0–312–17606–6

Library of Congress Cataloging-in-Publication Data
Mahon, Joseph.
Existentialism, feminism, and Simone de Beauvoir / Joseph Mahon ;
consultant editor, Jo Campling.
  p. cm.
Includes bibliographical references and index.
ISBN 0–312–17606–6 (cloth)
1. Beauvoir, Simone de, 1908–   . 2. Existentialism. 3. Feminist
theory. I. Campling, Jo. II. Title.
B2430.B344M34 1997
194—dc21   97–3279
                                                            CIP

This book is printed on paper suitable for recycling and made from fully managed and sustained forest sources.

10   9   8   7   6   5   4   3   2   1
06 05 04 03 02 01 00 99 98 97

Printed and bound in Great Britain by
Antony Rowe Ltd, Chippenham, Wiltshire

To Evelyn

Contents

Acknowledgements

I wish to thank Jo Campling, consultant editor for Macmillan, for her substantial help and advice with all stages of this book's preparation. My thanks also to Ezra and Sascha Talmor, editors of *The History of European Ideas* until 1995, for their sustained support for my research over fifteen years. Various members of my own family must also be mentioned: Evelyn, my partner by marriage, with whom I have had endless discussions; my son James, a graduate student of philosophy at Duke, who read sections of the final draft, and my daughter Alyce, completing a doctorate at the Courtauld Institute, for her help with the Bibliography, and the Notes section. Finally, I wish to thank several generations of students of philosophy at University College Galway who, by their written and oral responses to lecture material, have helped me shape the thoughts contained in these pages.

Preface

Twentieth-century philosophy has had its share of scandals, and among the more notorious has been the exclusion of Simone de Beauvoir from the major anthologies, and studies, of existentialist prose.[1] This exclusion is all the more extraordinary when one considers her long association with Jean-Paul Sartre, her philosophical essays of the 1940s, her role in the major debates concerning existentialist ethics in the immediate post-war period, as well as her substantial editorial role in, and contributions to, *Les Temps Modernes*. For these and other reasons, I shall argue here that de Beauvoir's writings, and especially her works of the 1940s, merit inclusion in the existentialist canon, and that to deny her a place in the pantheon is to do her a singular injustice.

In her memoirs, de Beauvoir speaks either modestly, or severely, of her philosophical monographs. Of all her books, she says, *The Ethics of Ambiguity* 'is the one that irritates me the most today'.[2] On the whole, she continues, she went to a great deal of trouble 'to present inaccurately a problem to which I then offered a solution quite as hollow as the Kantian maxims'.[3] The basic flaw in her argument had been to think that she 'could define a morality independent of a social context'.[4] Many commentators have accepted de Beauvoir's own appraisal of such works, Deirdre Bair observing that 'this is one of her least popular writings and one which scholars have generally tended to ignore'.[5] I shall argue, against this trend, that her philosophical monographs make a substantial contribution to existentialist thought, and particularly to existentialist ethics; that her critique of Heidegger in *Pyrrhus and Cineas* is not only convincing, but varies arguments found in *Being and Nothingness*; that many of the philosophical seeds of *The Second Sex* are to be found in her earlier philosophical essays; and that of the three major defences of existentialism offered in the immediate post-war period, viz. those of de Beauvoir, Sartre and Merleau-Ponty, hers is the most philosophically sustained and impressive.

Where de Beauvoir is concerned, the following orthodoxy has had a considerable currency: (1) that de Beauvoir, unlike Sartre, remained locked in the bleak isolation of existentialism;[6] (2) that, as Moira Gatens phrases it, 'the particular form of existentialism employed by de Beauvoir is that developed by Jean-Paul Sartre in *Being and Noth-*

ix

ingness';[7] (3) that Sartrean existentialism forms the philosophical basis of *The Second Sex*: as Genevieve Lloyd phrases it, 'De Beauvoir's idea of woman as other is articulated in terms drawn from the Sartrean struggle for dominance between the looker and looked at'.[8] I propose to challenge this orthodoxy in the following ways: (a) I shall demonstrate that the philosophical foundations of *The Second Sex* are to be located in de Beauvoir's earlier philosophical essays; (b) I shall demonstrate that de Beauvoir's philosophical thought differs extensively, and even profoundly, from that contained in contemporaneous works by Sartre, including the *Carnets* and the *Cahiers*; and (c) that de Beauvoir's attempt at constructing a normative ethics not only has no parallel in Sartre, but is a philosophical enterprise which he repeatedly repudiates.

Writing about *The Second Sex* in the third volume of her memoirs, de Beauvoir says: 'When all is said and done, it is possibly the book that has brought me the greatest satisfaction of all those I have written.'[9] Speaking of its popular success when first published in France, Webster and Powell write that 'de Beauvoir's revenge over narrow-minded intellectuals was crushing. *Le Deuxième Sexe* sold 22,000 copies in its first week of publication...De Beauvoir established her independence from Sartre and was to reinforce the message even more dramatically in her autobiography, *Mémoires d'une jeune fille rangée*. The two books were treated like the Old and New Testament of Women's Liberation.'[10]

This early public, if not always critical, success was soon to cross the Atlantic. 'In the sixties Simone de Beauvoir was seen as the theoretician par excellence on the condition of women', write Francis and Gontier in their biography. 'In the United States', they continue, '*The Second Sex*, published in paperback by Bantam Books, became the bible of feminism. Gloria Steinem, Kate Millett, and Betty Friedan drew inspiration from it. When American universities created women's studies departments, *The Second Sex* served as the basic text.'[11] Rosemary Tong, in her *Feminist Thought*, agrees: 'Clearly, *The Second Sex* has within a short thirty-year span achieved the status of a classic in feminist thought.'[12]

Yet this last sentence is preceded by an extract from the journal *Feminist Studies*, the opening sentence of which declares: 'De Beauvoir's analysis of women's oppression in *The Second Sex* is open to many criticisms: for its idealism – her focus on myths and images and her lack of practical strategies for liberation; for its ethnocentrism and androcentric view – her tendency to generalize from the experience of

European bourgeois women, with a resulting emphasis on women's historic ineffectiveness.'[13] In her full-length study *Simone de Beauvoir, A Feminist Mandarin*, Mary Evans argues that 'Her uncritical belief in what she describes as rationality, her negation and denial of various forms of female experience, and her tacit assumption that paid work and contraception are the two keys to the absolute freedom of womankind, all suggest a set of values that place a major importance on living like a childless, rather singular, employed man.'[14] Finally, the implications of imbuing her thought with patriarchal values and habits of mind extend to existentialism itself, argues Moira Gatens: 'If existentialism purports to be a theory of human being, yet its values emerge as sexually biased, then it must forfeit its status as a universal theory.'[15]

In view of the foregoing, *The Second Sex* may now be said to enjoy a somewhat suspect status, a ' "prehistoric" status relative to the movement of modern feminism', as Kate Soper puts it.[16] On the one hand, it is regarded as a feminist classic, indeed *the* feminist classic insofar as 'we have no theoretical source of comparable sweep that stimulates us to analyze and relentlessly question our situation as women in so many domains – literature, religion, politics, work, education, motherhood and sexuality'.[17] On the other hand, it has the historic, but marginal importance conveyed by Tong's sentence when she says that 'no introduction to feminist thought would be nearly complete without a discussion of this work, which has helped many feminists understand the full significance of woman's otherness'.[18] It is time, I suggest, to resolve the question of the status of *The Second Sex*, and in this book I propose to undertake a systematic revaluation, and defence, of its argument.

Humphrey Carpenter has criticized Deirdre Bair's biography of de Beauvoir on the grounds that it fails to give 'a proper account (either in the form of summary or criticism) of most of de Beauvoir's writings'.[19] He goes on to say 'Even *The Second Sex* scarcely gets discussed, and though existentialism is notoriously difficult to summarise or explain, Bair never even tries.'[20] I beg to differ, on at least one point: existentialism is not that difficult to summarize or explain, though it does require patient reconstruction of the primary sources. This activity of reconstruction is a pervasive feature of this book.

1 Early Philosophical Writing

In the 1940s Simone de Beauvoir published two strictly philosophical works, *Pyrrhus and Cineas* in 1944, and *The Ethics of Ambiguity* in 1947.[1] In the second volume of her memoirs she speaks of the first of these two philosophical works as follows. Early in 1943 Sartre had introduced her to Jean Grenier,[2] who asked her whether she was an existentialist. She recalls her embarrassment at the question, notwithstanding the fact that she had read Kierkegaard and was familiar with the expression *existential philosophy* which, she says, had been applied for some time to the writings of Heidegger. Yet she didn't, she confesses, understand the meaning of the word *existentialist*, a word which had only recently been coined by Gabriel Marcel. Besides, she adds, 'Grenier's question clashed with my modesty and my pride alike. I was not of sufficient importance, objectively considered, to merit any such label; as for my ideas, I was convinced that they reflected the truth rather than some entrenched doctrinal position.'[3]

But Grenier persisted, and asked her to contribute to an anthology he was editing. At first she refused, on the basis that Sartre's *Being and Nothingness* – which she had read in draft manuscript form – had said all that needed to be said on the subject of existentialism. At this stage Sartre intervened, telling her at least to try. She then thought, she says, of writing a play on the relationship of individual experience to universal reality. It would feature a city which would demand of one of its leading citizens that he sacrifice the life of someone who was dear to him in order to protect the public good. However, the plot became too abstract and the play never materialized, though she would return to a not too dissimilar theme in her 1945 play, *Les Bouches inutiles*. But, she continues, 'since someone was offering me a chance to deal directly with the problem on my mind, why not take advantage of the fact? So I began to write *Pyrrhus and Cineas*; I spent three months on it, and it swelled into a small book.'[4]

In her memoirs she introduces Part I of *Pyrrhus and Cineas* (to which I propose to confine my attention in this chapter) as follows:

If man is 'a creature of distances', why should be transcend himself just so far and no farther? How are the boundaries of his ambitions

1

to be defined? These were the questions I asked myself in the
early section. I rejected a merely *ad hoc* morality, and also all
those which involved eternity; no human individual can establish
a genuine relationship with the infinite, be it labelled God or
humanity. I showed the truth and importance of the idea of 'situation' which Sartre brought out in *Being and Nothingness*. I attacked
all moral alienation, and refused to admit that 'other people' could
be used as an alibi. I had likewise realized that in a world at war
every project is a matter of choice, and you must – as Blomart did
in *The Blood of Others* – consent to violence. The whole of this
critical exposé strikes me today as fair enough, though very summary.[5]

Part I of *Pyrrhus and Cineas* is subdivided into the following
sections: (a) 'Candide's Garden'; (b) 'The Moment'; (c) 'The Infinite';
(d) 'God'; (e) 'Humanity' and (f) 'The Situation'. In the coming pages
I shall reconstruct her argument in these sections; then in the second
and final part of this chapter I propose critically to review her
argument within the broader context of the standard concerns of
existentialist philosophy as such.

I

Candide's Garden

All human behaviour, writes de Beauvoir, may reasonably be
regarded as absurd, because no matter what we achieve there always
remains something else to be achieved. Yet despite the seemingly
derisory nature of our existence (though one which is sometimes
sufficiently tormenting to drive some people to suicide), we continue
to push forward and human existence retains its momentum. This
constancy, or steadfastness, in the face of folly and defeat may be
seen as the source of a basic truth about us.

There are two ways, fundamentally, she says, in which human
beings can react to the facts of human existence, viz. to death, grief,
separation, family life, mixing with other people, and so on. On the
one hand, you can refuse to acknowledge any meaningful connection
between human beings, in the manner of Camus' outsider, and for this
reason treat them with indifference. As far as he is concerned, the
relationship between two or more human beings is of no greater

consequence than the fact that I am standing on this piece of ground. I am here, it is there, and that's all there is to it.

Camus' outsider, says de Beauvoir, is correct to the extent that attachments are not given or established *a priori.*[6] Meaningful relationships with human beings are not given, but brought about; they have to be *created.* This is the alternative way of responding to other people, namely, to treat them with concern. They matter in your deciding to make them matter; otherwise, human attachments are a vain pretence.

'Each of us must cultivate her own garden'[7] says the eponymous hero of Voltaire's novella *Candide,* but that, says de Beauvoir, doesn't tell us the dimensions of anyone's garden. Some see it as a vast territory, waiting to be cultivated, while others find even a pot of flowers too much to work with. In any event, she concludes in this section, Candide's advice is really superfluous. Your life is always *your own* responsibility; no one else can lead it for you, and it carries your imprint from the moment you begin working on it.

The Moment

There is, says de Beauvoir, an ethics of enjoyment, of pleasure or satiation, propounded by, among others, Aristippus, Horace and André Gide in his novel *Les Nourritures terrestres,* which advocates abandoning the world in favour of relaxation and self-indulgence. But this, she soon adds, is a false concept of enjoyment, for relaxation soon induces boredom. The essence of enjoyment is that it is dynamic, active, and far-reaching; it always relates to things beyond itself. All enjoyable experience has a wealth of associations. As she puts it herself, 'Each pleasure is a project. It advances beyond the past towards the future, towards the world which is the frozen image of the future. To drink cinnamon chocolate, says Gide in his *Incidences,* is to imbibe the whole of Spain.'[8]

To withdraw from the world, then, is *ipso facto* to renounce all pleasure or enjoyment as well. The Epicureans and the Stoics, she says, understood perfectly well the connection between withdrawal and pleasure; by renouncing all activity, hence contact with the world, they realized that the only possible pleasure remaining would be that of immobility, of pure *ataraxia.*

Fundamentally, each human being is a *transcendence,* that is, oriented towards things beyond itself. '"Man is a creature of distances", as Heidegger has it, "he is always somewhere else".'[9] In other words, our hopes, longings, expectations, plans and ambitions all refer us to a future, to more or less distant events, to events *at a distance* from where we stand.

Because each human being is a transcendence, our happiness can be found only in further projects. The proof is that no sooner have we completed one project, than we set off to complete another. 'Pascal put it well when he said that what interests the hunter is not the hare but the hunt.'[10]

The Infinite

While each human being is essentially a transcendence, there is little to be gained, says de Beauvoir, from thinking of this transcendence as a transcendence towards the Infinite or the Universal. To aim at the Infinite is to aim to lose sight of the self. But the individual or self is the fundamental ontological datum: 'Man cannot escape his own presence.'[11] Flaubert thought he could rejoin the Universal when he wondered why he should bother himself with the proletariat of his day any more than the slaves of the distant past. But he didn't thereby escape his own time, or his own class, retorts de Beauvoir; on the contrary, he made himself a 19th-century bourgeois gentleman whose wealth, pleasures and vanity camouflaged his affinity with his period.

We cannot either diminish our being indefinitely, or expand it to infinity; we cannot have complete rest. All cessation is impossible, because transcendence is a perpetual surpassing. At the same time, an indefinite project is an absurdity because it doesn't end anywhere. Man cannot be God, 'But from the heart of his own situation couldn't he dedicate himself to the infinite?'.[12] With this question de Beauvoir introduces the topic of God, and man's relation to God.

God

It is tempting to turn to God for guidance, but, she warns,

> If God is infinite, and a plenitude of being, there is no distance between his project and his reality. What he wishes just is; he wishes things as they are. His will is simply the foundation of static being; one could hardly call it a will. Such a God is not a particular individual: he is the universal, the immutable and eternal being. And the universal is silence. It doesn't entreat us to do anything: it doesn't promise anything, it demands no sacrifice, it dispenses no

rewards or punishments, it cannot justify anything, and it cannot be the basis for either hope or despair. It exists, nothing further can be said about it. The perfection of its being leaves no space for man.[13]

De Beauvoir seems to be saying three distinct, but related, things in this complex passage. They are as follows. (1) There is a conception of God such that God has only to will X for X to exist or occur. God's perfection therefore leaves no room for human agency, for if God can do it simply by deciding to do it, then laborious human agency is a waste of time and effort. (2) Since for God willing is being, then the world as it is must also be the world as God wants it; for if He wanted a different world, it would *be* different, given God's omnipotent will. So, since God wants things as they are, and mere human beings have no hope of prevailing against God's will, there is, once again, no scope for a frail human agency. (3) If God is the immutable, universal and eternal being, then God is doomed to silence. The reason is that it is only particular beings who punish, promise, will, condemn and so on. But if God is doomed to silence, then human beings cannot, as a consequence, look to God for guidance.

The upshot of this whole line of reasoning is that we must choose between God and man, for if we turn to God there is either no meaningful role left to human agency and purpose, or else we are left with an eternal silence. As de Beauvoir puts it, 'If he [man] wants to give meaning to his actions, then he mustn't turn to this impersonal, indifferent and completed God.'[14]

There is, at the same time, she continues, a certain kind of Catholic naturalism which extends to everything the grace of God. We find its echoes, for example, in Claudel. Everything, on this view, comes from God and as such is good. But the orthodox Christian, says de Beauvoir, remains passive, and neglects to take this idea to its logical conclusion. There are two such implications. First of all, if everything is good, then all the human vices, such as gluttony, are good. The second is that if everything comes from God, then it is unnecessary to expend human effort on anything.[15]

But there is yet another way of looking at the relationship between God and man, says de Beauvoir. On this alternative perception, human beings are a *special creation*, brought into the world to fashion our own being, albeit in accordance with the wishes of the Creator. From this perspective, a human being is not a brute fact, but a free agent, and the will of God manifests itself as a call to freedom. Man is called upon to become what God would wish him to be, hence something which doesn't, as yet, exist. As such, there is space for becoming, for self-transcendence.

This concept of God has large-scale implications. In particular, God's will cannot be realized unless human beings choose to realize it, and God cannot force us to obey His will since He has created us free agents. De Beauvoir concludes that, on *this* concept of God, the fulfilment of God's will is contingent on human agency: 'This is what the German mystic Angelus Silesius meant when he said "God needs me just as much as I need him"'.[16]

We are exhorted to listen to the voice of God, but such an aspiration, says de Beauvoir, is naive: 'It is only by means of a human intermediary that God can make himself known, since we are incapable of understanding any other.'[17] The problem is: how do we tell the genuine emissary from the bogus?

The only way of telling the true from the false Messiah, she says, 'is by what they do'; and this is best decided on the basis of human welfare.[18] This is the fate of any moral code that claims a divine origin or backing: it ends up having to depend on accumulated human insight and experience to discern what God does and does not want.

She concludes her section on God with the following ringing words:

> Each society claims to have God on its side; it recreates him in its own image. It is the society that speaks, not God... Man cannot be illuminated by God; it is by way of man that one attempts to illuminate God. It is by way of human intermediaries that the voice of God will always make itself heard, and it is by means of human endeavours that we respond to that appeal. Thus if God existed, he would be powerless to guide human transcendence. Man always finds himself facing others like him, and this presence or absence at the base of the sky doesn't concern him at all.[19]

Humanity

If we look to humanity as a replacement for 'that absolute we sought in the sky',[21] we may well become demoralized, for 'if we see nothing else except the indefinite progression of each generation, it may well appear futile to take part in it'.[22] But, says de Beauvoir, we must not look on humanity in this fashion; rather we must see it as open and closed, as possibility and as actuality. It must be distinct from its destiny, 'for that's something we've got to accomplish'; at the same time, it has got to subsist, otherwise we would lack a base from which to venture forth into the future. Neither should we think of this humanity as a unity in which each and every person has a defined place, role or situation. To think in this way is to give credence to the myth of solidarity. We are not atomized parts of a solid mass, because we do get involved, we do question ourselves, we are free. We cannot, then, occupy a pre-defined place on earth; on the contrary, a human being will *take* his place 'by launching himself into the world, by making a life for himself by way of his projects among other human beings'.[23] The essential point is that the human world is a human construction which continually demands reconstruction, and in thus reconstructing the world I inescapably side with some human beings against others. Thus if I side with the proletariat, I oppose capitalism. Likewise, the soldier doesn't defend his country except by killing his adversaries. In these ways, 'The class and the country define themselves as a unity only by way of the unity of their opposition to the enemy. There is no proletariat except to the extent that there is a struggle against capitalism. A country doesn't exist outside its frontiers.'[24]

The Situation

So human existence may, then, be seen as a project, as a continuous shaping and reshaping of oneself, as a continuous choosing of objectives for oneself and a launching of oneself towards these same objectives. To refuse to choose is to refuse to be.[25] Yet there is a paradox attached to choosing oneself: one can always proceed beyond what one has already chosen for oneself, yet to venture beyond an end, one has had to aim at it as an end beyond which one cannot get. Human beings, concludes de Beauvoir, know no other way of living.

This leads her to reflect on death, and on the kind of limits it is capable of placing on our projects. She thinks it should not be seen as a grim reaper; on the contrary, the boundaries of any initiative, she believes, lie at the very heart of that initiative, not beyond it in death or anything else. She gives the following example:

A man goes on a journey; he hurries to reach Lyon this evening. This is because he is anxious to reach Valence tomorrow, so as to get to Montelimar the day after, then Avignon, and the day after that again, Arles. It's easy to mock him. His efforts were in vain; he'll have to return without having got to Nimes, Marseille. He won't have seen Bône or Constantinople. But that doesn't matter to him, he will have got where he wanted. That was his itinerary.[26]

Death, she concludes, will only put a halt to my efforts when I am dead ('qu'une fois que je suis mort') and laid out for others to gaze at. But death cannot touch me as a living thing; my project passes it by unhindered.

A human being is not, *pace* Heidegger, to be seen as a being-towards-death, nor is it the case that the only authentic existence lies in a recognition of ourselves as beings addressed to death. Heidegger, says de Beauvoir, is mistaken for two reasons: (a) Since we *are* mortal, we cannot *choose* death; as there is no avoiding death, or alternative to death, it doesn't make sense to speak of *choosing* death. (b) Existence isn't *for* anything, death therefore included. As she puts it herself, 'Being as being posits no end, it simply is. It's the project alone that posits its being as a being for such and such.'[27]

While we don't exist for any reason, neither do we exist in the manner of inert, inanimate objects. On the contrary,

> Man has to fashion what he will be. He continuously seeks to create himself, and that is what we call his project. Human beings exist in the manner of projects; these projects are not oriented towards death, but towards defined objectives. Man hunts, fishes, makes instruments, writes books. These are not mere diversions, mere escapism, but a movement towards being. Man accomplishes things so as to be.[28]

II

Existentialism, Anthropology and Ethics

I am interested in *Pyrrhus and Cineas* chiefly for the following three reasons: (i) I wish to assess its contribution to existentialist philosophy; (ii) I propose to use it as a base from which to track the subsequent twists and turns in de Beauvoir's writing, especially her works of the 1940s; (iii) above all, I wish to establish the extent to which it can be seen as a philosophical antecedent to *The Second Sex*.

If we take existentialism to be a kind of philosophy which is pre-occupied with the most salient and poignant features of human existence,[29] such as death, love, responsibility and despair, then it is clear that *Pyrrhus and Cineas* falls comfortably within the terms of that definition. It is preoccupied, as we have seen, with the subjects of human nature, freedom, religious belief, morality, death and commitment. These are, by my definition of the term, quintessentially existentialist themes. These themes are discussed in a language with which many readers will, at some stage, have become familiar, and for that reason de Beauvoir's prose may well seem to possess little in the way of originality. Students of 20th-century existentialism usually encounter such prose for the first time in Sartre's widely-read *Existentialism and Humanism*. We read there that

> Man is nothing else but that which he makes of himself. That is the first principle of existentialism...what do we mean to say by this, but that man is of a greater dignity than a stone or a table? For we mean to say that man primarily exists – that man is, before all else, something which projects itself towards a future and is aware that it is doing so.[30]

Later in the same work, when he seeks to distance true existentialism from triumphalist humanism, Sartre presents the alternative of existentialist humanism in the following words:

> Man is all the time outside of himself: it is in projecting and losing himself beyond himself that he makes man to exist; and, on the other hand, it is by pursuing transcendent aims that he himself is able to exist.[31]

Two years before these words were published Simone de Beauvoir had written in her *Pyrrhus and Cineas* that

> Man has to fashion what he will be. He continuously seeks to create himself, and this is what we call his project. Human beings exist in the manner of projects; these projects are not oriented towards death, but towards defined objectives. Man hunts, fishes, makes instruments, writes books. These are not mere diversions, mere escapism, but a movement towards being. Man accomplishes things so as to be.[32]

Unlike Sartre, de Beauvoir is not aggressively atheistic in *Pyrrhus and Cineas*, if indeed her discussion of the implications of religious belief can be correctly described as atheistic in the first place. Sartre proclaims himself an existential atheist,[33] maintains that 'there is no human nature, because there is no God to have a conception of it',[34] is dismissive of Christian ethics,[35] and concludes his address as follows:

Existentialism is nothing else but an attempt to draw the full conclusions from a consistently atheistic position . . . Existentialism is
not atheist in the sense that it would exhaust itself in demonstra-
tions of the non-existence of God. It declares, rather, that even if
God existed that would make no difference from its point of
view . . .[36]

Sartre stresses here the virtue of consistency, but does not himself
always manage to live up to the demands of this same virtue. Thus one
cannot claim *both* that the non-existence of God has demonstrable
implications for our concepts of freedom, human nature and morality,
and at the same time declare that even if God existed, that fact would
make no difference to the existentialist point of view. But for present
purposes I am more interested in discerning the ways in which de
Beauvoir's existentialism diverges from Sartre's than in identifying
inner inconsistencies in the latter's writing. De Beauvoir's approach,
in the work under consideration, is not to pursue the question: If God
doesn't exist, what are the implications of His non-existence? Rather,
she is more concerned to ask: If God *does* exist, what then are the
implications of His existence? She replies, in the main, that if there is a
God, then there is no space, or scope, left for human agency, and that
we are left marooned without moral guidance. There are, once again,
profound echoes of Sartre in these conclusions,[37] but de Beauvoir has
reached them in 1944, and from a different baseline of argument. De
Beauvoir's position is closer to that articulated by Rieux in one of the
theological debates in Camus' *The Plague*. Rieux himself doesn't
believe in God, but he readily acknowledges that very many people
do. At the same time they don't *really* believe in an all-powerful God,
not even those among them who are the most convinced they believe
in such a God. The reason we can be sure about this, he argues, is that
if we really did believe in an all-powerful God, then we would leave
everything in the hands of God: our health, welfare and so on. 'But no
one in the world believed in a God of that sort: no, not even Paneloux,
who believed that he believed in such a God. And this was proved by
the fact that no one ever threw himself on Providence completely.'[38]

De Beauvoir develops her argument concerning moral guidelines
differently, and less relentlessly, than does Sartre. She argues, quite
pithily, that if moral guidelines are thought to issue from God, then
that thought is mistaken. Of His nature, God, as an immutable and
eternal being, is incapable of issuing moral guidelines. Moreover, even
if it is rational to speak of the will of God, it is left to human beings,

and human institutions, at the end of the day to decipher it. But these human beings do not all read the message in the same way. If we are to decide among their interpretations, then we shall have to do so on the basis of human welfare. At the same time, what is distinctive about human nature is its unfolding as a project, as a constant surpassing of oneself towards something which one remains to be, and beyond which one will always need, in turn, to proceed. From this perspective, the concepts of human nature and human welfare must always be seen as open rather than closed.

Sartre reaches a not too different conclusion, but in a more aggressive fashion. In contrast to 19th-century secularism, he observes, existentialism is *truly* radical, that is, it doesn't believe in half-measures. It insists that one cannot logically dispense with God, but yet expect everything else to remain the same. God is not, so to speak, a veneer or a label which might be removed, leaving the underlying reality unchanged or intact. On the contrary, if God is removed from the picture, then the picture is comprehensively altered.[39]

In particular, we must revise our thinking about moral values. With the disappearance of God, there is no longer any supremely wise and perfectly good being to look to for moral guidance. To put it differently, there are no set rules, no rules devised for human conduct by someone who is uniquely qualified to do so. Dostoevsky once wrote, remarks Sartre, that if God did not exist everything would be permitted, a proposition which can be taken to mean that if there is no being who knows indubitably what ought to be done, who can communicate this knowledge to us, and would always do so without deceit or aberration, then we are bereft of moral guidance (and, in addition, we would have no supreme moral authority to answer to). This is what Sartre means when he says 'Everything is indeed permitted if God does not exist, and man is in consequence forlorn, for he cannot find anything to depend upon either within or outside of himself.'[40] This does not mean, as it has often been taken to mean, that morally speaking we are free to do as we please. Its true meaning is that we are bereft of moral guidance, that we have been left with no way of telling right from wrong, and that in consequence morality is something which we must, literally, invent.[41]

Like Sartre, de Beauvoir also rejects Heidegger's views on death, or at any rate what she takes to be Heidegger's views on death. Sartre does so on at least two separate occasions: first, in his short story *The Wall*, which, according to Philip Thody, 'refutes Heidegger's idea that man can live towards his own death and thus humanize it'.[42] Part of what Thody has in mind is that Sartre's short story – which features three prisoners from the Republican side, during the Spanish Civil War, who are awaiting execution – convincingly portrays the awfulness of death, the terror which it strikes even into the bravest of hearts, and the manner in which death, to use Sartre's own words, 'disenchants everything'. This last refrain is uttered by Pablo, the narrator, during their confinement:

> It was worth nothing because it was finished. I wondered how I'd been able to walk, to laugh with the girls: I wouldn't have moved so much as my little finger if I had only imagined I would die like this. My life was in front of me, closed, like a bag and yet everything inside of it was unfinished. For an instant I tried to judge it. I wanted to tell myself: this is a beautiful life. But I couldn't pass judgment on it; it was only a sketch; I had spent my time counterfeiting eternity. I had understood nothing. I had missed nothing: there were so many things I could have missed, the taste of manzanilla or the baths I took in summer in a little creek near Cadiz; but death had disenchanted everything.[43]

It is worth noting, however, that in contrast to Sartre's short story which treats of imminent, violent death, Heidegger writes neither of violent nor of imminent death,[44] but of death as indefinite certainty. For Heidegger we are certain about death. At the same time, we have all kinds of strategies for 'covering up' our certainty about death. Linguistically, we think of it coming, 'but not right away'. It is deferred until 'sometime later'. By such linguistic evasions it is possible to cover up what is distinctive about the certainty of death, namely, that death is possible at any moment. 'Along with the certainty of death goes the *indefiniteness* of its "when".'[45]

Because death is indefinite, that is, because it is possible for it to occur at any moment, this indefiniteness must be incorporated into the concept of a human subject. A human being is not simply a subject such that sometime it will die; rather it is an individual capable of dying *at any time*. It is a subject addressed to death as to its ownmost possibility. '*Death is*, as *Dasein's* end, in the Being of this entity *towards* its end.'[46]

Sartre launches a second, more convincing and vastly more technical offensive on Heidegger, some years later, in his *Being and Nothingness*. But he begins by pointing to some positive features of Heidegger's treatment. It is possible, he begins, to distinguish between the 'realist' and the 'idealist' concepts of death. On the realist view, death is the point of contact with the non-human; it is the link between the human and the non-human.[47] The idealist conception was promoted, he says, not by philosophers but by poets such as Rilke and novelists such as Malraux. On this view, death is the end, that is, the final stage, of life. It puts the final touch to life in the way that 'the resolved chord is the meaning of the melody'.[48] It was left to Heidegger, he continues, to give a philosophical account of this humanization of death. He does so by making death the peculiar possibility of each human being, so that human existence becomes a being-towards-death, one which is, so to speak, addressed to death. Then, inasmuch as each individual progresses towards death, it realizes its freedom to die 'and constitutes itself as a totality by its free choice of finitude'.[49]

Undoubtedly this is a seductive theory, admits Sartre, but we should not, he cautions, rush from the fact that death is a human event to the conclusion that death is, so to speak, a built-in feature of human existence. The first thing to be noted is 'the absurd character of death'. It has often been compared to the situation of the condemned man among other condemned men, who knows not the day of his execution but who sees each day that his fellow prisoners are being executed. Yet the comparison is misleading. 'We ought rather to compare ourselves to a man condemned to death who is bravely preparing himself for the ultimate penalty, who is doing everything possible to make a good showing on the scaffold, and who meanwhile is carried off by a flu epidemic.'[50] Death, in other words, is something which is to be expected, and yet it has the habit of confounding our expectations. Nevertheless, if the meaning of life becomes the expectation of death, then death, when it arrives, puts its seal on life. This, says Sartre, 'is basically the most positive content of Heidegger's "resolute decision"'.[51]

Unfortunately, Sartre immediately adds, it is easier to give Heidegger's advice than to follow it. This is because I can expect my own death, but not death itself. In the second place, death is not a uniquely personal event, since many other human possibilities have a personal character. Third, death can be expected only in the weak sense that there is a probability it will happen in a certain way at a certain time, and sooner rather than later. Moreover, if *chance* determines the character of death, then death cannot be considered my possibility; rather it is a nihilation which always lies outside my possibilities. Neither can death be seen in Christian terms as 'the closing of the account', for in that case death would decide the meaning of life and this is a function which cannot be assigned to it. Death cannot give meaning to life unless it is chosen. But, for the Christian, God chooses when we shall die; therefore we do not choose death and, as such, death cannot confer meaning on existence. Indeed, not only is death incapable of conferring meaning on existence, it has the very opposite effect in that it empties life of all meaning. It makes life retrospectively absurd in that it makes it impossible for us to make a complete or final evaluation of it. Death cuts short so many projects that we are left with an insufficiency of material on which to base our judgement of a person's endeavours.[52] Sartre is adamant on this point. He insists that 'death is never that which gives life its meaning; it is, on the contrary, that which in principle removes all meaning from life. If we must die, then our life has no meaning because its problems receive no solution and because the very meaning of the problems remains undetermined.'[53]

De Beauvoir's critique of Heidegger in her *Pyrrhus and Cineas* bears a strong resemblance to that of Sartre in his *Being and Nothingness*, but not to his earlier short story. The central refrain and argument of that short story is that it is not natural to die. This quite paradoxical idea makes its appearance in de Beauvoir's later writings, particularly in the closing paragraph of her account of her own mother's dying, *A Very Easy Death*, where she says 'There is no such thing as a natural death: nothing that happens to a man is ever natural, since his presence calls the world into question. All men must die: but for every man his death is an accident and, even if he knows it and consents to it, an unjustifiable violation.'[54] This short memoir also contains a rejection of Heidegger, especially in its opening sentences: 'But it is not true. You do not die from being born, nor from having lived, nor from old age. You die from *something*.'[55]

De Beauvoir takes a different approach in her *Pyrrhus and Cineas*, an approach that reminds us of, and varies, the argument of *Being and Nothingness*: we cannot *choose* death, she admonishes Heidegger, because we *are* mortal. This is not an entirely convincing argument, however; while we cannot choose to die (for want of a meaningful alternative), we can choose when, where and how to die. 'Sometimes I want to finish it all quickly so as to shorten the dread of waiting', she writes in *Force of Circumstance*,[56] but in the much earlier philosophical essay this possibility is not entertained. Heidegger, for his part, does not, strictly speaking, exhort us to choose death, since for Heidegger death is the ending of *Dasein*, and this ending is not simply

Being-at-an-end (*Zu-ende-sein*), but a Being-towards-the-end (*Sein zum ende*). So, for Heidegger, death is a matter of ending, but we end not in the mundane sense that we cease to be, but in the sense that from the moment that we begin to exist we are, so to speak, addressed to death. 'As soon as man comes to life, he is at once old enough to die.'[57] Heidegger asks us not to choose death but to have an authentic understanding of it. In this context he speaks, rather misleadingly, of death as a possibility, but he does so in order to make the point that death is uniquely impending. Death will be quite unlike anything else that befalls us. Not only does it sunder all relations with other human beings, it also evacuates the world of all further possibilities for oneself: death is the possibility of the absolute impossibility of *Dasein*. Ironically, this is an idea which de Beauvoir herself would articulate, with a more chilling resonance, in the third volume of her memoirs, some sixteen years later:

> When I cycled through the countryside and saw it drenched in sunlight and fresh life, my heart would contract at the thought of it going on when I was no longer there to behold it...Death is common to all of us, yet each individual faces it alone. While life still exists, we can die together; but in dying we pass beyond this world, to a place where the word 'together' no longer possesses any meaning.[58]

In her discussion of freedom and choosing oneself, de Beauvoir tends to lose sight of, or perhaps just ignores, distinctions which it is surely valuable to make, such as the difference between those choices which are guided by a unifying principle, those which are not, and choices which have quite unintended but far-reaching consequences. In short, one can distinguish between choosing a vocation or career, a one-off choice, and a choice having an unintended effect. Thus people choose to be teachers, sculptors, engineers, nurses, and so on, and, all going well, they emerge in these occupations following long periods of study, training or apprenticeship. People also choose to get married, and in doing so commit themselves to a whole way of life. Both kinds of choice, both these forms of choosing oneself, can and ought to be distinguished from the one-off choice, such as when one chooses from a dinner menu. And this in turn can be distinguished from the kind of circumstance where, say, one becomes a father by choosing to have unprotected sex with a member of the opposite sex, where one had no desire or intention of becoming a father.

De Beauvoir has also been criticized for ignoring, in her literary and philosophical writings of this period, the fact that women and men are not equally free to choose themselves. In this connection Mary Evans has this to say:

> Sartre's exhortation to others, his whole concept of being and of an authentic existence, were based on the rejection of the normal habits and assumptions of everyday life. What de Beauvoir was to realize – and here a significant shift occurs between her early and mature work – was that men have more freedom than women to make these crucial choices. In *She Came to Stay* and *The Blood of Others* the sexes are seen as equal in their capacity to make existential choices, yet only a few years later – in *The Second Sex* – de Beauvoir has recognised the constraints on women that inhibit their full participation in the world.[59]

It is interesting to note that de Beauvoir herself dates the moment of her critical awakening, of her movement from philosophical abstraction to feminist consciousness, much earlier than Evans allows, though she is honest enough to admit that it took some time before this feminist consciousness began to reflect itself in her work. In the second volume of her memoirs she recalls that in early 1944 Sartre and de Beauvoir had made several new friends, almost all of whom were former surrealists who had broken away from surrealism in the relatively distant past. She mentions Dora Marr, Picasso, Armand and Lucienne Salacrou, Georges Bataille and Georges Limbour. Mixing in these circles, she confides, gave her a clearer insight into the female condition. Prior to that, she had known very few women of her own age, and none who led 'normal married lives'. The much younger women she associated with, such as Colette Audry, had their share of problems, of course, but she perceived these problems as individual rather than generic. She knew that ethnic identity mattered enormously, but she had not yet recognized a female condition as such. Now, suddenly, she says,

> I met a large number of women over forty who, in differing circumstances and with various degrees of success, had all undergone one identical experience: they had lived as 'dependent persons'. Because I was a writer, and in a situation very different from theirs – also, I think, because I was a good listener – they told me a great deal; I began to take stock of the difficulties, deceptive advantages, traps, and manifold obstacles that most women encounter on their path. I

also felt how much they were both diminished and enriched by this experience. The problem did not concern me directly, and as yet I attributed comparatively little importance to it; but my interest had been aroused.[60]

But if, as she herself confesses, de Beauvoir had gone wrong on many points by sticking to abstractions, she would never leave the field of abstractions completely behind her. On the contrary, meeting women of her own age brought home to her the condition of women *generally*. She finds that they have all suffered in varying degrees the same experience of *dependency*, and she begins to take stock of the difficulties, deceptive advantages, traps and manifold obstacles that most women encounter on their path. If the above extract from *The Prime of Life* is any indicator, then de Beauvoir's later feminist writing will comprise an exciting and profitable mixture of abstraction and detail.

But it will be all the stronger for the fact that it will embrace two kinds of abstraction, that of abstract terms generally, and that of philosophical abstraction specifically. She will write that men are elevated to the status of *the Subject*, while women are relegated to the category of *the Other*. Women, she will allege, are confined to the domain of *immanence*, while men are favoured with the power of *transcendence*. Women perform *functions*, while men engage in *actions*. This dehumanization of woman, she will argue, is incompatible with her status as 'a free and autonomous being like all human creatures'. The point which I presently wish to press is that some of these abstract, philosophical concepts first appear, albeit in a different context and in an adumbrated form, in her early philosophical essay *Pyrrhus and Cineas*. I am thinking in particular of the concept of transcendence, as well as of the related concepts of the project and freedom. These will become, before the decade's end, part of the sturdy philosophical foundation of *The Second Sex*.

2 *The Blood of Others*: The Fictional Primer on Existentialism

This highly successful second novel, published in September 1945, was labelled a Resistance novel, and also an Existentialist novel, though its theme, de Beauvoir pleads in her memoirs, was a much more arid philosophical one, namely, 'the paradox of this existence experienced by me as my freedom and by those who came in contact with me as an object'.[1] But this philosophical intention was either ignored by the public, or, as de Beauvoir herself surmises, was simply not apparent to them.

The Blood of Others, dubbed by the American reviewer Richard McLaughlin 'the fictional primer on existentialism we have all been anxiously awaiting',[2] was, for the most part, written during the worst years of the war, throughout 1943 and 1944, and, as Deirdre Bair observes, much of the bleakness and uncertainty of that period pervades its background.[3] Yet it obviously stirred deep emotions among the reading public, because it created far more of a stir than de Beauvoir's first novel *She Came to Stay*. De Beauvoir herself reports that 'All the critics rated my second novel above my first; editorials expressing deep emotion were written about it in several newspapers. Both orally and by letter I received floods of compliments. Camus, though he liked the book, did not conceal his surprise at its success.'[4]

The structure of the present chapter will be as follows: in the first place, I shall reconstruct the narrative. Then I shall summarize the critical responses to this novel from a number of English-language critics. Finally, I shall reply to these critics and in the course of doing so I shall venture my own appraisal of it, giving special attention to its contribution to existentialist thought.

BLOMART AND HÉLÈNE

Blomart had come from a typical bourgeois family. His father owned a printing works, rarely socialized, and was opposed to the ideal of equality. Equalization, he maintained, merely reduced everyone to the same level; it would never elevate the masses, it would merely succeed in abolishing the elite.

Blomart's mother blamed poverty, slavery and war, 'as well as devouring passions and tragic misunderstandings',[5] on human stupidity. Had people but wanted a better world they could have achieved it, she believed. His father, by contrast, accepted the world as it was: 'in a dignified manner, he ran with the crowd, and exhortations failed to arrest his obstinate pace'.[6]

Blomart becomes increasingly alienated, not only from his father but also from his father's world, whose corrupt associations, he began to believe, 'infested' the whole town, indeed the whole earth. He temporarily joins the French Communist Party, decides to leave home, apprentice himself as a printer and begin to support himself. But the old workers, he finds, had difficulty accepting him as one of *them*, and they continued to treat him with deference. Yet Blomart persists, finds himself a one-room flat, and begins to make the transition to a more frugal lifestyle.

When Hélène meets Blomart, through her boyfriend Paul, he has left the Communist Party and has become an active trade unionist. She brings him food during a strike, sends him letters, and appears to him to want to embark on a passionate affair. Blomart later reflects that while he had tried to discourage her he had unavoidably managed to attract her: his eyes were his, his history was personal to him. He had now loomed up in her life, a presence from which she could flee, or which she could approach, 'but you could not prevent my existing in your consciousness'.[7]

At this stage in the novel Blomart and Hélène have a major philosophical argument, having to do with the possibility of finding good reasons for living. Hélène, interestingly, has marginally the better of this argument. When she was small, she confides, she believed fervently in God, and understood clearly her duties to God. Then she *had* to live, because otherwise it would have been impossible for her to fulfil these duties. Blomart replies that she is mistaken in thinking that reasons for living must descend from heaven; the truth is that we need to discover these reasons for ourselves. But Hélène is not impressed with this argument, on the basis that the reasons which we locate for ourselves are ones to which we have difficulty giving our allegiance. Blomart replies that the reasons we ourselves find for living become worthwhile ones in our committing ourselves to them by way of love or desire. But Hélène is not convinced, and counters with a Camus-like aphorism to the effect that death disenchants everything; or as she puts it herself, ' "How can we find within ourselves good reasons for living, since we die?" '[8] Blomart wonders why death should matter *that* much, provided one has lived the life one had wanted to live. But Hélène, concluding this philosophical exchange, maintains that a life, to be taken seriously, must be seen to be heading somewhere. However, as death, by definition, is an eternal nothingness, human existence is heading nowhere and, as such, cannot be considered meaningful.

WAR ARRIVES

Soon, however, they would find themselves caught up in the vast destructive movements of History. First, the Spanish Civil War broke out, and Blomart repeatedly finds himself called upon to make decisions for others, or decisions affecting others, but does not know, and cannot predict, the distant consequences of such decisions. This predicament causes him considerable moral anguish.

But the shadow of war hung not only over Spain; it menaced all of Europe. They had been introduced to Blumenfeld, a member of an illegal front conducting a clandestine struggle in Austria against the Nazis. Various possible responses to the encroachment of Nazi fascism are then broached. They are pacifism (Gauthier); 'organize meetings, a press campaign to inform your comrades of what's happening to us' (Blumenfeld), and inaction (Blomart) because of the grim consequences of action: 'Beyond the Pyrenees, the workers of Spain fell beneath the Fascist bullets – but could I redeem their blood at the price of French lives, at the price of a single life which was not my own life?'[9]

With the annexation of Austria, however, the moral pressure for involvement intensifies; Hélène insists that Blomart hasn't, in fact, created the world and, as such, isn't responsible for it. But he replies, ' "One day I read, 'Each of us is responsible for everything and to every human being.' " '[10] While we haven't originally made the world, we contribute to reshaping it at every instant. There is no stepping outside of History.

Hélène feels at this stage that she is becoming marginalized in Blomart's life. He, for his part, realized that she both wanted and needed his love. But he withheld that love on the pretext that he had undertaken to respect her freedom. ' "I love her, but I'm not in love with her"', he explains to his mother, when he introduces them. Yet soon afterwards he proposes marriage, and they even discuss, albeit briefly, the possibility of having children.

As war arrives Blomart sizes up the situation as follows: 'Gauthier was a pacifist. Paul was a Communist. Hélène was in love. Laurent was a working man. And I was nothing.'[11] Then war came, and his attitude to war no longer mattered.

Hélène manages to visit Blomart at the Front (much like de Beauvoir's own mission to Sartre), and she even contrives to get him posted back to Paris, an initiative that backfires because it precipitates Blomart into breaking off their engagement. Following the break with Hélène, Blomart returns to the Front and becomes an active participant in the war. He draws parallels between the killing fields and the fields of his childhood, where he had munched apples in a haze of pre-moral innocence. Here on the killing fields 'men were only means to an end, or obstacles or part of the scenery, and all the voices were silent, the whispering voices, the threatening voices, the voices of anxiety and guilt'.[12]

But the war begins to go disastrously for the French, Blomart is wounded in battle, and he is forced to contemplate the horror of the future that awaits them:

We are defeated; mankind is defeated. In its place a new race of animals proliferate over the earth; the blind heartbeat of life will no longer be distinguishable from the decomposition of death . . . There will be no more men.[13]

Gauthier, the pacifist, is for 'a loyal collaboration' so that new disasters can be avoided. Blomart recoils at the idea of collaboration, but recognizes that everyone collaborates after a fashion: he himself is walking about in Paris as if nothing on earth has changed! He resolves to fight, on the basis that existence is action, and that actions must be clearly visible. He has in mind acts of sabotage, munitions trains exploding, requisitioned hotels blowing up. The others – on this occasion Parmenthier and Leclerc – wonder whether he has considered the likelihood of frightful reprisals. Blomart replies that so far from fearing reprisals, he is actually counting on their occurring. Reprisals alone will galvanize the French into insurrection. ' "So you would allow innocent people to be shot down without a qualm?" ',[14] asks Parmenthier. ' "I've learned from this war" ', replies Blomart, ' "that there's as much guilt in sparing blood as in shedding it" ',[15] adding that they need also to consider all those lives their resistance will perhaps save. ' "Do you consider that all means are good?" ',[16] wonders Leclerc, to which Blomart replies, ' "On the contrary, all means are bad." '[17] He develops this line of reasoning as follows. He, too, had dreamed of justifying his actions with fine resounding reasons. But what reasons could be adduced with so much misery and carnage everywhere? On the one hand, one could say that the relevant calculations could not be made, because the objects of comparison – blood and tears – simply resisted all such comparisons. On the other hand, one could insist that all these human experiences are primitively calculable, so that 'every coin was current, even this one; the blood of others'.[18] Judged from this perspective, the price would never be too high. It would never be too high because ' "Anything is better than Fascism." '[19]

FINALE

Hélène, meanwhile, flees Paris, to stay at a house near Angers. Then she returns to Paris where she takes what she herself describes as a German 'client'. Herr Bergmann was in the rag trade, and he proposed a partnership which would be mutually beneficial: their 'collaboration' would be based on a marriage of German-produced fabrics and the innate French eye for design. But when they go dancing Hélène imagines the eyes of her friends all trained on her, and she experiences a dramatic change of heart. She thinks again of French defeat, of German victory, and of 'our prisoners'. She informs Herr Bergmann that she will not, after all, be accompanying him to Berlin.

The closing stage of the novel sees Blomart organizing a Resistance cell in a house in Meudon, from where he plans a series of attacks on German installations in Paris. The first such attack is excitingly successful, with eight Germans killed and an unknown number wounded. But when he dines with his parents, he learns that 12 hostages have been shot in retaliation. His father is proud of him, but his mother accuses the Resistance of having murdered the hostages. Blomart explodes: ' "Do you know what is happening in Poland? . . . They load Jews into trains, they hermetically close the trucks, and they send gas through the whole convoy. Do you want us to become accomplices to these massacres?" '[20] But his mother is not easily defeated in moral argument. She queries whether their bomb had succeeded in saving the life of a single Pole; as far as she can see, they have merely added to the aggregate of dead bodies. Her parting shot is that those who want to fight should be left to fight and shed their own blood. When he departs, Blomart is convinced she will die without forgiving him.

Hélène becomes involved with the Resistance as a consequence of helping her friend Yvonne, a Jewess, escape deportation. But on a particularly dangerous mission she is mortally wounded. The novel that opened with Blomart maintaining a vigil by her bedside closes by the same bedside, when she briefly regains consciousness.

CRITICAL RESPONSES TO *THE BLOOD OF OTHERS*

Existentialism, writes Maurice Cranston, considered itself a philosophy of crisis, so that it is not surprising then that 'both Simone de Beauvoir and Sartre should have made their names as writers during the most critical years of modern French history'.[21] In de Beauvoir's case, moreover, the reputation was thoroughly deserved, as *The Blood of Others* is the Resistance novel *par excellence*.[22] But it is also, thinks Cranston, a novel of considerable philosophical significance. He summarizes its philosophical content as follows: 'The main philosophical argument of the book, then, is first, that freedom is the supreme value in life; and second, that it demands great courage to be a free man.'[23] Cranston sees *The Blood of Others* as an essentially anti-determinist tract. It proclaims the future to be open, and the human will to be free. But man must be prepared to *assume* this freedom; he must *believe* that his will is free. Determinism is not merely a false philosophical doctrine, it is also psychologically menacing: 'Belief in determinism saps the resolution to make one's own fate, it breeds a kind of oriental fatalism. Simone de Beauvoir voices more than one objection to determinism. She not only considers it false; she considers it mischievous in so far as it encourages this attitude of passive resignation towards evil.'[24] This is the reason de Beauvoir prefers the writings of the 'scabrous' Sade to those of Zola: the latter, a 'thoroughgoing determinist', can neither praise nor blame, since 'he sees men as the creatures of circumstance who cannot be judged'. Simone de Beauvoir does not admire Zola. She prefers Sade, and in her essay 'Faut-il brûler Sade?' she claims for that scabrous writer 'a place among the ranks of the moralists precisely because he thought it essential to find a *justification* for all he did and said'.[25]

Determinism is a psychologically comfortable doctrine for it debars one from blaming others, and it also dispenses with the need to blame oneself. The libertarian or existentialist position, by contrast, allows no such ease of mind:

> To believe in the freedom of the will is to acknowledge one's own responsibility and one's own guilt. That is why courage is called for ... sometimes it is a heroic task to bear this responsibility. But there is no escaping from it. 'Chacun est responsable de tout devant tous' she quotes at the beginning of *Le Sang des Autres*, and these words of Dostoievsky's might serve as an epigraph to all her work.[26]

Mary Evans characterizes *The Blood of Others* as an attempt, at the level of prose fiction, to tackle 'the issue which she describes in *The Prime of Life* as having tormented her and Sartre during the war: the issue of German reprisals after acts of sabotage by the Resistance. Neither de Beauvoir nor Sartre was in any position to take up arms against the Germans, but they clearly perceived the dilemmas of those who did, and who in doing so brought about the death of innocent civilians.'[27] But the fictional resolution of the issue of moral responsibility is guided, she advises, by a philosophical principle contained in the following quotation from Dostoevsky which functions as a preface to the novel: 'Each man is responsible for everything before everyone.' Evans decodes this quotation as follows: 'we have responsibilities to other specific individuals, but over and above these are other responsibilities, crucially to the values of freedom and liberty. Unless we are prepared to fight for those general values, our particular commitments are nonsensical, since we are turning our backs on the creation and maintenance of those conditions in which the freedom of individuals can be realized.'[28] In the novel, then, as Evans reads it, Blomart feels, and cannot but feel, responsible for the death of Hélène. He has no reason to suppose that Hélène regrets her part in the Resistance, but he also knows that all of those involved in the consequences of his actions have not made the same choices as he has. Yet, according to Evans,

> rational thought, and political and ethical choice, all persuade him to another decision, that of continuing with his part in the Resistance. Despite the persuasive arguments in the novel against such action, the most telling of which is a remark by Blomart himself that 'it is easy to pay with the blood of others,' he decides that freedom for all can only be guaranteed by decisions and confrontations which sometimes jeopardize freedom and life.[29]

Chapter 4 of Evans's *Simone de Beauvoir: A Feminist Mandarin* is entirely devoted to an appraisal of de Beauvoir's fiction, and it, too, contains comments on *The Blood of Others* of both a direct and an indirect character. Here she divides up de Beauvoir's fiction into three distinct stages:

> the first is that of the existentialist novels (*She Came to Stay, The Blood of Others*, and *All Men are Mortal*), the second is that of the social novel (*The Mandarins*), and the third is that of what is perhaps best described as the stage of the novels of despair and moral anarchy: the collection of stories entitled *The Woman Destroyed* and the novel *Les Belles Images*.[30]

In all three stages, she advises, we can detect quite different kinds of heterosexual relationships, and very varied pictures of men and women. Thus in the first group of novels – which is what concerns me here –

> de Beauvoir portrays heterosexual relationships as intensely passionate, sexually expressive, and above all collaborative: men and women are brought together by common interests and values. For example, in *She Came to Stay*, Françoise and Pierre, like Jean and Hélène in *The Blood of Others*, are united by common intellectual and political commitments, mutual agreement about how to live, and a shared moral code that operates between them and in their dealings with the rest of the world.[31]

But regardless of whether de Beauvoir's novels depict equal or unequal couples, there are strong differences in all her novels between the *representations* of men and women, particularly in respect of their sexuality. What emerges as a pattern in *all* the novels, we are told, 'is that male sexual desire and expression are far less problematic than those of women. It is, moreover, men who show the greatest apparent inclination towards infidelity, or at least towards greater variety in their sexual partners than women.'[32]

I shall mention three other features of de Beauvoir's fiction which are noted by Evans. They are (1) 'that women do not, on the whole, behave particularly well towards each other'.[33] (2) Seen as exercises in feminist realism, de Beauvoir's novels would be highly rated, 'since she shows in fictional terms precisely those aspects of female emotional dependence on men which feminists have for so long attacked'.[34] (3) De Beauvoir's fiction, while acceptable as feminist realism, remains true to the patriarchal norms of the 19th-century linear novel. In particular, her fiction upholds the tradition of female attachment to, and confirmation by men. The issue here consists precisely of what women want, and get, from men that they cannot obtain from other women. In de Beauvoir's novels, according to Evans, the answer is not posed at a sexual or economic level, but at an intellectual one: women rely on men for their capacity 'to offer a coherent understanding of the world which women themselves are never portrayed as capable of. That is not to say that they are not competent, hard working, talented, and capable – in the case of Hélène of *The Blood of Others* or Françoise of *She Came to Stay* – of brave and determined action, but that they do not possess the same capacities for coherence and the systematization of the social world as the men with whom they are associated.'[35]

I turn next to Terry Keefe's appraisal, to which he devotes half of Chapter 8 of his book *Simone de Beauvoir: A Study of her Writings*. Keefe considers the narrative a technically complex one, not least chronologically; its description of Blomart's break with his family 'is convincing enough', and he finds 'great strength in the middle sections of the book, which give pointed embodiment to many of the theoretical problems raised in her moral essays'.[36] Once more in this novel, he maintains, de Beauvoir 'shows her gift for inventing and exploring concrete examples of the moral problems she discusses elsewhere. She squarely faces up to the difficult issues of sabotage and reprisals.'[37] Keefe, too, sees differences in the representation of the leading male and female characters: 'Above all, Hélène's perspective and values are totally different from those of Blomart, and it says much for Beauvoir that she not only foresaw our need for regular relief from the hero's convoluted and tortured thought-processes, but also succeeded in projecting us, in every other chapter, into the mind of a spoiled and selfish young woman.'[38] And yet, the contrast in personality and character, argues Keefe, never operates wholly in Blomart's favour, for 'Hélène has qualities that are almost entirely missing in Blomart – spontaneity, a zest for life, a capacity for certain emotions, perhaps even a certain kind of determination – and one to which he himself is quick to respond.'[39]

On the negative side, Keefe maintains that the end of the novel is contrived and 'closed', adding

> There is, of course, a certain historical justification for the way in which she has everyone pulling together in the Resistance: Blomart, Hélène, Communists, workers, Marcel, Denise, Madeleine, and the

French bourgeoisie as represented (somewhat caricaturally) by Blomart's father. But the ending does little more than paper over
certain conflicts that have been given great emphasis earlier in the
book... some of the questions asked in the novel are far better than
the answers Beauvoir felt obliged to give at the time. The objection
that if the Resistance fails, then those participating will have committed 'crimes inutiles' receives only the most inadequate of
responses.[40]

Finally, Elizabeth Fallaize devotes Chapter 3 of her book *The
Novels of Simone de Beauvoir* to a discussion of *The Blood of Others*,
a discussion which gives sustained attention to the thematics of the
text and its narrative structure. The interweaving of the personal lives
of its principal characters with the events of history mark a distinct
development in the thematic and narrative structure of this novel, she
observes, though for all that 'the anxieties exhibited in *She Came to
Stay* about the nature of our relations with others, and about the roles
women play, are just as present, manifesting themselves in the
obsessive imagery of blood and guilt, of nausea and the odour of
corruption which permeate the text'.[41]

Fallaize relentlessly, and convincingly, presses home the point that
Blomart is the dominant narrative power of the text. This status, she
argues, derives not just from the fact that his narrative is the longest,
and is voiced by himself, 'but from the fact that the central argument
of the text is made to rest heavily on the interpretation which Blomart
gives to the account of his past',[42] from the fact that 'Other characters
only appear in so far as Blomart presents and interprets them',[43] and
because 'The narrative stands of the two principal characters are far
from having equal weight in the novel.'[44] Blomart's narrative, she
further explains, 'encloses the one focussing through Hélène, since it
begins and ends the novel, and occupies seven chapters, in comparison
to Hélène's six. In addition, the chapters are of very uneven length,
with the result that Blomart's narrative in fact covers a third again as
many pages as the majority of the subsidiary characters, and has
to cover much wider time spans (as much as a decade or more in
Chapter 1).'[45]

Fallaize takes issue with the claim that *The Blood of Others* is
correctly considered to be a *roman à thèse*. She allows that 'It is
certainly possible to extract from the novel a more or less consciously
defined ideology',[46] noting that the Dostoevskian notion of responsibility functions as an unquestioned absolute in the text. At the same

time she wants to resist Susan Suleiman's claim that *The Blood of Others* is an 'authoritarian' text, that is, that it formulates and propounds 'a system of absolute values in an insistent and unambiguous manner; in its fictional universe "right" and "wrong" can be clearly and categorically distinguished'.[47] Fallaize argues that the text is not nearly as dogmatic or self-assured as this; thus 'even in the case of Resistance action, the argument for intervention is only arrived at after a series of refusals and hesitations. More importantly still, the arguments *against* the eventual solution are presented as serious and weighty ones.'[48] She points out that some of these arguments against defensive violence are actually left unanswered in the text: 'this is in particular the case of the point put forward by Blomart in his pacifist phase that there can be no point in struggling for man's happiness and dignity if human life is to be treated as a cheap resource'.[49]

While there is good reason for thinking that *The Blood of Others* is not an authoritarian text, it does, says Fallaize, deserve the status of 'an unmistakably committed novel'.[50] This it owes chiefly to the extensive range of arguments which it advances in favour of 'active resistance'.[51] Thus, for example, 'The pacifist case is disposed of by the portrait of Gauthier, the pacifist turned collaborator ... the fate of the Poles, the fate of those in prisoner-of-war and concentration camps is constantly raised as a reminder that the relative comfort and security of occupied Paris is only the more acceptable face of Nazi domination.'[52] Fallaize reasons, in fact, that 'In the climate of 1941–43, it is virtually unthinkable that she could have written about the Resistance in a noncommitted way, though she could have made the argument for commitment without taking it to the extremes of arguing that there must be "blood, newly shed, between us"'.[53]

The remainder of Fallaize's analysis has to do chiefly with the novel's representation of Hélène, the leading female character. 'Throughout the novel', says Fallaize, 'Hélène is characterised as strongly individualistic; it is this individualism, combined with a mood of nihilism resulting from the break with Blomart, which allows Hélène to view working with the Germans with indifference.'[54] Hélène is valorized in the novel for many of her traits, continues Fallaize, but especially for 'her zest for life and appetite for happiness',[55] and above all 'for the strength of her desires and the determination with which she pursues them. This is in strong contrast to the emotional vacuum which paralyses Blomart for the majority of the book.'[56] Finally, the representation of Hélène acquires a strongly allegorical character in the various scenes depicting her femaleness and the difficulties of the female condition; but it does so particularly in the abortion scene 'in which the blood of aborted childbirth is also made to suggest the blood of first menstruation'.[57] On this basis Fallaize suggests that *The Blood of Others* can be read as 'The Blood of *Women*': 'It is after all Hélène who has to shed her blood twice over in the novel.'[58]

REPLY TO CRITICS AND APPRAISAL

First I shall reply to the critics. As Cranston reads it, *The Blood of Others* propounds two related philosophical theses: that freedom is the supreme moral value, and that the exercise of freedom demands substantial courage. As a corollary, he further perceives *The Blood of Others* as an essentially anti-determinist tract. There is much to admire in this reading of the novel: freedom is exalted, particularly in the closing passage, and the price of freedom, it would have us believe, is an endless anguish: ' "You have not given me peace; but why should I desire peace? You have given me the courage to accept for ever the risk and the anguish, to bear my crimes and my guilt which will rend me eternally." '[59]

But even if the main philosophical argument of the novel is as Cranston has identified it,[60] it is by no means the only philosophical argument which it contains. Neither do its various philosophical theses all cohere. Thus if freedom is the supreme good, we are also informed that anything is better than fascism. We must find our own reasons for living, it is said, but the fate of countless human beings is decided by other human beings whom they do not even know. 'I am responsible for everything' is a constant refrain, but we are also reminded of how difficult it is to escape one's class inheritance. 'We only exist if we act' is yet another refrain, but the novel is a powerful reminder of the weakness of humans when confronted with History: millions of humans are scattered and mangled by historical forces (such as war and anti-Semitism) which individuals are powerless to resist. When we juxtapose all of these competing propositions, the novel is best seen, I submit, as a tormented response to the central human predicament: that human beings are free, but always in circumstances which are not of their own making and which relentlessly oppress and thwart them.[61]

Mary Evans presents the novel as a fictional treatment of the issue of German reprisals following acts of sabotage by the Resistance. If killing members of an occupying army were morally defensible, the same could hardly be said for causing the deaths of innocent hostages which was bound to follow. So what was one to do? This was a terrible dilemma, but it is hard to see it as the main or dominant theme of the novel for two reasons: (1) Few readers will fail to guess the decision that Blomart eventually reaches; in other words, the dilemma is too easily resolved. (2) Once the war has started, the moral reasoning of the main protagonists becomes visibly blunted. It yields, inexorably one feels, to the overwhelming presence of events, particularly to the overwhelming presence of Evil. In short, as the narrative unfolds, the dilemma palpably diminishes. Confronted with the facts about genocide, Blomart's mother (the voice of Cartesian heroism in the novel) is ultimately reduced to a kind of moral incoherence: she doesn't see how *further* killing will achieve any good (an understandable reaction), but she also says that the fighting should be left to those who *want* to fight, which is not only an acceptance of violence and aggression, but is also to ignore the realities of contemporary warfare.

Blomart, unquestionably the main character in the novel, articulates unequivocally the moral position that de Beauvoir herself would formulate, without apology or procrastination, in *The Ethics of Ambiguity*. Having reminded his friends that *everyone* collaborates after a fashion,[62] and that *all* means are bad, Blomart goes on to say not just that reprisals and therefore innocent deaths will cascade from their actions, but that he is *counting on them happening*. This, he proclaims, is the only way to maintain an absolute distance between occupier and occupied, the only way to undermine collaboration, the only way to ensure that 'France shall not slumber in a state of peace.'

In reply, then, to Evans, I should say that if *The Blood of Others* is to be seen as a fictional representation of the moral dilemmas of Resistance fighters, it does not portray them convincingly for the reasons cited. In defence of the novel, on the other hand, it could be argued that these dilemmas are often at their most excruciating, not during war, but before and after war, both for participants and non-participants alike. During war, moral considerations and scruples all too easily become marginalized. If the novel is seen as a treatment of this thesis, then, in my opinion, it is a much more convincing exercise.

Evans identifies the pattern of heterosexual relationships in the early existentialist novels as one of passionate reciprocity, but so far as *The Blood of Others* is concerned, this is too lazy a view to take of the matter. For one thing, there is the contrast drawn by Blomart between making love to Madeleine and making love with Hélène:

Madeleine made love passively, silently, and nearly always in the dark;
Hélène, by contrast, made love *freely*, because she consented to it, and
did not become submerged in the tumultuous coursing of her blood.
In his arms she was not 'a submissive body, but a living woman'.
Neither is the relationship between Blomart and Hélène as smooth
and untroubled as Evans implies. On the contrary, it evolves in the
following jagged fashion: Hélène grows tired of Paul, with whom she
also refuses to become sexually involved, but she is initially rejected
by Blomart, who is sexually involved with Madeleine. Rebuffed,
Hélène turns briefly to Petrus, by whom she becomes pregnant.
Wishing to terminate the pregnancy, she is forced to turn to Blomart
for help. The trauma of the abortion draws them closer, and they
begin to sleep together. They then become engaged; nonetheless,
Blomart insists that while he loves her, he is not *in* love with her, on
the pretext that he has undertaken to respect her freedom. Still, he
introduces her to his mother, and, *pace* Evans, they even discuss the
possibility of having children, albeit in a rather rarified philosophical
fashion.[63]

The war and the Occupation separate them, but she locates his
army unit and manages to meet him briefly. When she contrives to
have him posted back to Paris to a desk job, he breaks up with her,
returns to active service, is wounded in action and sets up a Resistance
group. Hélène, meanwhile, fraternizes with a wealthy German industrialist with whom she contemplates forming a business partnership.
But in a dramatic change of heart, she recognizes her obligations to
her friends and country, and she, too, joins the Resistance, and rejoins
Blomart. He falls intensely in love with her this time round, but their
reunion is short-lived, as she is mortally wounded on a rescue mission.
Then death separates them for ever. I submit that this is not the story
of a man and a woman 'united by common intellectual and political
commitments, mutual agreement about how to live, and a shared
moral code that operates between them and in their dealings with the
rest of the world'.[64] Rather, it is the story of a relationship which is
subjected to immense and varied external pressures (the attractions of
other men and women, family ties, war, survival, and so on), and to
internal difficulties (their different responses to rejection, war,
separation, responsibilities, and so on). Both sets of circumstances
combine to produce a relationship which is often uneasy, repeatedly
fractured, and also sometimes very tender. But it is really towards the
end of the novel only, when it is already too late, that the relationship
achieves that intense mutuality of which Evans speaks.

It seems to me that Evans is on safer ground with her remarks concerning the feminist realism of de Beauvoir's novel. By feminist realism she means the depiction of women as emotionally dependent on men and, as such, the achievement of an accurate portrayal of the social and emotional patterning of women's lives in patriarchal society. I am not sure whether 'emotional dependence' is the expression best suited to describe the different social identities possessed by the main protagonists in this novel, but it does give an important clue as to how these social identities actually differ. Thus if Blomart doesn't quite have a career, he does at least have a life-plan, albeit one which is repeatedly imposed upon by external events. Rejecting his bourgeois inheritance, he deliberately subjects himself to a downward social mobility by opting for a trade and taking up residence in a less salubrious part of town. He becomes politically active through membership of the Communist Party, and remains politically engaged when he later quits the CP and becomes involved in trade union work. When war breaks out he is wounded at the Front, but he evades capture and sets up a Resistance unit which he leads in acts of sabotage and assassination against the occupying army. In short, he is an activist, a leader, and the author of life-goals for himself. The goals in question are largely abstract: to abandon the bourgeoisie, to join the working class, to join the Communist Party, to become a trade unionist, to be a soldier, to fight the enemy, to lead a Resistance group. These goals are abstract in two senses: (a) they do not refer to any (other) single named human being, and (b) they relate, so far as they have an interpersonal dimension, to human *collectivities*. In short, they do not derive their meaning for their author from a commitment to any other particular human being. In a word, Blomart is *independent*.

By contrast, Hélène's interests often appear trivial, self-centred, or entirely grounded in a relationship, either real or sought-for, with a man. When we first encounter her, she is bored with life, but this turns out to be merely a boredom with her boyfriend Paul. She goes to elaborate lengths to steal a bicycle, and from an early stage is preoccupied with thoughts of Blomart and how she will make him hers. Having abandoned God, and, initially, having failed to capture Blomart, she is marooned between these two losses, the one divine, the other human, both male. She turns in desperation to Petrus, the ageing voluptuary, only to seek refuge again with Blomart for the purposes of procuring an abortion. When he is called up, she follows him to the Front and even gets herself arrested; later she flees to

Angers before the advancing German army, returning to Paris where she accepts a German protector, a male industrialist. Then one evening over dinner she experiences a sudden moment of truth. She recognizes the utter evil of Nazi fascism and joins the Resistance. But fate deals her a swift and crushing blow when, soon afterwards, she is mortally wounded on a Resistance mission.

The difference between this personal odyssey and that of Blomart is that Hélène's story cannot be told in its essential details without constant reference to another named human being: Paul, Blomart, Petrus, Blomart, Herr Bergmann, Blomart (as leader of the Resistance unit). It depends throughout for its meaning on the male correlate. In a word, Hélène is *dependent*, and to the extent that this kind of dependency typifies the social existence of the female in patriarchal society, *The Blood of Others* does quite accurately portray this condition.

I have two concluding comments to make about this novel. When Camus' post-war novel *The Plague* was awarded the *Prix des Critiques* in 1947, there were those who dissented from the general acclamation. Roland Barthes, for instance, argued that *The Plague* was an inadequate transposition of the problems of the Resistance, because Camus had replaced a struggle against men by a struggle against the imporoonal microbes of the plague.[65] Simone de Beauvoir echoes this line of criticism – that *The Plague* is an inadequate fictionalized account of the Resistance (or Occupation) because it descends to a sub-human level – when she writes as follows in the third volume of her memoirs:

> *The Plague* came out just at that time; here and there one could still hear the voice that spoke in *The Outsider*. It was Camus' voice and it touched us, but to treat the Occupation as the equivalent of a natural calamity was merely another means of escaping from History and the real problems. Everyone fell in too easily with the abstract morality expressed by this fable.[66]

This, I feel, is a rather harsh verdict on Camus' allegorical novel, since *The Plague* demonstrably posits four possible responses to Occupation. They are (i) Flight (the early Rambert); (ii) Collaboration (Cottard); (iii) Resistance (Rieux, Tarrou, Grand, Castel, the later Rambert and, eventually, Paneloux); (iv) Prayer (the early Paneloux). Simone de Beauvoir's own novel of the Occupation posits the following six responses: (1) Pacifism (Gauthier, Mme Blomart); (2) Non-Violent Resistance (Blumenfeld); (3) Inaction (Blomart); (4) Loyal

Collaboration (Gauthier); (5) Violent Resistance (Blomart, Hélène, Laurent, Madeleine, Denise, Marcel, M. Blomart); (6) War (the French Army). It is not, I submit, a forcing of the point to claim that these two novels do not differ to any marked extent in their treatment of the theme of Occupation and how to respond to it. Moreover, their convergence is hardly surprising when one recalls that both authors came out unequivocally in favour of resistance. De Beauvoir's harsh criticism of *The Plague* was therefore excessive, but it was possibly inspired more by Camus' postwar condemnation of violence than by anything conveyed in his allegory of the Occupation. De Beauvoir may well have been reacting, without admitting it, to Camus' *Combat* editorial *Neither Victims Nor Executioners*, in which he says: 'People like myself want not a world in which murder no longer exists... but rather one in which murder is not legitimate.'[67] This comes uncomfortably close to a public repudiation of de Beauvoir's Resistance ethic in *The Blood of Others*. ' "I've learned from this war that there's as much guilt in sparing blood as in shedding it" ', said Blomart, adding ' "Think of all those lives which our resistance will perhaps save." ' I personally have no quarrel with the ethics propounded in *The Blood of Others*, where de Beauvoir opts for an ethics of responsibility over an ethics of authenticity. But it may be that she herself remained uneasy about this difficult choice.

The Blood of Others may be seen as an exercise in feminist realism from an existentialist author; it may also be seen as an adumbration of an existentialist ethics, one which espouses an ethics of responsibility over against an ethics of authenticity.[68] But it is perhaps best seen as an outline statement of an existentialist theory of history.[69] This is the view that humans make history, that we humans are free, but this freedom is constantly imposed upon and often overwhelmed by such apocalyptic forces as war, fanaticism and the class struggle. This is a more pessimistic, but also a more realistic thesis than the Dostoevsky declamation – 'Each of us is responsible for everything and to every human being' – to which the novel purports to pay homage.

3 *The Ethics of Ambiguity*: An Existentialist Ethics

Simone de Beauvoir's *The Ethics of Ambiguity*[1] is a long philosophical essay published by Gallimard in 1947. De Beauvoir says she wrote it in response to requests, from Camus and others, for an essay on *action*, and with a view to defending existentialism against attacks from French Marxists such as Henri Lefebvre and Paul Naville. The essay is divided broadly into three sections, called respectively 'Ambiguity and Freedom', 'Personal Freedom and Others', and 'The Positive Aspect of Ambiguity'. Part I offers a defence of existentialism and, in particular, a defence of existentialist ethics. In Part II de Beauvoir offers a character ethics, that is, a series of profiles of human types; here she discusses, in the following sequence, the child, women, adolescence, the sub-man, the serious man, the nihilist, the adventurer, the passionate man, and the person who wills herself free. The section on the condition of women marks the first explicit and sustained recognition in her philosophical prose of an issue which will loom ever larger in her work as the decade progresses, culminating, of course, with the publication in 1949 of her feminist classic *The Second Sex*. Part III offers a detailed discussion of the ethics of violence; in it, de Beauvoir explores at length the philosophical basis of the ethical standpoints adumbrated in her Resistance novel *The Blood of Others*.

In this chapter I propose to concentrate on Part I of *The Ethics of Ambiguity*. In doing so I shall reconstruct her argument in accordance with the practices current in analytical philosophy. My main reason for doing so is to make her discussion more accessible.

AMBIGUITY AND FREEDOM

The human condition, says de Beauvoir, is marked by a 'tragic ambiguity';[2] this ambiguity consists, first of all, in the fact that each human being is both an object among other objects, and at the same time a privileged object in its possession of a cognizance of its situation. Philosophers have long tried to mask this ambiguity by reducing mind to matter, or matter to mind, 'or to merge them within a single substance'.[3] But the contemporary experience commands us

35

to feel acutely the paradox of our situation, namely, that we are both masters of our situation and yet completely vulnerable to outside forces. As de Beauvoir herself explains,

> The more widespread their mastery of the world, the more they find themselves crushed by uncontrollable forces. Though they are masters of the atomic bomb, yet it is created only to destroy them...There was Stalingrad and there was Buchenwald, and neither of the two wipes out the other.[4]

Existentialism from Kierkegaard to Sartre has acknowledged the ambiguity of our existence, that is, the fact that it is replete with contradictions. Yet it is held against existentialism that it is a philosophy of the absurd and of despair, that it encloses us in a sterile anguish, in an empty subjectivity. On the face of it, de Beauvoir allows, there may well appear to be some justification for these allegations, for 'Does not Sartre declare, in effect, that man is a "useless passion", that he tries in vain to realize the synthesis of the for-itself and the in-itself, to make himself God?'[5]

De Beauvoir replies that even the most optimistic ethical theories have their roots in an acknowledgement of failure. Nor could it be otherwise. The reason is that one does not propose moral standards to a being who is completely perfect and perfectly complete. Thus God has no need of an ethics, since there is nothing he has to be, no gap between what God is and what God ought to be: 'for a being who, from the very start, would be an exact coincidence with himself, in a perfect plenitude, the notion of having-to-be would have no meaning. One does not offer an ethics to a God.'[6] It follows that one can offer an ethics only to an agent who is less than perfect, someone we can exhort to *achieve perfection*; equally, this agent must be capable of some improvement, for there would clearly be no point in offering a moral education to agents who were both imperfect and incapable of improving themselves. In short, ethics is designed for human beings. In de Beauvoir's more technical prose, 'there can be a having-to-be only for a being who, according to the existentialist definition, questions himself in his being, a being who is at a distance from himself and who has to be his being.'[7]

But, it is said, existentialism doesn't offer such an ethics.[8] De Beauvoir takes this accusation to mean: Jean-Paul Sartre doesn't offer moral guidance in his *Being and Nothingness*. It is true, she replies, that Sartre declares that man is a useless passion. But, she quickly adds, Sartre also sees human beings as the source of *meaning* in the world.

Ambiguity arises also from the fact that a human being is both an epistemological subject and object, both in the world and yet capable of distancing themself from it, and conferring a meaning or identity upon it. It is this kind of ambiguity which Sartre acknowledges, and it is linked, she believes, with the kind of ambiguity which she herself has already identified. This ambiguity does not cause paralysis; rather it releases a succession of clashing emotions. As she explains,

> My contemplation is an excruciation only because it is also a joy. I cannot appropriate the snow field where I slide. It remains foreign, forbidden, but I take delight in this very effort towards an impossible possession. I experience it as a triumph, not as a defeat.[9]

This means that there is, so to speak, a constant tension in our being: a tension between success and failure, between being human and wanting to be superhuman, between negativity and positivity. The task facing each of us, thinks de Beauvoir, is to acknowledge and support this ambiguity which is characteristic of us: 'To attain his truth, man must not attempt to dispel the ambiguity of his being but, on the contrary, accept the task of realizing it.'[10]

The following is a summary of the discussion to date:

(a) Imperfect beings need an ethics.
(b) Human beings are ambiguous.
(c) Therefore human beings are imperfect.
(d) Therefore human beings need an ethics.
(e) Existentialism is capable of supplying such an ethics.

What comes next is de Beauvoir's attempt to convince us of the truth of (e), that is, of the closing proposition that existentialism does have an ethics to offer.

EXISTENTIALIST ETHICS

The first declaration of existentialist ethics is that we must reject all moral absolutes.[11] The following meanings may be assigned to the expression moral absolute: (a) universal moral standards: standards of conduct having, or thought to have, application to all moral agents (for example, 'It is wrong to steal'; 'Treat people as ends, never simply as means'); (b) an objective moral truth, that is, a moral belief which is true independently of whoever utters it (for example, 'Child abuse is wrong'); (c) an area of necessity in moral discourse, the idea that certain moral beliefs are true of necessity in that it would be incoherent or insane to deny them (for example, 'Murder is wrong'); (d) standards of perfection, sainthood, flawless behaviour (as indicated, perhaps, by the use of such words as 'holy', 'innocent', 'pure', 'saintly', 'just', and so on); (e) divine commands (for example, the Ten Commandments). It is meanings (d) and (e) that de Beauvoir primarily has in mind. We must reject all moral or foreign absolutes means, first of all, that we must reject all standards of perfection and sainthood for human beings. Her argument is a repeat of a previous idea:

'Absolute standards are for absolute beings.'[12]
Human beings are not absolute.
Therefore absolute standards are not designed for human beings.
Therefore human beings should reject such standards.

De Beauvoir also means that we must not take our moral standards from God. She reaches *this* conclusion as follows:

We must not deny our own freedom.
We do deny our own freedom if we take our moral standards from God, because to do so would be to imply that we do not have it within our own powers to devise moral standards, or because we hand over responsibility for moral standards to God.
Therefore we should not take our moral standards from God.

This is not exactly the same as saying (a) we should reject God's commandments, or (b) we should disobey God's commandments. In each case here the emphasis is entirely negative: we are, in effect, urged to reject God. De Beauvoir's intended emphasis, as I read it, is less negative: we are urged not to take our moral standards from God, but, by implication, to devise them for ourselves. Not so much to reject God as to assume responsibility for our own lives.

If we must not take our moral standards from God, then the only remaining alternative is that we must devise them for ourselves. De Beauvoir reaches this conclusion in this way also:

If we are *free*, we must be free to devise our own moral standards.
We are free.
Therefore we are free to devise our own moral standards.
Therefore we should devise them for ourselves.

We should devise them for ourselves, because the only remaining alternative – that we permit God to devise them for us – has already been excluded.

Not only are we free to devise our own moral standards, but freedom, understood as the power and the exercise of choice, is the *basis* of moral values. Things are desirable because we choose or have decided to desire them; things are valuable because we have put a value on them. As de Beauvoir herself phrases it,

It is desire that creates the desirable, and the project which sets up the end. It is human existence which makes values spring up in the world on the basis of which it will be able to judge the enterprise in which it will be engaged.[13]

Here is a summary of de Beauvoir's argument so far:

- The human condition is one of ambiguity.
- We must reject all standards of perfection for human beings.
- We must not take our moral standards from God.
- We should devise our own moral standards.
- The exercise of freedom is the foundation of moral values.

If we *should* devise our own moral standards, and if we *can* devise our own moral standards (because we are free), then can't we devise any standards we please, including therefore the most repugnant ones? Or, as Dostoevsky phrased it, 'If there is no God, isn't everything permitted?' On this view, God lays down the moral law and communicates the moral law to those of His creatures capable of comprehending it. He punishes those who transgress the law and rewards those who obey Him. It follows that if there is no God, then there are no rules laid down, and there is, *a fortiori*, no punishment for failure to obey the commandments.

'If there is no God, isn't everything permitted?' therefore means (a) if there are no rules laid down with sanctions attached to them, can't we do as we please without fear of punishment?; (b) if there are no rules laid down, can't we devise any rules we please?; (c) if there are no moral rules *a priori*, that is, existing independently of our having devised them, then can't we call anything at all good, including therefore the most (ostensibly) heinous deeds? At this point in the discussion de Beauvoir focusses on (a): she replies that we cannot evade responsibility, that we shall always have to answer to *ourselves* even if we don't have to answer to God. Man, she says,

bears the responsibility for a world which is not the work of a strange power, but of himself, where his defeats are inscribed, and his victories as well. A God can pardon, efface, and compensate. But if God does not exist, man's faults are inexpiable.[14]

In short, if there is no God, or if we choose to disregard God, the burden of morality is even greater, and it is entirely ours to shoulder. Yet what she calls the proponents of secular ethics charge existentialism with offering no objective content to the moral act. Existentialist ethics, she represents them as saying, 'is subjective, even solipsistic'.[15] De Beauvoir rejects this insinuation as well. She replies that by affirming that the source of all value 'resides in the freedom of man, existentialism merely carries on the tradition of Kant, Fichte, and Hegel, who, in the words of Hegel himself, "have taken for their point of departure the principle according to which the essence of right and duty and the essence of thinking and willing are absolutely identical"'.[16] Existentialism is a humanism, de Beauvoir implies, for the idea that defines all humanism, she goes on to point out, is that the world is not given but willed; it is the world we have sought to make in so far as what we will expresses our genuine reality.

Unlike Kant and Hegel, however, existentialism sees values emerging from 'the plurality of concrete, particular men projecting themselves towards their ends on the basis of situations whose particularity is as radical and as irreducible as subjectivity itself'.[17] As de Beauvoir sees it, the task for 'an ethics of ambiguity' will be to show whether separate individuals can be bound to one another, whether 'their individual freedoms can forge laws valid for all'.[18]

EXISTENTIALISM AND MARXISM

Marxism, too, says de Beauvoir, recognizes human separateness. It too rejects the idea of a moral law existing outside of, and independently of human subjectivity. Marx, too, 'does not consider that certain human situations are, in themselves, and absolutely, preferable to others'.[19] On the contrary, Marxism recognizes that it is the needs of people, the revolt of a class, which sets up aims and goals. What is desirable appears against the backdrop of, and in preference to what is rejected. Moreover, from this Marxist perspective,

> it is on the basis of a certain individual act of rooting itself in the historical and economic world that this will thrusts itself towards the future and then chooses a perspective where such words as goal, progress, efficacy, success, failure, action, adversaries, instruments and obstacles have a meaning. Then certain acts can be regarded as good and others as bad.[20]

So, are Marxism and existentialism saying the same thing? The answer is No, says de Beauvoir. The reason that they are not saying the same thing is that they hold radically opposed positions on the question of freedom, for even if it is the will which decides, Marxism *also* holds that the will is unfree. Here she quotes from the 1859 *Preface*: 'It is not the consciousness of men that determines their social existence, but their social existence that determines their consciousness.' As de Beauvoir reads it, this is a statement to the effect that human wills are the reflection of objective conditions by which the situation of the class, or the people under consideration is defined. Thus in the present moment of the development of capitalism, 'the proletariat cannot help wanting its elimination as a class. Subjectivity is reabsorbed into the objectivity of the given world. Revolt, need, hope, rejection, and desire are only the resultants of external forces.'[21]

It is precisely at this juncture that Marxism and existentialism go their separate ways, she says. Existentialism affirms human freedom, whereas Marxism denies it. Of the two, moreover, it is existentialism that sees things correctly, for in the end it is we ourselves who decide what to do with our lives. Indeed, it is not only individuals who are free, but classes also. The proletariat, for example, can *want* the revolution to be brought about by one party or another: 'It can let itself be lured on, as happened to the German proletariat, or can sleep in the dull comfort which capitalism grants it, as does the American proletariat. It may be said that in all these cases it is betraying; still, it must be free to betray.'[22]

Besides, says de Beauvoir, Marxism does not *always* deny freedom. The very concept of action would lose all meaning if history were a mechanical unrolling in which man appears only as a passive conductor of outside forces. Indeed, she continues, both by acting, and by preaching action, the Marxist revolutionary 'asserts himself as a veritable agent; he assumes himself to be free'.[23] Moreover, unlike Marx himself, contemporary Marxists, she alleges, feel no repugnance towards the edifying dullness of moralizing speeches; neither is it correct to depict these speeches as merely a matter of the expedient use of language. Even to admit that much is to concede that this language is *heard*, 'that it awakens an echo in the hearts of those to whom it is addressed'.[24]

MORALITY AND FREEDOM

What more can existentialism say about freedom? De Beauvoir replies that freedom is the source from which all values and all significations originally spring. Indeed, it is impossible to justify one's very existence, she thinks, unless one has freely assumed it. This leads her to conclude that the person who seeks to justify his life 'must want freedom itself absolutely and above everything else'.[25] And on this basis she further concludes that 'To will oneself moral and to will oneself free are one and the same decision.'[26] This conclusion can be read in either of two ways: (a) morality and freedom are identical (to choose to be moral is to choose to be free); (b) freedom is the supreme moral value; freedom is what we should aim at, or choose, in everything we do. By aiming at freedom, we effect the 'transition from nature to morality by establishing a genuine freedom on the original upsurge of our existence'.[27]

But how can we *choose* freedom if we *are* free? This is logically equivalent to asking: How can we choose death if we are mortal? (To choose death is to prefer it to some other alternative. But there is no other alternative to death. Therefore death cannot be chosen.) De Beauvoir gets out of this difficulty as follows. We can distinguish between two kinds of freedom: (i) freedom understood as a capacity for 'spontaneous' behaviour, which we all possess; (ii) freedom understood as a capacity for goal-directed behaviour, which is open to constant subversion by laziness, heedlessness, capriciousness, and so on. Morally good behaviour presupposes first-phase freedom, and must aim at second-phase freedom. Moral agents who acquiesce to laziness, capriciousness, and so forth, cannot hope to be morally good.

The following is a summary of this stretch of de Beauvoir's argument:

- We shall always have to answer to ourselves, even if we don't have to answer to God.
- The denial of freedom is incoherent, because everything that we do, including every commitment that we make, requires the exercise of that very freedom which Marxists (allegedly) have said we do not possess.
- Morality and freedom are the same.
- Freedom is the ultimate moral value, what we should always aim at.
- We have *spontaneous freedom*, but we must will ourselves free in the higher sense that we must be prepared to launch ourselves towards self-chosen goals; when we do so, we effect a transition from nature to morality.

To be free in the higher, second-phase sense of the word, it is necessary to have a developed sense of identity: you must be capable of setting yourself goals, launching yourself towards these goals, and keeping your progress under continuous scrutiny. It also requires that you exercise certain virtues, such as the virtue of *perseverance*. In this way de Beauvoir's existentialist ethics brings with it, or contains, a *character ethics*, understood in this context as a classification of virtues and vices, and an account of the basis of this classification. A virtue is a disposition to behave in a way that contributes to the enchancement of freedom; a vice, by contrast, is a disposition to behave in a way which diminishes the prospects of achieving freedom. Thus perseverance is a virtue, laziness a vice.

Stubbornness is not necessarily a virtue in that it can induce a readiness to persist with futile actions, with actions that contribute nothing to achieving the goals one has set oneself. De Beauvoir describes *resignation* as 'the saddest of virtues' principally because, as she sees it, resignation to a defeat condemns not only the defeat but also 'that whole part of ourselves which we had engaged in the effort. It was to escape this dilemma that the Stoics preached indifference,'[28]

There is a sense in which it is possible to preserve one's freedom by not attempting anything not within one's compass. But in that case, de Beauvoir advises, we manage to save only an 'abstract' kind of freedom. There are people who are so terrified at the prospect of failure that they keep themselves from ever doing anything; but, she adds, no one would dream of considering this kind of 'gloomy passivity' to be a triumph for freedom.

The only way for freedom to maintain itself against all obstacles, says de Beauvoir, is by giving itself a particular content. What this means is that freedom can, and will surmount defeat by constantly adopting new projects. Popular opinion is quite right, she says, 'in admiring a man who, having been ruined or having suffered an accident, knows how to gain the upper hand, that is, renew his engagement in the world, thereby strongly asserting the independence of freedom in relation to things'.[29] This renewal of freedom brings with it both heartbreak and joy: heartbreak with the collapse of certain projects, but also the joy of finding one's hands free again and ready to stretch out towards a new future.

Freedom is neither rescued nor renewed, she insists in an uncompromising rejection of Sisyphean heroism, by engaging in actions which have no meaning for the agent. As she rightly observes, there is no more obnoxious way of punishing someone than by forcing him to perform acts which make no sense to him, 'as when one empties and fills the same ditch indefinitely, when one makes soldiers who are being punished march up and down...This mystification of useless effort is more intolerable than fatigue.'[30]

A meaningful freedom, then, will neither seek to avoid constraints nor dissipate itself in useless effort. Rather it will 'absolutely reject the constraints which arrest its drive towards itself'.[31] But obstacles or constraints can be overcome either positively or negatively. The *prisoner* who escapes leaves the prison intact behind him, that is, changes nothing but his own situation. Likewise, *revolt* can be negative so long as it remains abstract. It becomes positive by means of 'action, escape, political struggle, revolution'.[32]

De Beauvoir addresses herself to one further question before closing this polemical section of her essay, namely, the question of how 'a bad willing' is possible. If acting morally is synonymous with acting freely, and we exercise our freedom whenever we act, then how is evil possible? This question can also be interpreted to mean: If you aim at freedom, then how does wickedness enter? The short answer is that wickedness enters by your aiming at the lesser of two freedoms, by your succumbing, in whole or in part, to laziness, caprice, resignation, and so on.

The Socratic tradition, says de Beauvoir, explains evil on the basis of ignorance. On this view, no one does wrong *knowingly*. So, if someone does behave wrongly, it is because they did not know it was wrong. In short, evil is the offspring of ignorance.

Socrates confuses (a) It is impossible to do wrong if you know it to be wrong (a *logical* claim analogous to 'It is impossible to be a legless ballet dancer') and (b) People can't bring themselves to do wrong knowing it to be wrong (a claim concerning human psychology). De Beauvoir rejects the Socratic answer on the basis that morality does not depend on knowledge; it depends on the will ('To will oneself moral and to will oneself free are one and the same'). This is not a good argument since it is perfectly possible to say 'If I'd *known that*, I wouldn't have done it'. So, knowledge does seem to come into it. De Beauvoir herself sees evil entering the human situation by way of weakness of the will: you can will yourself not to be free, or to be less free, and she likens this approach to that of the Christian tradition. Here she probably hears echoes from her childhood, such as 'Lead us not into temptation, but deliver us from evil'. But the

Christian tradition used to insist that three conditions had to be met for a grievous sin to occur (in the logical sense): they were grave matter, complete knowledge and full consent.

4 A Character Ethics

In the second section of *The Ethics of Ambiguity* de Beauvoir turns her
attention to further developing the character ethics[1] implicit in existentialism, and in doing so she comments at some length on the
condition of women. This will be the first sustained recognition in her
philosophical prose of an issue which will loom ever larger as the
decade progresses, culminating, of course, with the publication of *The
Second Sex* in 1949. In this section of the earlier strictly philosophical
essay, she discusses, in the following sequence, the child, the situation
of women, adolescence, the sub-man, the serious man, the nihilist, the
adventurer, the passionate man, and the person who wills herself free.
I shall now summarize her profiles of these human types, abiding by
the sequence which she herself adopted.

THE CHILD

De Beauvoir begins by quoting Descartes' dictum that man's unhappiness stems from his having first been a child. The child's situation is
characterized by the fact that he finds himself cast into a world which
he did nothing to help create, which has been fashioned without him,
'and which appears to him as an absolute to which he can only
submit'.[2] The world into which he is placed is both natural and
man-made, and yet he does not perceive any distinction between these
worlds, for in his eyes 'human inventions, words, customs, and values
are given facts, as inevitable as the sky and the trees'.[3] The child
belongs, then, to what de Beauvoir calls a *serious* world, because the
defining characteristic of the serious demeanour is to consider values
as having an *a priori* existence, that is, as existing necessarily, and
independently, of us. At his own level, of course, the child is not
serious: enclosed in his own child's circle, he feels that he can passion-
ately pursue and joyfully attain goals which he has adopted for
himself. But, says de Beauvoir, he can do so only because he implicitly
recognizes these goals as childish. The real world lies beyond his
puerile creations: this is the world of adults 'where he is allowed only
to respect and obey'.[4] The child is absorbed into this world by means
of rewards, punishments, prizes, words of praise and blame; all
conspire to instil in him the conviction that there exist 'a good and

evil which like a sun and a moon exist as ends in themselves'.[5] While the child waits to become an adult, he plays at being an adult, to the extent of even becoming a caricature of an adult. But no amount of play-acting can make him an adult, can burden him with freedom. The child escapes the anguish of freedom, the sense of complete and profound responsibility it brings with it, because he is not yet capable of leaving his mark on the world. His actions, as de Beauvoir puts it, 'do not weigh upon the earth'. So the child, if he wishes, can be lazy, recalcitrant, or whatever, but his whims and his faults will concern only him. There is no moral choice at the level of the child: since he cannot accomplish anything, the question 'What should I do?' simply doesn't arise.

WOMEN

The world of black slaves and white women is comparable to that of children, says de Beauvoir, for they too 'have no means of breaking the ceiling which is stretched over their heads'.[6] Like children, blacks and women can also exercise their freedom, but only within a universe which has been constructed before them, and without taking cognizance of their wishes. In the case of women, they have no option but to submit to the laws, the gods, the customs, and the truths which males alone have devised:

> Even today in Western countries, among women who have not had in their work an apprenticeship of freedom, there are still many who take shelter in the shadow of men; they adopt without discussion the opinions and values recognized by their husband or their lover, and that allows them to develop childish qualities which are forbidden to adults because they are based on a feeling of irresponsibility.[7]

The thoughtlessness, the gaiety of women, says de Beauvoir, which otherwise seems attractive as a pure and gratuitous taste for existence, has an unfortunate aspect to it, in that in many cases this thoughtlessness, this gaiety, these charming inventions, 'imply a deep complicity with the world of men which they seem so graciously to be contesting'.[8] So we should not be surprised, she continues, that when this male world which has sheltered them becomes unstable, these erstwhile sensitive and light-minded women 'show themselves harder, more bitter, and even more furious or cruel than their masters'.[9] It is then that we discover the difference between women and children: the child's situation is imposed upon him, whereas the woman (and here de Beauvoir again emphasizes that she is speaking about women in the Western world who do not participate in the paid labour force) 'chooses it or at least consents to it'.[10] The walls of ignorance and error that encircle women are every bit as impregnable as prison walls, de Beauvoir allows, but even within these walls, she holds, which are limiting like all human situations, an assertion of freedom is still possible. Moreover, once there appears a possibility of liberation, it is dishonest not to exploit this possibility. To deny or 'resign' the possibility of further freedom is a choice for which a woman bears responsibility. There is no liberation without consciousness of servitude, but as soon as this consciousness makes its appearance, so, too, does moral choice, and to refuse to acknowledge that choice is a renunciation of freedom, 'a resignation which implies dishonesty and which is a positive fault'.[11]

ADOLESCENCE

As childhood is left behind for adolescence, the child begins to discover himself as a subject among other subjects who seem less and less the gods they once appeared; on the contrary, the adolescent notices the contradictions among adults as well as their hesitations and weaknesses. Not only are these creatures fallible, says de Beauvoir, but, in addition, the adolescent sees that 'Language, customs, ethics and values have their source in these uncertain creatures.' The adolescent comes to realize that he, too, is going to be called upon to participate in this creation of values. He too is going to have to choose, and the gravity of this choice now begins to weigh heavily upon him. Herein, says de Beauvoir, undoubtedly lies the source of adolescent crises: 'the individual must at last assume his subjectivity'.[12] On the one hand, the collapsing of the 'serious' world of childhood is a deliverance, since the child felt himself helpless before obscure powers which directed the course of events. On the other hand, the adolescent now finds himself cast into a world which is no longer a ready-made world, but rather one for which he begins to have some responsibility. He finds himself abandoned, lacking a justification, the prey of a freedom which is no longer constrained. He has reached, on reaching adolescence, 'the moment of moral choice'.[13] He recognizes that he is free, and that everything will hinge on how he exercises that freedom.

This recognition of freedom is unfortunate for the adolescent in two distinguishable ways. First of all, his freedom was originally concealed from him, and as a consequence he will spend the rest of his days nostalgically recalling that time when he was blissfully unaware of freedom's burden. In the second place, while the child is not father to the man, it is on the basis of what he has been that he will decide what he wants to be. But what he has been is a child, so that his situation has been one in which 'He tranquilly abandoned himself to whims, laughter, tears and anger which seemed to him to have no morrow and no danger, and yet which left ineffaceable imprints about him.'[14]

The drama of original choice, says de Beauvoir, is that it goes on moment by moment for an entire lifetime, a freedom premissed on what one has been and, so far as one's childhood is concerned, premissed on what one has not already chosen to be. This 'contingency', she declares, is akin to 'the arbitrariness of the grace distributed by God in Calvinistic doctrine'.[15] But the existentialists, says de Beauvoir, unlike the Calvinists, think that man, no matter how disastrous his choices, can always be rescued from his choices. The situation of the human being is that he casts himself into the world by disclosing himself as a lack of being: a lack of being either in the sense of what he remains and hopes to be, but is not yet; or a lack of being in what he chooses *not to be*. This disclosure of the world, understood as what one aims to be, or what one might have been, constantly reinvests it with significance.

In this way each of us is personally responsible for creating a world of values, for investing the world with laudable human properties; as de Beauvoir puts it, 'What is called vitality, sensitivity, and intelligence are not ready-made qualities, but a way of casting onself into the world and of disclosing being.'[16] No doubt this plunge into the world is accomplished by means of a body, but the body is not simply a brute fact with which we have to cope. It is the *means* by which we relate to the world, and an *expression* of that relationship. The human body is a weight, a burden, and also a means of contact; that, says de Beauvoir, is why it is 'an object of sympathy or repulsion'.[17] The body does not determine behaviour; on the contrary, if there is (bodily) vitality, it is because we commit ourselves generously and maintain such a commitment in the face of adversity.

THE SUB-MAN[18]

At this stage of her dissertation de Beauvoir invokes the idea of a kind of 'hierarchy' among men, and arising out of the idea of vitality as a function of the spontaneous commitment or projection of the human subject into the world, places those making the least commitment to anything 'on the lowest rung of the ladder'. These are the 'sub-men' who are characterized by *apathy*, by a kind of metaphysical blindness and deafness, by a rejection of that 'passion' which is the human condition, described here as 'the laceration and the failure of that drive towards being which always misses its goal, but which thereby is the very existence which he rejects'.[19]

The sub-man finds about himself a dull and insignificant world, to which he contributes little or nothing, so that it constantly and inevitably fails to meet his expectations. Yet by his very limited commitments he shows himself to be a human being. At the same time by the incoherence of his plans, by virtue of his haphazard whims or by his indifference, 'he reduces to nothingness the meaning of his surpassing'.[20]

If the sub-man were nothing but a brute fact, he would merge with other inert objects in the world and he would provoke no reaction from us. But we do react to him, he does provoke our contempt, and he is responsible for his refusal to assume responsibility.

It is impossible, says de Beauvoir, completely to escape the fate of being human, since 'nobody can know the peace of the tomb while he is alive'.[21] Caught, then, between a failure to engage or disengage, the sub-man is led to take refuge in the ready-made values of the serious world. In this way he will proclaim certain opinions; he will take shelter behind a label; and to hide his indifference 'he will readily abandon himself to verbal outbursts or even physical violence'.[22] Because of this proneness to sudden and erratic attachments, he is easily led into becoming 'One day, a monarchist, the next day, an anarchist... more readily anti-semitic, anti-clerical, or anti-republican'.[23] Yet precisely because of this capacity for erratic attachments, the sub-man is far from harmless; on the contrary, he fulfils himself in the world as a blind, uncontrolled force which anybody can get control of. De Beauvoir makes much of this factor: 'In lynchings, in pogroms, in all the great bloody movements organized by the fanaticism of seriousness and passion, those who do the actual dirty work are recruited from among the sub-men.'[24]

Ethics, thunders de Beauvoir, is the triumph of freedom over facticity; in other words, ethics is the choice of freedom over acquiescence; instead of resisting the projects of human individuals it involves combining with them to 'aggrandize' the reign of the human. The penalty for inertia, flight and negation is that the sub-man finds himself in a world which is 'bare', 'incoherent', a 'desert'. He experiences 'bewilderment' and 'fear' in the face of war, sickness, revolution, fascism and bolshevism. The extremity of his predicament lies in the fact that the more indistinct these dangers are, the more fearful they become. The sub-man, says de Beauvoir, is not very clear about what he has to lose, which is understandable since he has nothing; but this very uncertainty reinforces his terror: 'Indeed what he fears is that the shock of the unforeseen may remind him of the agonizing consciousness of himself.'[25]

THE SERIOUS MAN

The attitude of the serious man is not too far removed, says de Beauvoir, from that of the sub-man; this is because the serious man, in his own way, also denies his freedom. He does so by his acceptance of certain values or ends as 'unconditioned', as 'absolute'. It is hardly surprising, she adds, that this attitude is so widespread, since it has its psychological basis in childhood. For having lived 'under the eyes of the gods, having been given the promise of divinity, one does not readily accept becoming simply a man with all his anxiety and doubt'.[26] A common occurrence, then, is that following a more or less crisis-ridden adolescence, 'the young man' either turns back towards the world of his parents and teachers, or else he adheres to values which are new but seem to him to have the same degree of authority. But unlike the child, says de Beauvoir, the serious man's acceptance of values as absolute is marked by *dishonesty*. The difference between them is that whereas values are given to a child, the adult gives them to himself, and the serious man's dishonesty derives from the fact that he must ceaselessly renew the *denial* of this freedom.

De Beauvoir allows that there are certain adults who are capable, in all honesty, of living in the world of the serious, such as those who are denied all instruments of escape, those who are enslaved or those who are mystified. She explains that the less that economic and social circumstances allow an individual to act upon the world, the more this world will appear to that same individual as given. And it is precisely this situation in which *women* find themselves. They inherit what she calls a long tradition of submission. She goes on to say that while there is often 'laziness and timidity in their resignation',[27] nonetheless some freedom and honesty remains available to them. As ignorant and powerless individuals they know they are not responsible for the world they are required to accept, but by the same token they also know that under altered circumstances they could contribute to shaping it to their own ends:

> They can, in their situation of ignorant and powerless individuals, know the truth of existence and raise themselves to a properly moral life. It even happens that they turn the freedom which they have thus won against the very object of that respect; thus, in *A Doll's House*, the childlike naivete of the heroine leads her to rebel against the lie of the serious.[28]

By contrast, the man who possesses the means to escape from the prison of ready-made values, but does not use such means, consumes his freedom in not using them. This individual, says de Beauvoir, *makes himself* serious; he hides his subjectivity 'under the shield of rights which emanate from the ethical universe recognized by him; he is no longer a man, but a father, a boss, a member of the Christian Church or the Communist Party'.[29]

The serious man is not only dishonest, he is also the slave of those values which he himself has made valuable. He forgets that each goal is simultaneously a point of departure, and that freedom is the supreme moral value, the unique end towards which all human behaviour should be directed. But the serious man will not question anything, least of all those values he accepts as absolute. Thus for the military man what is absolute is the army; for the colonial administrator the highway under construction; for the 'serious' revolutionary the revolution. In this way, she says, we get 'army, highway, revolution, productions becoming inhuman idols to which one will not hesitate to sacrifice man himself'.[30]

Because his values become idols, the serious man, like the sub-man, is dangerous. As de Beauvoir explains, the colonial administrator who has raised the highway to the status of an idol will have few scruples about assuring its construction when the price is a greater number of native lives: 'for what value has the life of a native who is incompetent, lazy, and clumsy when it comes to building highways?'[31] Not surprisingly, this conclusion leads very rapidly to the further conclusion that the serious attitude leads to a fanaticism which is as formidable as the fanaticism of passion. It is, she says by way of illustration, 'the fanaticism of the vigilantes of America who defend morality by means of lynchings. It is the political fanaticism which empties politics of all human content and imposes the State, not *for* individuals, but *against* them.'[32]

There are two doleful consequences arising out of seriousness for the serious man. The first is that the world lying outside that world on which he places an absolute value becomes a lost world, 'a faceless desert', so that once he leaves behind him the world of the serious his life loses its meaning. De Beauvoir gives the example of an old general who becomes dull on retiring from the army: 'ruined, dishonoured, this important personage is now only a "has been". He joins the sub-man, unless by suicide he once and for all puts an end to the agony of his freedom.'[33]

The second doleful consequence awaiting the serious man – besides suicide or ignominy – is that he will fall into a state of constant worry or preoccupation. His absolute belongs to the external world, and is constantly threatened by other forces in that world over which he has no effective control. The upshot, says de Beauvoir, is that he will always be expressing disappointment, for his wish to have the world harden into a thing is belied by the very movement of life. He will find that 'The future will contest his present successes; his children will disobey him, his will will be opposed by those of strangers; he will be a prey to ill-humour and bitterness.'[34] With this threat of failure and reversal a constant menace, the serious man is liable to succumb to the thought that nothing really matters, and it is at this very moment, says de Beauvoir, that 'There then blazes forth the absurdity of a life which has sought outside of itself the justifications which it alone could give itself.'[35]

THE NIHILIST

Nihilism, as it is understood here, is the desire to *be* nothing, and this desire manifests itself either at the onset of adolescence when the individual, seeing his child's universe flow away, 'feels the lack which is in his heart'; or later on, when his attempts to fulfil himself have resulted in failure. At all events, says de Beauvoir, the desire to be nothing arises among men who wish to rid themselves of the anxiety of their freedom by denying the world and by denying themselves. This radical denial of the world and of oneself is yet compatible with the retention of a kind of affection for it. Sartre, she points out, describes Baudelaire's rancorous rejection of the values of his childhood, a rancour from which scorn alone was able to rescue him.[36] Yet Baudelaire would have been unable to scoff at the world he rejected unless it had continued to exist for him.

Rejection can, of course, take more extreme forms than scorn, as happens when someone gives himself to a cause which he knows to be lost, condemning himself by immersing himself in this condemned world. Such a condemnation, she believes, occurred in the world of art with the emergence of what she calls 'Dadaist incoherence'. Yet rejection itself has a tendency to harden into something positive, and serious: either the act of rejection is itself elevated into the supreme value, or certain values are rejected in favour of others. Again de Beauvoir illustrates her point by reference to the world of art: the surrealists who sought to subvert all positive and serious values ended up by reinstating the rule of unruliness: 'We have been present at the establishment of a new Church, with its dogmas, its rites, its faithful, its priests, and even its martyrs; today, there is nothing of a destroyer in Breton; he is a pope.'[37]

Nihilism, as de Beauvoir sees it, forces the recognition of a certain truth. It is true, she says, that the world in itself possesses no meaning, and it is true that in himself the individual is nothing. But the world can be *given* a meaning, and one can *make* something of oneself. It is, in any event, impossible to escape the logic of existence, the fact that every rejection of existence itself entails or presupposes existing. Thus the nihilist rejects existence without managing to eliminate it: 'He denies any meaning to his transcendence, and yet he transcends himself.'[38]

THE ADVENTURER

Unlike the nihilist, the adventurer throws himself into living, even in the absence of a justification for living. He likes action for its own sake; it is not the ends he achieves, but the achieving of them that he values. As de Beauvoir explains, 'He throws himself into his undertakings with zest, into exploration, conquest, war, speculation, love, politics, but he does not attach himself to the end at which he aims; only to his conquest.'[39] Whether he succeeds or fails, the adventurer forges ahead, throwing himself into each new enterprise with the same indifferent ardour. This realization of freedom as an independence in relation to the serious world, this constant *challenge*, as it were, to the serious world conforms, says de Beauvoir, to the requirements of ethics, and if existentialism were solipsistic, she adds, 'it would have to regard the adventurer as its perfect hero'.[40]

There are also *impure* forms of adventurism. Thus certain individuals give the impression of caprice but, behind all their caprice, are deadly serious about achieving their goals. They declare themselves uninterested in politics, and in this way they readily allowed themselves, she says, to be collaborationists in 1941 and to become communists in 1945. Another kind of impure adventurism occurs when the spirit of adventure is suffused with an attachment to those values that typify the world of the serious. Here de Beauvoir cites the example of Cortez and the conquistadores who 'served God and emperor by serving their own pleasure'.[41]

But adventurism always leads to the adventurer having to make a choice about how he will treat others. This is because he finds himself in a world peopled with other human subjects; the conquistador meets the Indians, every day Don Juan is confronted with Elviras. Either he respects their freedom, and tries to help them free themselves, or he remains indifferent to them. If he respects their freedom, if his goal is their liberation as well as his own, then, says de Beauvoir, this agent no longer deserves the name of adventurer: 'One would not dream, for example, of applying it to a Lawrence, who was so concerned about the life of his companions and the freedom of others, so tormented by the human problems which all action raises. One is then in the presence of a genuinely free man.'[42]

The true adventurer, by contrast, is indifferent to the fate of others; he thinks he can assert his own existence without taking any heed of the existence of others. Thus, she holds, the massacres of the Indians meant nothing to Pizarro and Don Juan was unmoved by Elvira's tears: 'Indifferent to the ends they set up for themselves, they were still more indifferent to the means of attaining them; they cared only for their pleasure or their glory.'[43]

While the true adventurer will stop at nothing to reach his goal, he cannot impose his tyranny unaided; he needs money, arms, soldiers, or the assistance of the police and the law. So it is not a matter of chance, says de Beauvoir, but a 'dialectical necessity' which leads the adventurer to be complacent regarding all regimes which defend the privileges of class and party, and makes him particularly complacent towards authoritarian regimes and fascism.

THE PASSIONATE MAN

The passionate individual elevates certain objects or goals into absolutes which he *alone* will adore and sanctify. This is the difference between the serious and the passionate man: the former recognizes certain values as absolutes in an objective fashion, as existing for *all* to recognize as absolute, whereas the passionate man infuses his absolutes with subjectivity. They exist for his sake alone. De Beauvoir recognizes that there are, as she calls them, transitions between the serious and the passionate worlds. As she explains, 'A goal which was first willed in the name of the serious can become an object of passion; inversely, a passionate attachment can wither into a serious relationship.'[44] But real passion is saturated with subjectivity: in amorous passion the lover does not want the object of his love to be admired objectively, but prefers instead to think her unknown and unrecognized: 'the lover thinks that his appropriation of her is greater if he is alone in revealing her worth'.[45]

Passion is infused with, and animated by, subjective impulses. But there are both *generous* and *maniacal* passions, and the latter involve a deformation of freedom. The defining characteristic of the maniacal passions is *possessiveness*: it causes rare objects to appear in the world, but also depopulates it.

The passionate man is at once tragic, admirable and horrifying. Tragic, in that his whole life's involvement is with an object which can continually escape him; admirable, in that we admire 'the pride of a subjectivity which chooses its end without bending itself to any foreign law and the precious brilliance of the object revealed by the force of this assertion'.[46] But at the same time, such passion inspires a kind of horror as well, a horror at the solitude which the passion imposes on its subject who, having withdrawn into his own world, can realize his freedom only as a separation.

Because the passionate man has withdrawn into his own solitary world, he inevitably appears as a stranger, and as an obstacle to those who desire what de Beauvoir calls 'a communion of freedom'. Such a person, to whom de Beauvoir also refers as 'an opaque resistance' and 'an inert facticity', appears not only as strange, but also as an obstacle and as an attenuated tyrant. Since the object of his passion is the only end or ideal which he values, everything and everyone else in the world is easily relegated by him to the status of means towards this end: 'Not intending his freedom for men, the passionate man does not recognize them as freedoms either. He will not hesitate to treat them as things.'[47]

But de Beauvoir holds out some hope for the passionate man: a conversion from passion to love is always possible. To love another, as opposed to possessing or wanting to possess that other, is to recognize that person as a free subject in her own right, and therefore as strange, forbidden, and always capable of escaping all attempts to possess her. In short, love is the antithesis of passion, in that love demands renunciation of all possession: 'And to love him genuinely is to love him in his otherness and in that freedom by which he escapes. Love is then renunciation of all possession.'[48]

MORALITY AND FREEDOM

As she closes this section of her essay, de Beauvoir starts to show her own hand in a series of broad strokes designed to shed light on the concept of the truly ethical individual. Her thesis here may be summarized as follows:

(a) It is impossible to fulfil oneself except in association with other human beings.

(b) To be dependent in this way on others is frightening, and causes problems.

(c) Intellectuals have sought to surmount this 'ambiguity of their condition' in critical thought or creative activity. But the critic remains ambiguous and particularized, no matter what degree of truth and insight he attempts to impose upon his subject-matter: 'His criticism falls into the world of particular men. He does not merely describe. He takes sides.'[49]

(d) The artist, likewise, attempts to pin down existence and make it eternal. But even if he succeeds, he does not thereby become eternal *himself*.

(e) It is impossible to escape existence *in* the world, and it is in this world that we are faced with having to realize ourselves morally, making sure to avoid what she calls 'the pitfalls' delineated earlier, that is, doing what we can to avoid succumbing to nihilism, adventurism, passion, seriousness, thoughtlessness and resignation.

(f) Realizing oneself morally implies, negatively, avoiding the vices just mentioned; positively, acting morally means enhancing the value of freedom by acting in ways which freedom itself makes possible.

(g) Enhancing the value of freedom requires not only willing freedom for oneself, *but also for others*. Other human subjects both steal the world from me – by virtue of what they do to it, or make of themselves – and make a donation of the world to me. They invest it with meaning and turn it into a place where *my* self-realization

becomes possible. So, each of us needs the freedom, the inter-
ventions, of other individuals: 'Only the freedom of others keeps
each one of us from hardening into the absurdity of facticity.'[50]

(h) Thus the charge against existentialism, that it is a radical individualism, a Nietzschean will to power, is either profoundly
mistaken, or else simply malicious. Existentialism does *not* exalt
the individual who both creates his own values and imposes them
on others. The behaviour that leads to this kind of tyranny is
rooted in passion, in pride, and in the spirit of adventure and, de
Beauvoir reiterates, 'existentialist ethics condemns them'. Existentialist ethics acknowledges as 'an irreducible truth' the fact that 'I
concern others and they concern me.'[51]

(i) In conclusion, if freedom is the fundamental moral value, it has to
be respected and promoted *both* in oneself *and* in others. There is
no escaping this dual obligation: 'To will oneself free is also to will
others free.'[52] But this principle, while it is not an abstract one, will
inescapably raise difficulties. In particular, how can one will free
those to whom one is *opposed*?

5 Ethics for Violence

The third and longest section of *The Ethics of Ambiguity* is called 'The Positive Aspect of Ambiguity', and in it de Beauvoir attempts to demonstrate exactly how the principle of freedom can function as a guideline for human behaviour. This third section is itself subdivided into the following five subject areas: (i) 'The Aesthetic Attitude'; (ii) 'Freedom and Liberation'; (iii) 'The Antinomies of Action'; (iv) 'The Present and the Future'; (v) 'Ambiguity'. In this chapter I shall reconstruct her argument in each of these sections following the sequence which she herself has established.

THE AESTHETIC ATTITUDE

What de Beauvoir calls the aesthetic attitude is an attitude of *detached contemplation* towards the world and towards history; it is born in part of a demoralized consciousness, a consciousness in awe of the scale of history and the consequent finitude of the individual when viewed on this scale. The aesthetic attitude also involves a withdrawal from this world, a neutral positioning in the worst sense of that word: 'outside of time and far from men, he faces history, which he thinks he does not belong to, like a pure beholding... Thus, the lover of historical works is present at the birth of Athens, Rome and Byzantium with the same serene passion.'[1]

De Beauvoir is dismissive of the aesthetic or contemplative attitude: while we cannot recover the past, the present is not yet to be regarded as merely a potential past. On the contrary, the present is the moment of choice and action. We cannot avoid living it through a project and there is, she holds, no project which is purely contemplative since one always projects oneself towards something. To refuse to participate, or take sides, is itself to step into history; she adds, with some severity, that 'those French intellectuals who, in the name of history, poetry, or art, sought to rise above the drama of the age, were willingly its actors; more or less explicitly, they were playing the occupier's game'.[2]

FREEDOM AND LIBERATION

In the section entitled 'Freedom and Liberation' de Beauvoir meets head-on the charge against existentialism that its moral precept of the will to freedom is a hollow one, that it prescribes no course of action in particular and, as such, is useless as a guide to behaviour. She replies that freedom exists in and by means of action in the world, that to will freedom and to will the disclosure of being are one and the same choice, and that as a result of the disclosure of being we have discoveries, inventions, industries, culture, paintings and books which 'people the world concretely and open concrete possibilities to men'.[3]

If the exercise of freedom consists of thus opening up, or disclosing the world, then what, if anything, are we *forbidden*? The answer, implicit almost in the question, is that whatever cuts us off from our goals is forbidden or morally wrong. In a word, what is forbidden is *oppression*. De Beauvoir makes the following series of observations about oppression. (a) Oppression emanates from other human beings. (b) The awfulness of oppression lies in the fact that it divides the human world into two groups: those who enlighten humankind by showing it the future, and those who are condemned to mark time hopelessly in order merely to support the collectivity. (c) The oppressed have but one remedy available to them – to revolt against their oppression. (d) There is a greater *urgency* about liberation for those who are oppressed than there is for those who have escaped it. The oppressed individual will therefore be more *totally* involved in the struggle than those who, though at one with him in the effort to eliminate servitude, do not themselves experience it. But, she is quick to add, 'every man is affected by this struggle in so essential a way that he can not fulfil himself morally without taking part in it'.[4] (e) To the objection that under the pretext of freedom the oppressor is denied *his* freedom (in effect, the freedom to oppress), de Beauvoir replies that we must respect freedom 'only when it is intended for freedom, not when it strays and resigns itself. A freedom which is interested only in denying freedom must be denied.'[5]

THE ANTINOMIES OF ACTION

In the section entitled 'The Antinomies of Action' de Beauvoir discusses at some length the ethics of violence. Her general line of argument is that violence against freedom is not justified, but that violence against a freedom which occupies itself in denying freedom to others is another matter. She holds that we are obliged to destroy not only the oppressor 'but also those who serve him, whether they do so out of ignorance or out of constraint'.[6]

To defeat oppression, she says, it may even be necessary to cease serving, however temporarily, certain worthwhile causes. She explains that ordinarily, for instance, one would support anti-colonial rebellions in the British Empire; but as these were supported by fascist regimes and would, if successful, weaken the anti-fascist alliance, one could not wish them to succeed. It can thus come about that one can find oneself 'obliged to oppress and kill men who are pursuing goals whose validity one acknowledges [one]self'.[7]

Tyrants do not pursue oppression as a universal principle, advises de Beauvoir, but much more selectively. They target Jews, or Negroes, or native Indians, whom they isolate in separate categories. Furthermore, to win the allegiance of his troops the tyrant will be careful not to appeal to the rights or the liberation of man, since he needs to instil a contempt for certain categories of men. Instead, he will propose the merits of a project which is far larger than the individual, such as the future of the class, or of the socialist state, so that 'if the individual is taught to consent to his sacrifice, the latter is abolished as such, and the soldier who has renounced himself in favour of his cause will die joyfully; in fact, that is how the young Hitlerians died'.[8]

In the aftermath of a war or some such time of mass destruction, it is sometimes irritating to find the wheels of justice beginning to grind slowly again. It seems faintly absurd to conduct long-drawn-out judicial inquiries, especially when those who have been brought to trial for war crimes were not themselves so indulgent towards their victims. Yet it is precisely by way of such cumbersome court procedures, says de Beauvoir, that 'the sacred character' of human life gets rediscovered. The aim, she explains, is 'to re-establish the individual within his rights';[9] democracies, she insists, 'must restore to their members the sense of their dignity, the sense of the dignity of each man'.[10] The soldier must become a citizen again so that 'the city may continue to subsist as such, may continue to deserve one's dedicating oneself to it'.[11]

To engage in violence, says de Beauvoir, is to engage in crime, in the cancelling out of unique human lives. One can try to evade responsibility for this crime by insisting that the violence is 'necessary', in which case, she says, it becomes not a crime, but a fatality. But to argue this way constitutes evasion, she insists, for even if the end is necessary, the means used to achieve it must be chosen. What she calls 'historical materialism' evades the anguish of choice, she alleges, by its insistence that there is not just one end but also just one means of achieving it. In that event, she says, since the unrolling of history is inexorable, 'there is no longer any place for the anguish of choice, or for regret, or for outrage; revolt can no longer surge up in the heart'.[12] She allows that the partisans of violence may well agree with this line of thought, but still want to insist that this violence is useful. The utility of violence, she says, is upheld by a wide diaspora of opinions and ideologies. The means–end distinction is brought into play here: the end sets up the means which are subordinated to it. From this perspective sacrifices will still have to be made, but they can now be justified. What is repugnant is not so much the crime as the arbitrariness of the crime. But once allocated a place within the historical enterprise, 'one escapes from the anguish of decision and from remorse'. There is, however, one proviso, namely, that the campaign must be successful: 'victory gives meaning and utility to all the misfortunes which have helped bring it about'.[13]

De Beauvoir replies to *this* defence of the means–end principle by pointing out that war and politics differ from all other techniques in that the material used is a human material. Men fight for ends which they themselves value, so that the most disciplined soldier would mutiny if skilful propaganda did not persuade him that he was dedicating himself to the cause of man, 'to his cause'. Utilitarianism, she continues, tries to identify the cause of each man with the cause of mankind, and it is precisely here that we encounter the ambiguous truth of the matter: each of us does indeed belong to humanity, and yet 'each one exists absolutely as for himself'; each is interested in the liberation of all, 'but as a separate existence engaged in his own projects'.[14] There are only particular persons, and we are bound to them by way of our own particular projects. In the area of human conflict the practical implication of this truth is that inevitably we shall find ourselves fighting for some members of the human race *against others*. The question then is: How do we decide which side to support?

The matter can, of course, be settled *numerically*, as when one decides that ten thousand lives are more valuable than one. This solution, she agrees, is 'logical', even if 'this logic implies an outrageous absurdity, to prefer the salvation of the greater number'.[15] The logical solution is also rather abstract, 'for one rarely bases a choice on pure quantity. Some humans will be judged more favourably, as more useful, etc. if such hard decisions have to be made, as happened in the concentration camps.'[16] We seem to have turned full circle, she concludes, since we have come back to the view that what appears useful is to sacrifice those who are less useful. The only escape from this unwelcome conclusion is to reconsider the human subject from the perspective of the *future*. Man is the future of man in the sense that, denied the possibility of transcendence, he is reduced to nothing. Man fulfils himself by his projects, and he justifies himself on the basis of those ends at which he aims. If we are to make further headway in delineating an ethics for ambiguity, we must look more closely at this 'sovereign affirmation of the future'.

THE PRESENT AND THE FUTURE

In the section headed 'The Present and the Future' de Beauvoir returns to the means–end question, which she locates within the broader compass of a discussion on the future and its relationship to the present. She distinguishes between the future as the direction which my particular actions are taking,[17] and the Future understood as the goal and the fulfilment of human endeavour, as the End or Destiny for which human beings have long been waiting. In the context of Christian eschatology this Future was almost stripped of its temporal character altogether, notwithstanding the fact that it was promised to the faithful only at the end of their days. The secular humanism of the 18th century brought the idea down to earth again and, via the idea of progress, the two concepts of the future became fused, so that 'the future appeared both as the meaning of our transcendence and as the immobility of being: it is human, terrestrial, and the resting-place of things. It is in this form that it is hesitantly reflected in the systems of Hegel and Comte.'[18] It is in this form also, says de Beauvoir, that it is often invoked in contemporary times as the unity of the world, or as a finished socialist state: 'In both cases the Future appears as both the infinite and as Totality, as number and as unity of conciliation; it is the abolition of the negative, it is fulness, happiness.'[19]

From this concept of the Future – as abolition of the negative, as fullness and as happiness – it is a relatively short step to seeing the Present in negative terms, as that which needs to be annihilated in order to achieve 'the permanence of future being'. The present is transitory, and made to be abolished. Reduced to itself, the present is nothing, and with this conclusion, advises de Beauvoir, we come to see one distinct meaning of the means–end principle, viz. in themselves, the means are indifferent, of no moral value; their value is derived from the value of the End which they serve. Thus it comes about, she says, that some serenely think that 'the present oppression has no importance if, through it, the World can be fulfilled as such: then, within the harmonious equilibrium of work and wealth, oppression will be wiped out by itself'.[20]

De Beauvoir refuses to accept the means–end principle thus conceived. She has at least six objections to it. (1) Even Hegel could not accept the idea of a stationary Future, on the basis that as the mind is forever restless, the struggle will never cease. (2) Marx did not see socialism as the end of history, only as the end of pre-history. (3) Man is originally a negativity; a human subject exists as a human subject by making itself a lack, by, among other things, envisaging possibilities of being which do not as yet exist. (4) The fundamental ambiguity of the human condition means that humans will always find themselves presented with opposing choices. (5) The idea of perfect Happiness, Harmony, and so on is at odds with the known facts: 'the world has always been at war and always will be; if man is waiting for universal peace in order to establish his existence validly, he will wait indefinitely: there will never be any *other* future'.[21] (6) Our hold on the future is limited; we can see only so far into the future. Beyond that perceived future there is only Darkness, and this darkness justifies *none* of our present actions.

If our grasp on the future is fragile, what, then, can be said concerning the *ethical basis* of our actions? The choice, says de Beauvoir, does not rest between Totality and Nothingness. Our grasp on the future may be fragile, and the presence of the individual finite, but yet without that finite individual there would be no world. Finite forms 'stand out through time and space'. The implications for ethics and action are (a) that we must make our decisions on the basis of a limited knowledge, while (b) the means chosen must harmonize with the end, otherwise the end itself is absurd and valueless.

AMBIGUITY

In the fifth and final section of a long third chapter, de Beauvoir returns to the theme of ambiguity, and tries to show what kind of difference an existentialist ethics would make in practice. In doing so she takes up clear-cut positions on some of the large political and moral questions of the immediate post-Occupation period, such as what was to be done with collaborators. I shall, once again, summarize her discussion before commenting on it at a later stage. *Ambiguity* is to be distinguished from *absurdity*. To claim that existence is absurd is to deny that it can ever be given a meaning, whereas to claim that it is ambiguous is to say that its meaning is never fixed. Absurdism and ethics are mutually exclusive, but what de Beauvoir calls 'the finished rationalization of the real' would likewise leave no room for ethics. Ethics emerges in and for a world which, like art, will never be finalized. Each activity, no matter what, has elements of success and failure built into it; likewise 'painting is not given completely either in Giotto or Titian or Cézanne; it is sought through the centuries and is never finished'.[22]

The analogy with art works also in the following way: each artist strives to produce a finished work of art, not a work which would merely be a prelude to Art itself. Likewise, each person realizes the value of freedom in himself 'if, in aiming at itself, freedom is achieved absolutely in the very fact of aiming at itself'.[23] What this means is that freedom is achieved if and when there is nothing in the action which denies the value of freedom. From this perspective de Beauvoir is led immediately to distance existentialism from, as she labels it, 'political realism'. In the name of existentialist ethics, she says, 'we condemn a magistrate who handed over a communist to save ten hostages, and along with him the Vichyites who were trying "to make the best of things"'.[24] They opposed the political realism of the Vichyites because they sought not a rationalization of the present, such as it had been imposed by the German Occupation, but an unconditional repudiation of that Occupation. The Resistance did not aspire to a positive effectiveness; it was a negation, a revolt, a martyrdom, 'and in this negative movement freedom was positively and absolutely confirmed'.[25]

In a general way, the end towards which freedom works must be confronted at each moment on the basis of the absolute end of Freedom itself, and it is in this context that the means used to achieve each end should be evaluated. But de Beauvoir herself recognizes that this is far too abstract a position for the purposes of ethics. Practically speaking, then, what should we do? Ethics, she replies, 'does not furnish recipes any more than do science and art. One can merely propose methods.'[26] The first such 'method' is that of the value of each individual: 'the individual as such is one of the ends at which our action must aim'.[27] De Beauvoir then acknowledges, without embarrassment, that with this kind of emphasis existentialism is indistinguishable from 'Christian charity, the Epicurean cult of friendship, and Kantian moralism which treats each man as an end'.[28]

Treating others as ends in themselves does not oblige us to love literally *every* other human being; specifically, it does not oblige us to extend the hand of friendship to oppressors. But in other cases the matter is not so easy. Do we physically restrain the would-be suicide, or do we permit this attempt 'against his own freedom'? We are challenged, she maintains, with finding a way between two extremes: between indifference to heedlessness, caprice, mania and passion on the one hand, and denial of an individual's right to assert his own freedom on the other. If we forbid someone to fulfil his own existence we as much as deprive him of life itself. It follows that both fascism and heavy-handed paternalism are unacceptable: fascism because it seeks to fashion the happiness of the individual from without, and paternalism 'which thinks it has done something for man by prohibiting him from certain possibilities of temptation, whereas what is necessary is to give him reasons for resisting it'.[29]

Having argued against paternalism de Beauvoir now formulates her second 'method'. It is to the effect that the good of an individual or group of individuals requires that it be taken as an absolute end of our actions, 'but we are not authorized to decide upon this end *a priori*'.[30] What she means is that no action has its moral value already inscribed on it, so that 'one of the concrete consequences of existentialist ethics is the rejection of all the previous justifications which might be drawn from the civilisation, the age and the culture'.[31] Moral evaluation must proceed on the basis that the other is to be treated *as a freedom whose own end is freedom*. This principle will not necessarily make the activity of moral evaluation any easier; on the contrary, it may well complicate it. De Beauvoir gives the example of a young woman who takes an overdose, but is rescued in time and later becomes a happy mother. She comments that 'her friends were right in considering her suicide as a hasty and heedless act and in putting her into a position to reject it or return to it freely'.[32] But de Beauvoir also points out that in 'asylums' one sees depressed patients who have attempted suicide at least 20 times, whose freedom is consumed in 'seeking the means of escaping their jailers and of putting an end to their intolerable anguish'.[33]

Returning to the means–end discussion, she reiterates the general principle that the means can no more be judged in detachment from the end than vice versa. Ends such as the Revolution must not be seen as immediate totalities, but as goals which are hastened or retarded in their coming. The implication for the discussion on *violent* means is that it doesn't follow that the revolutionary 'must retreat from violence'; equally, 'he must not regard it as justified *a priori* by its ends'.[34] Violence can be neither condemned nor justified *a priori*; each act of violence must be considered in its own right. But *sometimes* the moral status or legitimacy of the violent act presents no problem. Thus 'In an underground revolutionary movement when one discovers the presence of a stool-pigeon, one does not hesitate to beat him up; he is a present and a future danger which has to be gotten rid of.'[35] However, if the person is merely *suspected* of treason, that is not a sufficient warrant for harming him, merely for placing him under arrest until the matter has been thoroughly investigated. At the same time, de Beauvoir makes no bones about saying that 'If a questionable individual holds the fate of other men in his hands, if, in order to avoid the risk of killing one innocent man, one runs the risk of letting ten innocent men die, it is reasonable to sacrifice him.'[36]

At the abstract level, then, the method she proposes consists of confronting, in each case, the value realized with the values aimed at. More concretely, she holds that 'an action which wants to serve man ought to be careful not to forget him on the way'.[37] This ethics, she insists in the Conclusion, is individualistic, but not solipsistic; it accords the individual 'an absolute value', and recognizes in 'him alone the power of laying the foundations of his own existence'. She adds that 'It is individualism in the sense in which the wisdom of the ancients, the Christian ethic of salvation, and the Kantian ideal of virtue also merit this name.'[38]

6 Other Defences of Existentialism: De Beauvoir and Merleau-Ponty

Simone de Beauvoir's *The Ethics of Ambiguity* is one of three sustained defences of existentialism which were offered in the 1940s.[1] The remaining two defences were furnished by Maurice Merleau-Ponty and Jean-Paul Sartre. Merleau-Ponty's defence is to be found chiefly in his essays 'The Battle over Existentialism', *Les Temps Modernes*, No. 2, November 1945, 'Metaphysics and the Novel', *Cahiers du Sud*, No. 270, March 1945, and 'A Scandalous Author', *Figaro Littéraire*, 6 December 1947, but also, if to a less obvious extent, in the essays 'The War Has Taken Place', *Les Temps Modernes*, No. 1, October 1945, and 'The Metaphysical in Man', *Revue de métaphysique et de morale*, Nos 3–4, July 1947. I shall now summarize the main lines of thought in these essays – from the general perspective of the defence of existentialism – before comparing Merleau-Ponty's defence with that of Simone de Beauvoir.

'The Battle over Existentialism' (1945) presents existentialism as a worthy philosophical attempt at constructing a philosophical anthropology. There are two classical, contrasting views on human nature, says Merleau-Ponty: on the one hand, man is seen as 'the result of the physical, physiological, and sociological influences which shape him from the outside and make him one thing among many';[2] on the other hand, man appears as 'an a-cosmic freedom . . . in so far as he is spirit and represents to himself the very causes which supposedly act upon him'.[3] Thus, on the one hand, man is part of the world, whereas on the other he is the constituting consciousness of the world. As Merleau-Ponty sees it, existentialism tries to chart a *via media* between these philosophical extremes; it tries to find, in the concept of *existence*, a way between these two classical polarities. It does so as follows. Man exists in and through a body; he is inserted into the world by means of a body; through it he is involved with the world; by means of it he knows the world and accomplishes things in it. So, man is not *simply* in the world, as are material objects; rather he is involved in a continuous *exchange* with it; but this exchange would not be possible if he were nothing but a pure or disembodied consciousness. In 'Metaphysics and the Novel' (1945) Merleau-Ponty offers a defence of Simone de Beauvoir's first novel, *She Came to Stay*, against the accusation of amoralism. What is held against her characters, he says, is not that they flagrantly break the rules of society, for 'The sinner is always accepted, even in the strictest societies, because he is part of the system and, as a sinner, does not question its principles.'[4] What is held against them, rather, is their lack, or apparent lack, of a moral sense: 'What one finds unbearable in Pierre and Françoise is their artless disavowal of morality, their air of candour and youth, that absolute lack of gravity, dizziness and remorse.'[5] But it would be a mistake, he continues, to identify existentialism with amoralism. There *is* an existentialism 'which leans towards "skepticism", but it is certainly not that of *l'Invitée*.[6] This 'skeptical' existentialism, he says, can be located in some of Camus' best known works, such as *The Outsider*, where 'on the pretext that human acts lose all their meaning when detached from their context and broken down into their component parts... one concludes that all conduct is senseless'.[7] But de Beauvoir's novel does not follow this path. In her novel, existence is suspended between the private and the public, the temporary and the eternal.

The novel, says Merleau-Ponty, does not offer *solutions* to human problems, and is the better for not doing so. There is no perfect solution to human problems: what seems like the solution now may not seem like the solution at some time in the future. Indeed, all human projects are 'contradictory because they simultaneously attract and repel their realization'.[8] For example, in loving someone one hopes for recognition from the object of one's love; and yet one wants this recognition to be freely bestowed. But if it is to be freely given, it can never be possessed. True morality, he concludes, does not consist in scrupulously following bidden rules, adding that 'there are no ways to *be* just or to *be* saved'.[9] True morality consists, rather, in 'actively being what we are by chance, of establishing that communication with others and with ourselves for which our temporal structure gives us the opportunity and of which our liberty is only the rough outline'.[10]

In 'A Scandalous Author' (1947) Merleau-Ponty defends Sartre's *literary* works against the accusation that they are replete with ugliness. Art is not necessarily to be defined on the basis of the beauty of its objects, replies Merleau-Ponty, adding that it is nothing new to call a man a combination of angel and animal, but that most critics lack Pascal's boldness in doing so: 'They are reluctant to mix the angelic and the bestial in man. They need something above and beyond human disorder, and if they do not find this in religion, they seek it in a religion of the beautiful.'[11] What separates Sartre from his critics, advises Merleau-Ponty, is that he values human imperfection, whereas they don't. On the Sartrean view, man is not part of the natural world alongside sky, harvests and animals. Unlike them, he has no fixed interests, no still point of equilibrium and repose; in fact, under human observation these self-same durable objects lose their self-sufficiency and self-evidence 'and, in a sudden reversal, appear arbitrary and superfluous'.[12] Thus it comes about that 'Ugliness is the collision of man as nothingness or freedom with nature as plenitude and fate.'[13]

In 'The War Has Taken Place' (1945) Merleau-Ponty argues against what he calls a Cartesian pacifism, which held that there is no *world* at war, with democracies on one side and fascist states on the other; rather there were men on both sides who were ready for freedom, prepared for happiness, 'always able to attain them under any regime, provided they took hold of themselves and recover the only freedom that exists: their free judgment'.[14] On this view, war was the only evil, and there was essentially only one choice to be made: either war or peace. Merleau-Ponty retorts that the issue was not so simple as choosing between bellicism and Cartesian heroism; rather the basic, recurrent choice was one between degrees and kinds of compromise, since even to remain *living* was itself a kind of acquiescence. So, one could either stop living, 'refusing that corrupted air, that poisonous bread, or one could continue, which meant contriving a little hide-out of private freedom in the midst of the common misery; and this is what most of them did, putting their consciences to rest by means of some carefully weighed sacrifices'.[15] Compromise did not, of course, extend as far as acquitting 'the traitors who called this regime down upon us, aided it more than was absolutely necessary, and were the self-appointed keepers of the new law'.[16] What it meant was that no one could protest complete innocence, and that no one could be judged 'in the name of a morality which no one followed to the letter'.[17] This conclusion leads Merleau-Ponty to contrast two moralities: on the one hand, a pure morality or ethical innocence, and, on the other, 'a kind of vulgar immoralism', which latter, he insists, is healthy. The moral individual does not want to dirty his hands, but this kind of purity is possible only 'because he usually has enough time, talent, or money to stand back from the enterprises of which he disapproves and to prepare a good conscience for himself.[18] But this luxury is not widely available, and therefore the morality which it supports cannot be recommended. In wartime, at any rate, the only practicable and desirable morality is a morality of compromise:

> The common people do not have that freedom: the garage mechanic had to repair German cars if he wanted to live... We are in the world, mingled with it, compromised with it... One cannot get beyond history and time; all one can do is manufacture a private eternity in their midst, as artificial as the eternity of the madman who believes he is God.[19]

Finally, in an essay entitled 'The Metaphysical in Man' (1947) Merleau-Ponty links metaphysical and moral consciousness together, associating both with discovery, lived human experience, contingency, acceptance of paradox, and 'a lived familiarity with whatever threatens... knowledge'.[20] The core thought here is that 'Metaphysical and moral consciousness dies upon contact with the absolute.'[21] A contrast is drawn between 'system' and 'metaphysics'; system is 'an arrangement of concepts which makes all the aspects of experience immediately compatible and compossible'.[22] To this construction of concepts Merleau-Ponty opposes metaphysical and moral consciousness, which 'has no other objects than those of experience: this world, other people, human history, truth, culture'.[23]

At this stage we are in a strong position to compare Merleau-Ponty's defence of existentialism with that of Simone de Beauvoir in her *The Ethics of Ambiguity*. These two defences have much in common; indeed, it would be surprising were this not the case, since one of Merleau-Ponty's articles is written in defence of Simone de Beauvoir. Her existentialism is not an amoralism, he argues; but neither does her novel *She Came to Stay* offer *solutions* to human problems, and it is the better for not attempting to do so. There is no perfect solution to human problems, because all human projects have elements of success and failure built into them. True morality does not consist in scrupulously following moral rules; there are no ways to *be* just, or to *be* saved. We encounter what are basically the same ideas in de Beauvoir's discussion of ambiguity. Ethics, she insists, emerges in and for a world which, like art, will never be finalized. Ethics, she adds, does 'not furnish recipes any more than do science and art. One can merely propose methods.'[24]

When writing about violence and the Occupation, or in their use of material relating to the Occupation, both of these authors are refreshingly frank in their stances. Both espouse an ethic of responsibility over an ethic of authenticity;[25] that is, both accept the reality of evil, as well as the necessity of opposing evil with force, on moral as well as political grounds. As far as Merleau-Ponty is concerned, the ethic to be adopted in wartime, or in times of crisis, is an ethic of compromise: one has to dirty one's hands, often purely to survive. Cartesian heroism is not a realistic, nor even a realizable choice: there is no morally pure or neutral position in such circumstances. Compromise does not require acquiescence; on the contrary, traitors must be dealt with. Compromise means both a readiness to accommodate the forces of evil when this becomes necessary for survival, as well as a readiness to lay aside the principles of tolerance and respect for human life when faced with despotism. Here, too, Simone de Beauvoir says essentially the same thing. For example, she writes that 'In an underground revolutionary movement, when one discovers the presence of a stool-pigeon, one does not hesitate to beat him up; he is a present and a future danger who must be gotten rid of.'[26] She then proceeds to articulate and defend the principle of the lesser of two evils, accepting fully the scale of the horrors such a principle may carry with it.

Finally, both these authors are resolute in their rejection of absolutes (or at any rate *some* absolutes in de Beauvoir's case, a point I shall return to later). So far as Merleau-Ponty is concerned, 'Metaphysical and moral consciousness dies upon contact with the absolute',[27] while further on he describes metaphysics, or the metaphysical in man, as 'the experience we have of these paradoxes in all situations of personal and collective history and the actions which, by assuming them, transform them into reason'.[28] Simone de Beauvoir doesn't speak of paradoxes but of ambiguity, but she, too, rejects absolutes. Absolute standards are for absolute beings such as God, she insists. We must create our own moral values, for not to do so is to deny our freedom. This freedom does not license apathy, indifference or recklessness; on the contrary, what becomes of ourselves and our world is entirely our own responsibility. The burden of morality is greatest when it has to be self-imposed.

There are, nevertheless, some differences between the defences of existentialism offered by Simone de Beauvoir and Maurice Merleau-Ponty. Philosophically speaking, his defence is more far-ranging, treating at some length of anthropology, ethics, metaphysics, aesthetics, epistemology, politics, Marxism and the theory of history. He is clearly more familiar with the Marxist classics, and at this point in time more sympathetic to Marxism.[32] The main difference between their respective defences, as I see it, is de Beauvoir's concentration on the development of a distinctively existentialist *ethics*, and judged from this perspective her defence of existentialism is by far the more impressive of the two. Her detailed attempt at constructing a character ethics in Section II, coupled with her lengthy disquisition on oppression, and analysis of the means–end question, to my mind make *The Ethics of Ambiguity* the single most sustained and impressive attempt at forging an existentialist ethics which is available. Her closest rival for this title is not, however, Merleau-Ponty, but her longtime philosophical and social associate, Jean-Paul Sartre.

7 Other Defences of Existentialism: De Beauvoir and Sartre

Having already considered the defences of existentialism provided by Simone de Beauvoir and Maurice Merleau-Ponty, I shall now consider the defence of existentialism which was provided by Jean-Paul Sartre. What is more, since producing a defence of existentialism has, in effect, come to mean producing an *existentialist ethics*, I shall have to consider a number of works by Sartre, including some of his posthumous publications. I propose, then, to consider the following works, in the following sequence: the *War Diaries* (written between November 1939 and March 1940), *Being and Nothingness* (1943), *Existentialism and Humanism* (1946) and, finally, *Notebooks for an Ethics* (written in 1947 and 1948).

SARTRE'S *WAR DIARIES*

Sartre's posthumously published *War Diaries*[1] is subtitled 'Notebooks from a Phoney War, November 1939–March 1940'. The expression 'a Phoney War' refers to the eight-month period between September 1939 and April 1940 when, following the German invasion of Poland on 1 September 1939, German and French troops entrenched in their respective fortified lines faced each other along several hundred kilometres of common frontier with little more than an occasional perfunctory exchange of shelling.

In his 'Self-Portrait at Seventy', Sartre speaks as follows about the war:

> The war really divided my life in two. It began when I was thirty-four and ended when I was forty, and that really was the passage from youth to maturity. At the same time, the war revealed to me certain aspects of myself and the world...You might say that in it I passed from the individualism, the pure individual, of before the war to the social and to socialism. That was the real turning-point of my life.[2]

74

Characteristically, says Sartre's English translator Quintin Hoare, 'Sartre's way of living that turning-point in his life was to write about it. To write about it prodigiously.'[3] In the few months which intervened between his call-up in September 1939 and his capture by the advancing German forces in late June 1940, Sartre produced, says Hoare,

> notebooks, of which the present volume contains about one third; letters, of which the 550 printed pages published in 1983 by de Beauvoir represent only a small part... and his novel *The Age of Reason*, plus a few lesser literary experiments when the first draft of this was completed. In all, perhaps one million words.[4]

'I must', declares Sartre on 7 December 1939, 'set my ideas about morality in order.'[5] The following is a summary of these ideas. (a) Morality is 'a system of ends'.[6] (b) The end to be pursued is entirely human in its dimensions. (c) All moral precepts are inescapably human. (d) The problem of conduct exists only for human and, as such, limited beings. (e) The end posited by morality cannot be God, because God is 'the eternal and transcendent being'.[7] (f) Since morality concerns human beings alone, it follows that God doesn't come into it; the moral question keeps God 'at a distance'. (g) It is impossible to 'derive values from facts'.[8] (h) In particular, it is impossible to derive values from facts about human nature, because there are no such facts, because 'human reality is not a fact'.[9] (i) Human behaviour can be evaluated morally because human behaviour is the behaviour of an agent seeking 'to be its own foundation'.[10] (j) This search to be its own foundation is doomed to failure because it is constantly defeated by 'death', 'deceit', 'jealousy', and the very hopelessness of that quest to be the author of those features of yourself for which you cannot possibly be responsible (for example, your genetic inheritance). (k) There is no escape from the burden of freedom; that is, we are responsible no matter what, even under the most atrocious of circumstances.

None of these propositions is articulated or defended at any significant length in the *War Diaries* and, as such, they cannot be considered a rival existentialist *ethics* to that supplied by de Beauvoir in *The Ethics of Ambiguity*. De Beauvoir herself does consider and develop a few of these same ideas, such as the idea that the end posited by morality cannot be God since God is the eternal and transcendent deity. But in general de Beauvoir follows a very different route in her attempt at producing an existentialist ethics, and her philosophical interests diverge sharply from those of Sartre. Her interest in the virtues and vices finds no echoes in Sartre, nor does her emphasis on the *dignity* of the individual as a core moral and political value surface in his early wartime writings. De Beauvoir is also far more comfortable with the concept of human nature, or at any rate with the concept of a human *psychological* nature. (She herself, it should be noted, is not always consistent in her treatment of this topic. For example, in her December 1945 essay 'L'Existentialisme et la sagesse des nations', she declares that for existentialism the self doesn't exist (*le moi n'est pas*[11]), and she goes to some lengths to distance existentialism from what she calls 'the philosophy of immanence'.) Both de Beauvoir and Sartre place an emphasis on the value of freedom, and on the burden of responsibility which freedom carries with it. But unlike Sartre, de Beauvoir recognizes and discusses a range of philosophical problems raised by the principle of freedom, such as the problem of conflicting freedoms, whether all uses of freedom are permitted, and, if not, on what basis are we justified in curtailing oppressive uses of freedom. Above all, perhaps, de Beauvoir has a vivid sense of *evil*, and seeks both a psychological and an ethical explanation of its occurrence. There is, at this stage, no evidence that Sartre has any interest in this topic.

FROM *BEING AND NOTHINGNESS* TO *EXISTENTIALISM AND HUMANISM*

In his *Existentialism and Humanism* Sartre declares that 'Existentialism is nothing else but an attempt to draw the full conclusions from a consistently atheistic position.'[12] But since he also declares, just a few sentences later, that 'even if God existed, that would make no difference from its point of view',[13] we are justified in searching elsewhere for the philosophical origins of his controversial lecture. *Existentialism and Humanism* is, in fact, much more accurately described as an attempt to work out the full implications of the few remarks on ethics which are to be found in *Being and Nothingness*. One of these occurs during Sartre's analysis of anguish, when he identifies a sub-species of anguish called 'ethical anguish'. Ethical anguish appears 'when I consider myself in my original relation to values'.[14] As Sartre sees it, value derives its being from its exigency, rather than drawing its exigency from its being. Values do not deliver themselves to a contemplative intuition which recognizes them *as being values*; on the contrary, values are revealed to an active freedom which makes them exist as values by the sole fact of recognizing them as such. In short, nothing is valuable without first being valued, just as nothing is desirable without being desired. It follows, for Sartre, that 'my freedom is the unique foundation of values, and that *nothing*, absolutely nothing, justifies me in adopting this or that particular value, this or that particular scale of values'.[15] Since I am the unique source of values, it follows that there can be no pre-existing values on which I can base my own particular choice of values. The result is that 'My freedom is anguished at being the foundation of values while itself without foundation.'[16]

Sartre returns to this theme in the closing section of the book, entitled 'Ethical Implications'. Ontology, he begins, cannot formulate ethical precepts, but it can 'allow us to catch a glimpse of what sort of ethics will assume its responsibilities when confronted with *a human reality in situation*'.[17] Negatively, this ethics will repudiate 'the spirit of seriousness', which considers values to be 'transcendent givens independent of human subjectivity'.[18] He gives as an example of this spirit of seriousness the belief that bread is desirable because it is *necessary* to live, and because bread *is* nourishing. This, he says, 'is an ethics which is ashamed of itself and does not dare to speak its name. It has obscured all its goals in order to free itself from anguish. Man pursues being blindly by hiding from himself the free project which is this pursuit.'[19] Sartre then returns to an earlier refrain: that ontology and existential psychoanalysis 'must reveal to the moral agent that *he is the being by whom values exist*. It is then that his freedom will become conscious of itself and will reveal itself in anguish as the unique source of value and the nothingness by which the world exists.'[20] *Existentialism and Humanism* represents Sartre's attempt at explaining and vindicating this argument in a more accessible philosophical prose.

In his *Existentialism and Humanism* Sartre says that 'the first principle of existentialism' is that 'Man is nothing else but that which he makes of himself.'[21] He explains that this merely means that man is not to be compared to a table or a stone. Man is before all else a project, a being 'which propels itself towards a future and is aware that it is doing so'.[22] The first *effect*, then, of existentialism is that 'it puts every man in possession of himself as he is, and places the entire responsibility for his existence squarely upon his own shoulders'.[23]

What is more, each of us is not just responsible for his or her own individual self, but for all others as well. Sartre defends this second, larger claim as follows. (1) What I become depends on what I do or fail to do now. (2) The things that I do or fail to do proclaim the things that I value or believe in. (3) Thus the individual is not just the architect of his own future; he is also a mediator of values, a source of proposals for others as to how they, too, should lead their lives. As Sartre puts it, 'For in effect, of all the actions a man may take in order to create himself as he wills to be, there is not one which is not creative at the same time of an image of man such as he believes he ought to be.'[24]

But to what *extent* are we responsible for others? Sartre gives two diverging answers to this question: (i) the individual in choosing for himself indicates what he would *like* everyone else to be; (ii) the individual in choosing for himself *decides* what everyone else will be. The evidence for this second, stronger response is found in the following passage concerning anguish:

> When a man commits himself to anything, fully realising that he is not only choosing what he will be, but is thereby at the same time a *legislator* [my emphasis] deciding for the whole of mankind, in such a moment a man cannot escape from the sense of complete and profound responsibility.[25]

Sartre concedes that there are many indeed who show no such anxiety. He replies that they are merely disguising their anguish, or are in flight from it. Yet sensing, perhaps, the incipient dogmatism of this response, he goes on to develop his point in the following Kantian-sounding fashion. He argues that 'one ought always to ask oneself what would happen if everyone did as one is doing',[26] and then reminds his readers that a refusal to pose this question is, in its own way, an anguished recognition of its importance.

Sartre has argued, at this early stage of his lecture, that if there is no God, then the notion or hypothesis of a human nature must also be rejected.[27] Now he argues that if there is no God, then the consequences of his absence must be drawn 'to the full'. What he means is that there are additional conclusions to be drawn from the fact, or at any rate the hypothesis, of God's non-existence, that these conclusions must be comprehensively documented, and that they must then be incorporated into the mainstream of existentialist philosophy.

Much like the retention of the human nature hypothesis, these inferences were also ignored by French secularism, he says. The French secularists of the late 19th century, according to Sartre, dispensed with God, that is, no longer saw God as a basis, anchorage or fundamental reference point for an understanding of the human world. But they did not for all that dispense with an absolutist, or what Sartre calls an *a priori* scheme of values. They did not, that is to say, dispense with the notion that there are certain standards to which we ought to conform *no matter what*, or *come what may*. For if, as Sartre paraphrases them, we are to have a moral code, a society and a law-abiding and peaceful world, then it is essential that certain values should be taken with the utmost seriousness. So seriously that it must go *without saying* that one should be honest, that one should not lie, that one should not beat one's wife, and that one should not abnegate one's duties towards one's children. The upshot of this way of thinking, says Sartre, is that God is dispensed with, while everything else remains the same! And this, he adds with scarcely concealed sarcasm, is what is known as 'radicalism' in France.[28] By contrast, existentialism is truly or properly radical, he says, that is, it doesn't believe in half-measures. It insists that one cannot (logically) dispense with God, but yet expect everything else to remain the same. God is not, so to speak, a veneer or label which might be removed, leaving the underlying item or reality intact. On the contrary, if God is removed from the picture the whole composition is comprehensively altered.

In particular, we must revise our thinking about moral values. With the disappearance of God there is no longer any supremely wise and perfect being to look to for moral guidance. There are *no set rules*, no rules devised and prescribed for human conduct by someone who is competent to do so. Dostoevsky once wrote, says Sartre, ' "If God did not exist, everything would be permitted" ', meaning that if there was no being who knew indubitably what should be done, who could communicate such knowledge to us, and would always do so without deceit or aberration, then we would be bereft of all moral guidance (and, in addition, we would have no supreme moral authority to answer to). This is really what Sartre has in mind when he says 'Everything is indeed permitted if God does not exist, and man is in consequence forlorn, for he cannot find anything to depend upon either within or outside himself.'[29] This does *not* mean, as it is often taken to mean, that we can do whatever we like. Its true meaning is that we are bereft of all moral guidance, that we have no way of telling right from wrong.

Anxious to pre-empt a predictable response to this new element in existentialist philosophy, Sartre now recalls his earlier anti-essentialism. The predictable response is to the effect that even if there is no God it still doesn't follow that we are bereft of all moral guidance. We might, for instance, look to *human nature* for the purpose of moral guidance. That is, if all human beings have a common, as distinct from an identical, nature, then should it not be possible to find 'inscribed' in that nature some guidelines, or clues, as to what would be appropriate behaviour for individuals of that type? This argument, amounting to a natural law hypothesis of a rudimentary kind, has made a very poor impression on the contemporary mind,[30] and Sartre's response to it is unexceptional. Man, he replies, discovers that he has nothing to fall back on: no God *nor* any human nature. Human nature cannot serve as a norm for human behaviour because there just is *no* human nature.

Are there, then, no other, remaining guidelines besides God and human nature? Sartre is, in fact, prepared to consider other possible foundations for moral belief. The first of these is what he calls 'the power of passion'. The existentialist, he advises, does not believe in the power of passion. This is because he considers passion itself not a cause, but an effect; not a source of human behaviour but a consequence of such behaviour. As Sartre concludes, 'He thinks that man is responsible for his passion.'[31]

The second alternative that Sartre considers is a minimalist Christian ethics understood as an ethics of brotherly love, while the third is the Kantian ethics of treating other human beings as ends, never simply as means. These ethical codes are uncertain, he claims. They are still too abstract for the purpose of discerning, or establishing, the morality of any particular case. He gives as proof the example of a pupil of his who couldn't decide whether to go to England to join the Free French Forces (and avenge his elder brother who had been killed in the German offensive of 1940), or whether to stay near his mother at home and help her to get by. He fully realized, says Sartre, that this woman lived only for him and that his disappearance – or perhaps his death – would plunge her into despair. He found himself, then, confronted by two very different modes of action, 'the one concrete and immediate, but directed towards one individual only; the other, an action addressed to an end infinitely greater, a national collectivity, but for that very reason ambiguous, or a lot less concrete – and it might be frustrated on the way'.[32] Neither the Christian nor the Kantian ethical codes could help this student out of his dilemma, argues Sartre, and on this basis he concludes, yet again, that we are lost for moral guidance. The moral codes in question may be capable of setting up very general horizons of value;

but this is totally inadequate for the purpose of helping us to cope with life as we have to live it on a day-to-day basis.

Could we not, finally, trust in what Sartre calls 'instincts' at one point, and 'feelings' at another? As his own pupil put it to him: 'In the end it is feeling that counts...If I feel that I love my mother enough to sacrifice everything for her...then I stay with her. If, on the contrary, I feel that my love for her is not enough, I go.'[33] Sartre replies that this argument assumes that feelings are distinguishable from and instigative of action. But the relationship between them is, if anything, the very reverse, since the only evidence of what one feels is located in what one does. Thus there is no love apart from the deeds of love, no feeling of anger apart from angry outbursts.

All that remains to us, therefore, is freedom or the power of choice. In coming to me, says Sartre, the student 'knew what advice I should give him, and I had but one reply to make. You are free, therefore choose – that is to say, invent. No rule of general morality can show you what to do: no signs are vouchsafed in this world.'[34]

There are major differences between this and de Beauvoir's defences of existentialism, despite some evidence or appearances to the contrary. The resemblances are to be located mainly in the polemical and closing stages of de Beauvoir's essay. In the polemical section she rejects absolute standards as appropriate only for absolute beings, and she sees morality weighing down heavily on human shoulders in the absence of God. At the same time, her essay lacks those shrill, aggressive assertions of atheism which are such a notable feature of Sartre's lecture.

Sartre and de Beauvoir both acknowledge, but seek also to distance themselves from Marxism in these documents. However, they do so in different ways. De Beauvoir rejects the Marxist theory of history, which she perceives as determinist and therefore as incapable of attaching true significance to human freedom and human projects. Marxism as presented by Sartre emphasizes class solidarity as essential to the liberation of the individual. Outside of his class the individual has too many obstacles and limitations to overcome, thus making his individual project a vain mystification. Sartre replies that he shall always count on his comrades-in-arms so long as they are committed to the same cause as he is; but, he adds, he cannot in the end count upon men he does not know, nor can he base his confidence 'upon human goodness or upon man's interest in the good of society, seeing that man is free and that there is no human nature which I can take as foundational'.[35]

In the closing stages of her section on character ethics, de Beauvoir acknowledges that enhancing the value of freedom requires not just willing freedom for oneself *but also for others*. This immediately reminds us of Sartre's 'in choosing for himself he chooses for all men'. But de Beauvoir does not develop her idea in the same way as Sartre. As she sees it, what must always be remembered is that I concern others and they concern me. This is quite different to Sartre's idea that others concern, or should concern me. De Beauvoir moves even further away from Sartre when she says that existentialism does not exalt the individual who both creates his own values and imposes them on others. She sees this kind of behaviour culminating in tyranny, as rooted in passion, in pride, and in what she calls the spirit of adventure, all of which are *condemned* by existentialist ethics as she sees it.

De Beauvoir launches a very different kind of attack against Marxism in the closing stages of *The Ethics of Ambiguity*, one which has no echo or parallel in Sartre. A collectivist ethic, she alleges, can assign to individuals nothing but 'an abstract identity', one which merely authorizes 'a comradeship between them by means of which each one is likened to each of the others'.[36] Because human subjects are thus understood as merely abstract identities, no one ever really dies. His or her place is easily taken in the group, in the marching, in the choral singing, by yet another abstract individual. If, on the other hand, one recognizes the radical heterogeneity of human individuals, as does *her* existentialist ethics, then one's perspective on death will radically alter. From this perspective death (in war) is not just a terrible sacrifice, an irreparable loss, but also an occasion for refusal and revolt: 'why with *my* blood rather than with another's? Why was it *my* son who is dead?'[37]

When, some pages further on, de Beauvoir writes that ethics 'does not furnish recipes any more than do science and art. One can merely propose methods',[38] it is tempting to compare this to Sartre's 'Nor, on the other hand, if God does not exist, are we provided with any values or commands that could legitimise our behaviour. Thus we have neither behind us nor before us in a luminous realm of values, any means of justification or excuse. We are left alone, without excuse.'[39] But Sartre concludes from this passage, and the difficulty posed by the moral dilemma facing his pupil, that 'values are uncertain', that they are still 'too abstract to determine the particular, concrete case', and that Christian doctrine and the Kantian ethic both fall into this category. Simone de Beauvoir, for her part, concludes that the first 'method' furnished by ethics is that of the value of each individual, that 'the individual as such is one of the ends at which our actions must aim',[40] and that to this extent existentialist ethics is indistinguishable from 'Christian charity, the Epicurean cult of friendship, and Kantian moralism which treats each man as an end'.[41] In her February 1946 essay 'An Eye for an Eye' she goes even further. There she argues that there are occasions when no redemption is possible because the evil which has been perpetrated is an absolute evil – *un mal absolu*; that when, quite deliberately, someone sets about degrading another human being, reducing him to the status of a mere object or thing, then a scandal has been caused for which no mercy can be entertained. That is why she had refused to sign the petition on behalf of Brasillach.[42]

It is when she returns to a discussion of the morality of violence that de Beauvoir's philosophical distance from Sartre is, once again, at its most visible. She begins from a standard Sartrean position, namely, that violence can neither be justified nor condemned *a priori*, but she quickly moves to assure us that the moral status of some violent actions is immediately unambiguous. Thus, 'In an underground revolutionary movement when one discovers the presence of a stool-pigeon, one does not hesitate to beat him up; he is a present and a future danger which has to be gotten rid of.'[43] Other cases are more complicated, she allows, but she proposes that all cases should be evaluated on the basis of 'the values realized with the values aimed at'. Sartre's *Existentialism and Humanism* not only refuses to furnish guidelines, principles or 'methods' of this kind; it repeatedly vilifies all efforts at doing so. There is therefore no basis for identifying, for treating as essentially the same, the approaches to ethics of Sartre and de Beauvoir at this stage in their writings.

SARTRE'S *NOTEBOOKS FOR AN ETHICS*

According to the translator David Pellauer, it is difficult to establish with certainty when exactly Sartre's *Notebooks for an Ethics* were written, but some of the references contained therein should, he maintains, 'allow the reader some sense of the period when they were written, beginning it seems in the spring of 1947 and ending sometime toward the autumn of 1948'.[44] On one view of the matter, the *Notebooks* represent the fulfilment of a promise, one made in the conclusion to *Being and Nothingness*, where Sartre announced that he would devote a subsequent work to ethics.[45] Another view, propounded by Sartre's adopted daughter Arlette Elkaim-Sartre, is that the project for an ethics dates back to before *Being and Nothingness*. 'Sartre', she claims, 'was already very much caught up in research for it in 1939 – cf his *War Diaries*.'[46]

Sartre distinguishes, on the very opening page, between *doing* good and *being* good. Being good is 'a certain mode of ontological being',[47] and it is conferred on those who do good in the eyes of God. For those who believe in God, it is a question of *being* moral in God's eyes, and in that event 'the subordination of doing to being is legitimate'.[48] However, when God dies the 'ontological individualism of the Christian' makes no difference since, *ex hypothesi*, there is no longer any God to recognize one's moral perfection. Morality, says Sartre, must aim at the world, not at the self; you should act helpfully, not so as to be the helpful type, but because people need your help.

The *Notebooks* contain a huge number of scattered remarks about ethics, but chiefly the following. The only worthwhile ethics, says Sartre, is a concrete ethics, that is, an ethical theory which combines the universal and the historical. Kant's ethics fails to accomplish this merger of the universal and the historical because it offers us no help with concrete moral choice, for example, with the problem of collaboration or resistance. To resolve this issue it is necessary to have a developed *historical* intelligence, not an 'abstract universal' one. For example, says Sartre, 'I expect it of a Frenchman that he should refuse to collaborate in 1940. I am much less sure in the case of a nobleman in the thirteenth century.'[49]

Ethical theories can be either *tough* or *tender*, and Sartre says that he personally favours an ethical theory of the tough variety. By 'tough' he means an ethics which is not premissed on hope, but on *honesty*: on the honest recognition that humans are ignoble. 'We have to love them', he adds, 'for what they might be, not for what they are.'[50]

Ethics today, continues Sartre, 'must be revolutionary socialist ethics',[51] but the atmosphere of ethics, he remarks on the previous page, is that of *failure* and *mystery*. He elaborates as follows on the aura of mystery attached to ethics: it is necessary not only to change the world, but also to discover it. This discovery will occur when it is changed. So it is a matter of 'being ethical *in ignorance*'.[52]

Contrary to what Merleau-Ponty would have us believe, Sartre is not over-enamoured of Pascal, at least not of some of Pascal's declarations on human nature. He takes issue, for instance, with

Pascal's claim that 'The heart of man is cruel and foul'. This is the way that human beings appear to us, says Sartre, and we do not know this about them in advance. These are not vices which they carry with them from birth, but facts about the way they behave. In this sense, there is '*a priori* neither good nor evil'.[53]

Sartre's scarcely concealed antagonism towards ethics surfaces once again with a remark which he borrows from Lenin, to the effect that a revolutionary has no *ethics* 'because his goal is concrete and his obligations are made known by the end he proposes for himself'.[54] Ethics, claims Sartre, is irretrievably abstract: it is the goal you give yourself when you lack a goal, and it proposes a certain way of behaving towards others with whom you have no concrete relationship in the first place. Because its content is purely formal, says Sartre, ethics 'can only be conceived of in terms of some status quo'; for example, 'What relations should one have with the family, *assuming* that the family exists and that one wants to preserve it (or not change it, which comes down to the same thing)?'[55] The historical agent moves beyond ethics, forced to ignore it since it merely represents 'a purely formal game between judicial persons. It appears where political action, religious life, history has stopped.'[56] At the same time, Sartre is forced to acknowledge that the concrete goal which the historical agent proposes for himself 'presupposes a certain conception of man and of values',[57] what Sartre is pleased to call 'a concrete ethics that is like *the logic of effective action*'.[58]

In the closing pages of the *Notebooks* Sartre returns again to the subject of ethics, this time in the context of a discussion of the alienating, that is, destructive powers of 'mental activities'. He lists among these activities religion, ethics and art. The ethical life, he remarks, is dominated by the spirit of seriousness, by the admission that values already exist. There is an ethical order waiting to be realized, but on the ethical outlook we already know what it will look like. Passions and failings stand in the way of the Good; 'The ethical life is therefore a struggle against Evil that is constantly being reborn. The Good is the partial destruction of Evil.'[59] What is missing from these activities, says Sartre, from religion, ethics and art, is the quintessential human activity of *creation*; instead we have human beings who obey, discover and awaken things. The upshot is that man becomes the inessential, while the world becomes essential. The world takes priority; man tends it as he would a garden: 'Man is essential only in that he is indispensable, in his very inessentialness, to the universe. He is its gardener.'[60]

Sartre makes the following points about the means–end 'maxim of violence', as he calls it. (1) Violence is inflicted only on 'organized natures' such as 'living organisms, tools, human establishments, and men'.[61] (2) Violence is possible 'only when the form that is opposed to you is destructible'.[62] (3) Violence is not one means among others for attaining an end, but, by deliberate choice, the attaining of that end *'by any means whatsoever'*. (4) This is why 'the maxim of violence is "the end justifies the means"'.[63] But this formula is 'profoundly ambiguous', says Sartre. Its condensed meaning is that *all* the means that contribute to bringing about the end are justified (including therefore violent means). But what we are to understand by this depends on whether the means are intrinsic or extrinsic to achieving the end in question. For example, a man dying of thirst is justified in breaking the neck of a bottle if he cannot otherwise gain access to its contents. But, says Sartre, this is not really violence at all since it was the only remaining means of securing the overriding objective. On the other hand, if the same means are used to open a bottle at a social function, then the means transform the end from one of social drinking into one of repudiation of such conviviality. 'Violence (breaking the bottle's neck) changes the end by breaking the social bond.'[64]

In his 'Translator's Introduction' David Pellauer distinguishes between four positions which it is possible to adopt on the status of the *Notebooks*. (1) We can say that the project of publishing an ethical sequel to *Being and Nothingness* 'was inherently impossible, given the description of inter-subjectivity developed in *Being and Nothingness*'.[65] (2) We can say that 'the general outlines of a Sartrean ethics' are evident in the *Notebooks*, 'and can even be filled in in considerable detail'.[66] (3) We can take the revisionist position that 'a Sartrean ethics is possible if one moves beyond the limits of *Being and Nothingness*, something it is sometimes suggested Sartre himself did over time, especially in his *Critique of Dialectical Reason* and the accompanying introductory essay called "Search for a Method"'.[67] (4) Finally, there is the position which, says Pellauer, is nearest his own 'after having translated these notebooks... that while Sartre does offer a number of interesting discussions of topics relevant to an ethics developed on the basis of his ontology... any overall synthesis is lacking and in the last analysis is unobtainable'.[68] My own view is that the *Notebooks* contain the rudiments of an ethical theory, but nothing else that would be of interest to a contemporary moral philosopher. So to some extent I disagree with Pellauer's claim that 'nowhere does Sartre really discuss what he means by an ethics, at least not in terms familiar to English-speaking philosophers'.[69] The *Notebooks*, as I said, contain a huge number of scattered remarks about ethics, adopt a Humean position on facts and values, offer a critique of Kantian ethics, and make repeated attempts to explain Marxist criticisms of morality. But none of this is done in a way which is sufficiently elaborated or sustained to make it a valuable contribution to moral philosophy, and quite a bit of it marks a mere re-working of familiar Sartrean positions. There is nothing in the *Notebooks*, I submit, to threaten the status of de Beauvoir's *The Ethics of Ambiguity* as *the* existentialist text on ethics.

8 De Beauvoir's *Ethics*: A Critical Appraisal

In the previous chapters I have identified three main defences of existentialism which were offered in the 1940s: those issuing from Simone de Beauvoir, Maurice Merleau-Ponty and Jean-Paul Sartre. In the works examined, defending existentialism more or less came to mean establishing the capacity of existentialist philosophy to produce an ethics for a shattered postwar world. I have argued that Simone de Beauvoir rose to this challenge with greater authority than her contemporaries, and in the process distanced herself philosophically from Sartre to an extent that is oceanic. But it is time now to consider the merits of her moral philosophy in its own right, and not merely as a divergent philosophy to that presented by Sartre.

The Ethics of Ambiguity is divided into three parts, which are not at all alike. There is, first of all, a polemical section (to employ de Beauvoir's own terminology), followed by an attempt at formulating a character ethics (as I have chosen to call it), and, finally, there is a detailed exploration of the ethics of violence and, in particular, discussion of the means–end principle. In later years de Beauvoir herself remained supportive of the polemical section (if unsupportive of the work as a whole): it still seemed valid, she wrote in 1963. It remained valid because in the immediate postwar period 'Existentialism was being treated as nihilist philosophy, wilfully pessimistic, frivolous, licentious, despairing and ignoble.' Some defence had to be made, she says, notwithstanding the fact that she herself considered the reproaches against existentialism to be absurd.

Undoubtedly the reproaches cited *were* absurd and to that extent any defence of existentialism was bound to sound convincing. However, if we look at the defence on its own merits, that is, as a contribution to philosophical knowledge, then, as de Beauvoir herself suspected, it is not nearly as impressive.[1] The polemical section has four main weaknesses, relating to (i) its account of evil, (ii) its renunciation of absolutes, (iii) its claim that value derives its being from its exigency, and (iv) its critique of Marxism.

Evil is not the offspring of ignorance, argues de Beauvoir, but comes from weakness of the will. You can will yourself not to be free, or to be less free, or you can allow yourself to yield to temptation, to laziness, stubbornness, resignation or any of a plethora of minor vices. However, if evil is primarily a matter, not of a failure to reach certain standards for yourself, but of a failure to respect certain standards in one's behaviour towards others, then de Beauvoir's answer, in the polemical section of her essay, will not suffice. In her contemporaneous article 'An Eye for an Eye', de Beauvoir identifies one category of evil as an absolute evil (*un mal absolu*), and she defines it as the degradation of human beings into disposable objects. She implies that no one can reasonably fail to be aware of this fundamental standard for human conduct, that everyone retains the capacity to meet this standard in his or her behaviour, and that therefore the failure to respect the dignity of human beings is something which cannot be pardoned. From this perspective, evil in its most palpable form is a consequence of a refusal to respect the dignity of human beings, by reducing them to the status of disposable objects. 'For human life to have meaning', she writes, 'human beings must be held responsible for the evil they do as much as for the good', and that, she continues, is why she refused to sign the petition on behalf of Brasillach. Here evil is explained (a) by the existence of a category of absolute evil, (b) by the fact, or supposition, that no human agent can fail to know what absolute evil is, (c) by the capacity of any human agent to resist absolute evil, and (d) by the readiness of some human agents to descend to these levels of depravity. This is a more satisfactory account of evil than that presented in the polemical section of *The Ethics of Ambiguity*.

De Beauvoir is adamant that absolute standards are for absolute beings, and that as human beings are suffused with ambiguity absolute standards are not for them. In one sense this is a very reasonable claim to make: human beings could behave better, to say the least, but if we set our moral expectations too high we are unlikely, ever, to see these standards met, and the task of moral education will become an impossible one. But the word *absolute* has other connotations, as I noted at the time, and de Beauvoir herself does not hesitate to utilize these additional meanings. Thus *The Ethics of Ambiguity* is replete with references to standards which ought not to be transgressed and limits which ought not to be violated. We are informed, for example, that the individual as such is one of the ends at which our actions must aim; that one must will oneself free; that freedom is the source of all values, and that an action that wants to serve man ought to be careful not to forget him on the way. In the contemporaneous essay 'An Eye for an Eye', de Beauvoir writes that 'to the extent that the social order rejects tyranny, and strives to recover a lost human dignity, we claim it as ours'.[2] These claims are absolutist in two senses: (a) they give priority to certain values, or principles, over others, irrespective of whether this is the way that moral agents themselves view the matter; (b) they proclaim that there are standards of behaviour which must be adhered to *no matter what.* In general, in these writings de Beauvoir expresses a concern for the dignity or value of the human being; torture, internment, extermination and brutality are unequivocally condemned as absolutely evil on the basis that they degrade human life in the most fundamental way, namely, reduce human beings to the status of disposable objects. This is an admirable, if not exactly original, contribution to ethics; at the same time, it sits uneasily with other sections of de Beauvoir's ethics, not least her repudiation of absolutes. It is also difficult, to say the least, to square this deeply humanitarian ethics with the claim, made at an advanced stage of *The Ethics of Ambiguity,* that no action has its moral value *already* inscribed on it. Of course, this could be the perfectly legitimate, innocuous claim that we cannot have any idea of the moral status of an action without first being familiar with its features. But core existentialist pronouncements are never intended to be that innocuous, so de Beauvoir must be read as (a) saying that we cannot *know* what moral status to assign to any action regardless of whatever else we know about it, and (b) making the less sceptical claim that we can ourselves confer on it what moral status we choose it to have. It is impossible to square this kind of thinking with the view that there is an absolute evil which consists of the degradation of human beings into objects, and that anyone who is guilty of such evil deserves to get it (literally) in the neck.

It is desire that creates the desirable, argues de Beauvoir (not unlike Sartre); in other words, things are desirable because they are desired, rather than their being desired because they are desirable. In one sense, this is nothing more than the trivial claim that whatever is desired is capable of being desired, but it is intended to make the stronger claim that nothing is desirable in its own right, that is, independently of its being desired. Health, for example, would not be desirable if no one desired it. But clearly health would be desirable *for* human beings even if it were not desirable *to* human beings. It is not the case therefore that desire creates the desirable, since the two are quite independent of each other. What is desired relates to what human beings want; what is desirable relates to what human beings need, to what it is palpably in their interest to have. Individual human beings are the best judges of the former, but have no special competence, still less an overriding competence, in what concerns matters of interests.

De Beauvoir's broadside against Marxism is perhaps the weakest part of the polemical section of her essay. As with all such overgeneralized attacks, one can rarely be sure just who or what she is attacking: it could be the classical Marxists, French Communist Party leaders, or Marxist intellectuals either inside or outside the Party. There are very few references to named texts, nor is there anything remotely approaching a sustained analysis of any text that is named. The result is a fusillade of clichéd criticisms, in particular the claim that Marxism is a determinism and that therefore it can find no meaningful role for the self-chosen actions of human agents. No theory of history, she argues, can afford to deny the contribution made by the behaviour of human agents to the unfolding of events; but if Marxism is a determinist theory of history then it cannot, fundamentally, assign any efficacy to the actions of self-directing individuals or classes since, *ex hypothesi*, entities of this type simply do not exist. So Marxism requires as a theoretical premise a recognition of the phenomenon of freedom, a recognition which another of its theoretical premises explicitly disavows.

There are many problems with this argument. To begin with, de Beauvoir herself, almost reluctantly, acknowledges that Marxism does not *always* deny freedom; but she makes this assertion not on the basis of any textual evidence, but on the basis that Marxism cannot *afford* to commit itself to a denial of human freedom. To paraphrase her, the very notion of action would lose all meaning if history were a mechanical unrolling in which man appears only as a passive conductor of outside forces. Merleau-Ponty, as it happens, writes with greater delicacy and textual authority on these matters. In his 1946 essay 'Marxism and Philosophy' he observes that a Marxist conception of human society, and in particular economic society, cannot subordinate it to permanent laws such as those of classical physics, 'because it sees society heading towards a new arrangement in which the laws of classical economics will no longer apply'.[3] Marx's entire effort in *Das Kapital*, he says, is directed precisely to showing that these famous laws, often presented as the permanent features of a 'social nature', are really 'the attributes (and the masks) of a certain "social structure", capitalism, which is evolving towards its own destruction'.[4] For Marx, he adds, the vehicle of history, and the motivating force of the dialectic is none other than 'concrete human

intersubjectivity, the successive and simultaneous community of exis-
tences in the process of self-realization in a type of ownership which
they both submit to and transform, each created by and creating the
other'.[5]

In more recent years two eminent Marx scholars, G. A. Cohen and
Alan Wood, have addressed the issue of Marxism and determinism,
and their contribution gives us yet another vantage point from which
to appraise de Beauvoir's efforts. Cohen turns to this topic in Chapter
4 of his book *History, Labour and Freedom*, a chapter entitled 'Inevit-
ability and Revolutionary Agency'; but for present purposes I shall
confine my attention to Wood's more wide-ranging remarks on the
topic in his book *Karl Marx*. Wood observes, first of all, that while
historical materialism has often been described as economic determinism, Marx himself never employed this expression. Second, while
Marx does say that the 'economic basis' of society 'conditions' and
even 'determines' its political and intellectual life processes, 'this is not
incompatible with saying that the "conditioned" and "determined"
aspects of social life cannot also have some influence on the economic
sphere'.[6] (In fact, Wood neglects to mention that in the 1859 *Preface*
Marx speaks of the thought processes of individuals being determined
by their social existence only 'in a general way'.)

In the chapter entitled 'Materialism, Agency and Consciousness',
Wood returns to the question of whether historical materialism is a
species of causal determinism, and as such incompatible with libertar-
ianism, 'the view which affirms that human choices are free and denies
that they are determined'.[7] Wood argues that while Marx's words
easily lend themselves to the construal that historical materialism is
committed to causal determinism, no philosophical determinism is
implied by the terms he uses. Thus Marx holds that 'economic circumstances dominate people by placing obstacles in the way of their
achieving a fulfilling way of life and by subjecting them to illusions
which prevent their setting meaningful goals for themselves'.[8] But as
Wood quickly remarks, even extreme libertarians admit that people
are sometimes prevented by external obstacles from doing what they
want to, and that ignorance or error sometimes stands in the way of
their formulating rational aims. Wood further points out that 'One of
Marx's primary objectives is to free people as much as possible from
the social relations and ideological illusions which dominate and
imprison them. If Marx's belief that people in class society are so
dominated is a species of determinism, then it is one of Marx's chief
practical aims to make this determinism cease.'[9]

De Beauvoir herself judged *The Ethics of Ambiguity* to be least successful in its attempt at constructing a character ethics, that is, in its attempt at identifying the virtues and vices, as well as identifying the types of persons in whom these same virtues and vices reside. In her memoirs she dismisses this section of her philosophical tract as derivative (borrowing excessively from Hegel), and as lacking a social basis. She is, arguably, too severe on herself, though her character ethics is not without flaws. An obvious lapse of concentration occurs when she assigns women (who *form* a sex) to the same category as nihilists, adventurers and other disreputable types (who merely *belong* to a sex). The same goes for children: childhood is a stage through which all adults must pass, whereas the same, mercifully, cannot be said for nihilism, adventurism and acquiring the spirit of seriousness.

De Beauvoir identifies far more vices than virtues. The vices she identifies are those of laziness, childishness, thoughtlessness, recalcitrance, complicity, light-mindedness, ignorance, dishonesty, resignation, cruelty, bitterness, arbitrariness, apathy, indifference, whimsicality, submissiveness, timidity, naiveté, hardness, unscrupulousness, incompetence, clumsiness, seriousness, rancour, caprice, adventurism, subjectivity, mania and possessiveness. Clearly, this is not an exhaustive listing of the vices, but it is comprehensive, and it lends credence to Renee Winegarten's view (with which I concur) that de Beauvoir 'was marked by Catholicism for life, not only by *timor mortis* but by the high standards of strict soul-searching, by the desire for and satisfaction in rectitude, by the quest for absolute perfection, and by a deep awareness of the vanity of all human endeavour'.[10]

De Beauvoir provides interesting, and up to a point valuable profiles of certain personality types, but she makes no attempt to establish how representative these types are, whether class background is a feature of their make-up, whether movement from one personality type to another is possible (except in the case of the passionate man, who can reject possessiveness for love), and the extent to which the vices they possess are gendered. It is true that de Beauvoir ascribes a plethora of vices, such as submissiveness, timidity and thoughtlessness, to women alone, and the female attributes in question have that seductive familiarity which is the hallmark of all successful stereotyping. At the same time de Beauvoir repeatedly challenges women to liberate themselves, and this liberation would presumably include ridding themselves of those vices which are supposed to be inalienable parts of their nature. So de Beauvoir's position would seem to be that certain vices are gendered (have an exclusive or predominant association with the female sex), but the gendering in question is historical and therefore alterable.

I shall conclude by commenting on an argument from the third and final section of *The Ethics of Ambiguity*, an argument which in its more extended ramifications could not, I believe, have come from any other existentialist except de Beauvoir. Treating others as ends in themselves does not oblige us to love literally *every* other human being, argues de Beauvoir; specifically, it does not oblige us to extend the hand of friendship to oppressors. But in other cases the matter is not so easy. Do we physically restrain the would-be suicide, or do we permit 'this attempt against his own freedom'? In reply to this question de Beauvoir first adduces the following two principles: (a) it is no more necessary to serve an abstract ethics obstinately than it is to yield without due consideration to impulses of pity or generosity; (b) violence is justified only if it opens concrete possibilities to the freedom which one is trying to save. Thus we are justified in practising painful medicine if it will succeed, or has reasonable hope of succeeding in restoring an individual to good health. Likewise, if the would-be suicide is a victim of depression, or is in some way calling for help, and there is a preparedness to supply him with appropriate care and treatment, then we are justified in blocking his exercise of freedom in would-be self-destruction. However, de Beauvoir goes on to make the considerably more controversial claim that the permissibility of intervention is a function of our *closeness* to the main actor. At times she merely means that the closer we are to the main actor the better positioned we are to interfere with his or her behaviour. But de Beauvoir wants also to make the stronger, moral claim that the more *responsibility* we have for someone, the more entitled we are to obstruct that person's intentions, especially where these are of a self-destructive kind. She speaks in this connection of the responsibilities of parents, and of members of the caring professions such as nurses and doctors, and she claims that the more seriously someone accepts her responsibilities the more acceptable becomes the 'strictness' of her decisions. This line of thought culminates with the vaguely sinister statement that 'love authorizes severities which are not granted to indifference'.

I am uneasy about the passage in this whole argument from the claim that closeness to an actor facilitates interference with her behaviour to the further claim that responsibility for an actor authorizes severities which are not permitted to strangers. This latter claim can itself be understood as saying either (a) responsibility is a *burden* and therefore the carer must be granted certain additional rights which are to be denied to strangers, or (b) that those who work *hardest* at meeting their responsibilities have a more substantial entitlement to interfere with the lives of those to whom they have a duty of care. Interpretation (b) gives strict, neurotic, and obsessive parents and carers excessive moral authority over those they are 'closest' to, offering them a licence to transform their charges into prisoners, or obedient pets. Interpretation (a) is less fascist, in the sense that, *prima facie*, it seems fair to say that those burdened with responsibilities should be compensated in some way. But in what way? If the responsibility has been freely undertaken, then why should it be paid for? A plausible case can be made for saying that if a socially necessary function is performed in the process, then some compensation is in order even if the responsibility has in fact been freely undertaken. But it is another matter to claim that compensation should take the form of authorizing 'strictness' and 'severities' in parental/carer behaviour. Many a childhood and adolescence has been blighted by these same severities, de Beauvoir's own adolescence included. It is ironic that she should seek a justification for practices from which she personally suffered at a vulnerable age, and which one way or another would shadow her for the remainder of her days.

9 The Historical Background to *The Second Sex*

The third volume of Simone de Beauvoir's memoirs,[1] on which much of this chapter is based, covers the period from August 1944 to March 1963. It begins with the Liberation and ends with meditations on old age and death. In a liberated Paris she participated in and witnessed what she calls 'an orgy of brotherhood'.[2] The streets were full of American soldiers, and everyone felt that Europe would soon be cleansed of fascism.

There was little occurring in the world of publishing, according to de Beauvoir, just Aragon's *Aurélien*, which bored her,[3] and Malraux's *The Walnut Trees of Altenburg*, which had the same effect. But her own philosophical essay *Pyrrhus and Cineas* was published in 1944, and because the reading public had been 'starved for ideology and literature for four years, this slender essay was very well received'.[4]

In 1943 Sartre, de Beauvoir and Merleau-Ponty had conceived two projects: an encyclopedia and a review. The encyclopedia never materialized, but the review did. In September 1944 they formed an editorial committee, whose composition she documents as follows: 'Camus was too absorbed by *Combat* to be a member; Malraux refused; it was made up of Raymond Aron, Michel Leiris, Merleau-Ponty, Albert Ollivier, Jean Paulhan, Sartre and myself; in those days, none of these names clashed.'[5] It was Sartre who gave the review its title *Les Temps Modernes*, a play on the Charlie Chaplin film *Modern Times*; but the name, as Deirdre Bair explains, was also 'a reference to the hoped-for changes in postwar society'.[6]

In February 1945 de Beauvoir got the opportunity to visit Spain and Portugal, and she could scarcely believe the affluence of Spain compared to the wretchedness of France. The French, she reminds her readers, had no stockings, oranges or negotiable currency; Spanish women, by contrast, had silk stockings, while shops in Spain and railway buffets were crammed with food. But Spain, she further discovered, was pervasively fascist. She was stopped short by a window display of 'superb photographs with captions underneath extolling the heroism of "the women of Germany during the war", the heroism of the *Volkstürm*.[7] De Beauvoir hoped, with hindsight we can say naively, that the Americans would regain Spain for democracy and put Franco to flight. Meanwhile, she reported reprisals against communists, and the routine torture in the prisons of opponents of the dictatorship.

The main purpose of her trip to the Iberian peninsula was to visit her sister and brother-in-law Lionel de Roulet in Lisbon, as well as to deliver a number of lectures on the Occupation. She had been given an assignment by *Combat* to report on social conditions in Spain and Portugal, but so as not to compromise Lionel – then attached to the French Institute in Lisbon – she wrote her Portuguese articles under the assumed name Daniel Secrétain. She saw, on a trip to the Algarve, 'earth the colour of Africa covered with mimosa, bristling with aloes; I saw steep cliffs breasting an ocean calmed by the soft sky, white-washed villages, baroque churches statelier than the Spanish ones'.[8] But she also witnessed great deprivation and indigence, for under their bright clothes the people remained hungry. They went barefoot, she reports, had stony faces, and in the false gaiety of the villages she could detect 'the dulled look in the men's eyes; under the terrible weight of the sun, they were consumed by a wild fire of despair'.[9] In Oporto she witnessed little girls in rags digging avidly into the trash cans. But on the positive side, she had valuable talks with members of the Portuguese opposition to fascism, and was told that the two dictators would find the defeat of the Axis powers a very minor inconvenience indeed.

De Beauvoir published her articles and inaugurated, it is said, a new kind of investigative journalism in French newspapers.[10] But the Portuguese embassy intervened, Camus was in North Africa, and when Pascal Pia, who was replacing him at *Combat*, halted publication of the series, Camus was unable to intervene on her behalf. However, the series was continued and concluded in *Volontés*.

In September 1945 *The Blood of Others*[11] was published, and it created more of a stir than her first novel *She Came to Stay*.[12] 'All the critics rated my second novel above my first', she says; 'editorials expressing deep emotion were written about it in several newspapers. Both orally and by letter I received floods of compliments. Camus, though he liked the book, did not conceal his surprise at this success.'[13] It was labelled not only a Resistance novel, but also an Existentialist novel. Henceforth, this label would be affixed automatically to anything written by herself or Sartre. Like Sartre,[14] she rejected the title at first, but their protests were in vain; in the end, she reports, they took the epithet that everyone assigned to them and exploited it for their own purposes.

In fact, they soon found themselves launched on what she calls an existentialist offensive. The publication of her novel was followed, a few weeks later, by the publication of Sartre's *The Age of Reason*, and *The Reprieve*, as well as by the first issue of *Les Temps Modernes*. Sartre gave a lecture on the topic 'Is Existentialism a Humanism?', while de Beauvoir herself lectured on the theme of the novel and metaphysics. Her play *Les Bouches Inutiles*[15] opened, and suddenly her life overflowed its boundaries. She was pushed out into the limelight, but more, she adds with typical self-deprecation, because of her association with Sartre than for any accomplishments of her own. Newspapers and journals, such as *Combat* and *Terre des hommes*, reported faithfully on anything they said or wrote, while at the Flore people stared at them and whispered.

There were basically two reasons for the acclamation: (1) France, in a period of decline, was busy exalting her two most characteristic national products, *haute couture*[16] and literature; (2) existentialism was exactly what their readers wanted. Speaking, yet again of Sartre, de Beauvoir claims that his petit bourgeois readers had been shattered by the war: they had lost their faith in peace, progress and immutable essences. They had, as she puts it, 'discovered History in its most terrible form'.[17] What they needed was a philosophy which would acknowledge all the recent horrors and, at the same time, offer them beliefs they could still cling to. Existentialism arrived to fill that intellectual and psychological void: 'Existentialism, struggling to reconcile history and morality, authorized them to accept their transitory condition without renouncing a certain absolute, to face horror and absurdity while still retaining their human dignity, to preserve their individuality. It seemed to offer the solution they had dreamed of.'[18]

In 1946 she published yet another novel, *All Men Are Mortal*,[19] and in it tried to rework a theme which had made its appearance in *She Came to Stay*, that of the will to be everything. This had been the devouring hope of Françoise in de Beauvoir's first novel. De Beauvoir later regretted not having shown this illusion and its demise in a clearer light, and for this reason had decided to rework that theme in her third novel. In *All Men Are Mortal* her new hero would 'seek identification with the universe and then discover that the world resolves itself into individual liberties, each of which he is unable to retain. While in *The Blood of Others* Blomart believes himself responsible for everything, this man would suffer the incapacity to do anything. In this way, his story would be a complement to my first novel and the antithesis of my second.'[20]

In 1947 she published a second philosophical work, *The Ethics of Ambiguity*.[21] The idea for this work came from defending *Being and Nothingness* against attacks by Gabriel Marcel. 'Of all my books, it is the one that irritates me the most today', she writes in 1963. 'Existentialism was being treated as nihilist philosophy, wilfully pessimistic, frivolous, licentious, and ignoble; some defence had to be made.'[22] But in 1963 she harshly judges her defence as having the hollowness of the Kantian maxims, and reproaches herself for having thought she could devise a normative ethics independently of a social context.

Their relations with Camus were becoming strained. One day Sartre had rebuked Camus by saying that his newspaper *Combat* had become too preoccupied with moral issues at the expense of political ones. De Beauvoir adds that existentialism – at any rate as they understood it – irritated him, and that he had offered no more than 'a few acid observations' on her *The Ethics of Ambiguity*. Camus had said that when he was with them he couldn't help sympathizing with them, but that when he was away from them they angered him.

In January 1947 de Beauvoir went to America, of which she had high hopes since it had helped save Europe from fascism. But in America she found that their anti-communism verged on neurosis, and that their attitude towards Europe was one of arrogant condescension. She reports that 'From Harvard to New Orleans, from Washington to Los Angeles, I heard students, teachers and journalists seriously wondering whether it would not be better to drop their bombs on Moscow before the USSR was in a position to fight back. It was explained that in order to defend freedom, it was becoming necessary to suppress it: the witch-hunt was getting under way.'[23]

Yet it was in America that she began her second major relationship with a man,[24] the author Nelson Algren, a relationship which would endure for several years and would not be fully extinguished until his death in 1981.[25] Algren lived in semi-squalor in Chicago. Their first day together, she confides in her memoirs, was very much like the one Anne and Lewis spend together in *The Mandarins*: 'embarrassment, impatience, misunderstanding, fatigue, and finally the intoxication of deep understanding'.[26] Before she left America she told Algren that her life was permanently fixed in Paris. He believed her, she says, without at all understanding what she meant. In 1948 she published an account of her American trip under the title *L'Amérique au jour le jour*.[27]

Back in Paris she found that Sartre and Camus had been temporarily reconciled, and that Sartre was under attack from Communist Party intellectuals.[28] In September 1947 she returned to Algren. On this occasion he introduced her to his Chicago, to 'the prisons, the police stations and the line-ups, the hospitals, the stockyards, the burlesque houses, the slums with their empty lots and their nettles'.[29] She met very few people, she says, partly because the purge of communists and liberals was spreading panic in the media and the film industry, where some of Algren's friends were employed; the rest were 'dope addicts, gamblers, whores, thieves, ex-convicts or outlaws; they were all escapees from American conformism; that is why Algren liked to be around them; but they were not particularly friendly'.[30]

Once again Algren asked her to stay with him in America, for good, and once again she declined. But on this occasion, she confides, they parted less sadly than in May, because the following spring they planned to take a trip lasting several months, down the Mississippi and then to Guatemala and Mexico.

She returned to America in 1948, but stayed for only two months instead of the scheduled four. She loved the wide landscape of the Mississippi, but Algren grew distant when she announced her intention of returning home. He even declared his preparedness to marry her, but to no avail. The main problem was that even if Sartre hadn't existed, she wasn't prepared to live in Chicago, while Algren needed to stay rooted in America, in his own city, in the world he had created for himself. As the Irish biographer, poet and playwright Ulick O'Connor put it, 'He felt his writing power came from his presence in the city. It was a cruel twist of fate then that he should have found a lover who wouldn't leave her own city for the same reason.'[31]

Since the beginning of May 1948 sections of her essay on Woman – to which she had been making the odd passing reference in her recollections of that period – had been appearing in *Les Temps Modernes* under the title *La Femme et les Mythes*. However, she was informed by Leiris that Lévi-Strauss had been critical of the sections on primitive societies. He was just finishing his thesis on *Les Structures élémentaires de la Parenté*, and she asked him to let her read it. It confirmed her, she says, in her view of woman as *Other*: 'it showed how the male remains the essential being, even within the matrilinear societies generally termed matriarchal'.[32]

Volume 1 of her work on Woman was finished in the autumn of 1948, and she decided to hand it over to Gallimard straight away. She thought of various titles for it, such as *The Other*, *The Second*, and

The Other Sex. Bost[33] suggested *The Second Sex*, and on reflection it was decided that that was exactly right.[34]

Volume 1 of *The Second Sex* was published by Gallimard in June 1949, and Volume 2 appeared in November of that same year. In it she sets out to describe the condition of woman in general. To do so, she first considered the myths forged by men about woman through all their cosmologies, religions, superstitions, ideologies and literature. She tried, she says, 'to establish some order in the picture which at first appeared to me completely incoherent; in every case, man puts himself forward as the Subject and considered the woman as an object, as the Other'.[35]

She was not saying there was no difference between women and men; on the contrary, writing the book had made her even more aware of the differences between them. What she firmly believed, however, was that these differences were cultural rather than natural. On this basis she undertook to 'recount systematically, from childhood to old age, how they were created; I examined the possibilities this world offers women, those it denies them, their limits, their good and bad luck, their evasions and their achievements. That was what I put into the second volume: *L'Expérience vécue.*'[36]

The first volume was well received: 22,000 copies were sold in the first week. The second volume also sold well, but it shocked people. De Beauvoir was accused of indecency, and received all manner of insult: 'Unsatisfied, frigid, priapic, nymphomaniac, lesbian, a hundred times aborted. I was everything, even an unmarried mother.'[37] The illustrious Mauriac wrote to one of the contributors to *Les Temps Modernes*: ' "Your employer's vagina has no secrets from me" ', which shows, she observes, 'that in private life he wasn't afraid of words'.[38]

The violence and level of the reactions left her perplexed. Among the Latin races, she recalls, Catholicism was known to encourage masculine tyranny verging on sadism. Italian men combined such tyranny with coarseness, their Spanish counterparts with arrogance, but the sort of meanness she had encountered seemed quintessentially French. She reasons that the French male felt threatened by female competition, and that as soon as his innate sense of superiority came to be challenged, he resorted to the vilification of women.

It is worth recalling, at this juncture, that even in 1949 women, and particularly married women, were very much second-class citizens in France. As Webster and Powell summarize their situation, married Frenchwomen lived under male tutelage. A woman was obliged to give up all her financial and legal rights on marriage under laws which treated her like a juvenile or a mental defective. Even with the introduction of a female suffrage in 1945, women were excluded from any part in national reconstruction despite the fact that many played a crucial, voluntary role in the Resistance. A general atmosphere of intolerance persuaded women like the author, Marguerite Yourcenar, who became the first woman member of the Académie Française in 1980, to settle in the United States and take out American citizenship.[39]

In view of this lack of recognition, and interest in, women's rights, it is hardly surprising that a two-volume work in defence of women's rights, particularly to a career and to independence, should occasion controversy, even among her friends and acquaintances. One of these latter, an unnamed academic, stopped reading her book and threw it across the room. Camus, she recalls,

in a few morose sentences accused me of making the French male look ridiculous. A Mediterranean man, cultivating Spanish pride, he would allow woman equality only if she kept to her own, and different, realm; also, he was of course, as George Orwell would have said, the more equal of the two. He had blithely admitted to us once that he disliked the idea of being sized up and judged by a woman: she was the object, *he* was the eye and the consciousness. He laughed about it, but it is true that he did not accept reciprocity.[40]

Her adversaries, she declares, created and maintained many misunderstandings about the book. Her views on maternity came in for particularly bitter attack. Many men disputed her right to discuss women, since she hadn't given birth. But neither had they, she retorts. It was alleged that she had refused to attach any value to the maternal instinct and to love, but she denies that this was the case: she had simply demanded that women should experience maternity and love truthfully and freely, 'whereas they often use them as excuses and take refuge in them, only to find themselves imprisoned in that refuge when those emotions have dried up in their hearts'.[41] She was accused of promoting sexual promiscuity, but she denies that she had done so. What she had advised, on this subject as on others, was that all decisions concerning sexual involvement should be made 'independently of institutions, conventions and motives of self-aggrandisement'.[42] Moreover, she claims, if the motivation for sex does not synchronize with sexual activity itself, 'then the only result can be lies, distortions and mutilations'.[43]

There were those who defended the document on Woman: she mentions by name Francis Jeanson, Nadeau and Mounier. She adds that it proved to be a very controversial work, bringing her floods of correspondence. But when all is said and done, she concludes, 'it is possibly the book that has brought me the greatest satisfaction of all those I have written. If I am asked what I think of it today, I have no hesitation in replying: "I'm all for it." '[44]

I propose to leave the last word on the biographical background to *The Second Sex* to Webster and Powell, who round off their commentary on this particular episode in French cultural history as follows:

... but de Beauvoir's revenge over narrow-minded intellectuals was crushing. *Le Deuxième Sexe* sold 22,000 copies in its first week of publication and became an international bestseller throughout the world. More than a million copies were sold in the United States alone. De Beauvoir established her independence from Sartre and was to reinforce the message even more dramatically in her autobiography, *Mémoires d'une jeune fille bien rangée*. The two books were treated like the Old and New Testament of women's liberation.[45]

10 The Philosophical Foundations of *The Second Sex*

Part of the argument of this book is that *The Second Sex* is a philosophical as well as a feminist work. The purpose of the present chapter is to document, with as much precision as possible, what that philosophical structure or content actually is. My approach shall be as follows: the preceding chapters have shown, I hope, that Simone de Beauvoir had already published a substantial amount of philosophy *before* she wrote and published *The Second Sex*. I shall therefore begin with a summary of what her philosophical thoughts to date have been. I shall then ask: Which of these philosophical thoughts which predate *The Second Sex* reappear in it, and what new, that is, hitherto unpublished, ideas does it contain? In this way I hope to establish, not merely that *The Second Sex* is a philosophical work, but, further, that it has an assignable place in the itinerary of de Beauvoir's philosophical thinking.

I

In *Pyrrhus and Cineas* de Beauvoir argues (1) that, fundamentally, a human being in a transcendence, that is, oriented towards things beyond itself; (2) that to appeal to the Infinite is to lose sight of the self; (3) that turning from God to Humanity will not solve the problem of furnishing moral guidance, since Humanity itself is never completed; (4) that human existence is a project, and as such paradoxical: one can always proceed beyond what one has already chosen for oneself, yet to go beyond an objective or end one has to aim at it as an end beyond which one cannot get; (5) finally, we don't exist for any purpose, including therefore death. Death will put an end to my efforts when, and only when, I am dead.

II

In *The Blood of Others* de Beauvoir argues that: (1) Each of us is responsible for everything and to every human being. (2) There are reasons for living, but they do not fall ready-made from heaven; rather we must locate them for ourselves. (3) While we haven't originally made the world, we contribute to reshaping it at every instant. There is no stepping outside of history. (4) Anything is better than fascism. (5) Freedom is the supreme good.

III

In *The Ethics of Ambiguity* de Beauvoir argues that there is a constant tension built into our being: a tension between success and failure, between being human and wanting to be superhuman, between negativity and positivity. The task facing each of us is to acknowledge and support this 'ambiguity' which is so characteristic of us.

We must, she continues, reject all moral absolutes. We must do so because absolute standards are for absolute beings, and humans are finite and fallible, never absolute. Neither should we accept moral standards from a God, since to do so would be to deny our own freedom. It follows that if we are not to deny our own freedom, we must acknowledge *ourselves* as the source of moral values.

We are free, she says, in the weak sense that we have 'spontaneity', and in the strong sense that we can *will* freedom. To convert spontaneity into true freedom, we must assume our projects positively.

Human unhappiness, says de Beauvoir, taking her cue from Descartes, comes from our first having been children. The *child's* situation is characterized by the fact that it finds itself cast into a world which it did nothing to help create, and which appears to it as an absolute to which it must submit. The world of black slaves and white women is comparable to that of children, for they too have no means of breaking the ceiling which is stretched over their heads. In the case of women, they have no option but to submit to the laws, the gods, the customs and the truths which men have created. The *difference* between the situation of children and that of women is that whereas the child's situation is imposed on it, the 'Western woman of today' chooses it, or at least consents to it.

There are two kinds, or levels, of existence available to human beings: those of perpetuating life, and surpassing it. If living is nothing more than the maintenance of life, 'then living is only not dying, and human existence is indistinguishable from an absurd vegetation'.[1]

The oppressed have only one option available to them: to revolt against their oppression. We are obliged to respect freedom 'only when it is intended for freedom, not when it strays and resigns itself. A freedom which is interested only in denying freedom must be denied.'[2]

Ambiguity is to be distinguished from *absurdity*. To claim that existence is absurd is to deny that it can ever be given a meaning, whereas to claim that it is ambiguous is to say that its meaning is never fixed. Absurdism and ethics are mutually exclusive, but an ambiguous world does not exclude ethics; on the contrary, ethics emerges in and for a world which will never be finalized.

IV

I shall now turn to *The Second Sex*, a work which is teeming with material drawn from social history, with cultural (as distinct from philosophical) anthropology, with literary criticism and passionate advocacy of women's liberation. But all of this is cast in a philosophical mould or framework. This philosophical framework is itself made up of three philosophical distinctions and a philosophical anthropology. They are as follows: (1) The distinction between the Subject and the Other. (2) The distinction between transcendence and immanence. (3) The distinction between actions and functions. (4) A philosophical anthropology which sees the human individual as a free, autonomous, historical being, one who is inserted into the world by means of a body but who is not, for all that, chained to a fixed and unalterable destiny. I shall now look at each of these sections of the philosophical foundation of *The Second Sex* in greater detail.

(1) The Subject and the Other

The distinction between the Subject and the Other as found in *The Second Sex* owes a certain amount, but by no means everything, to the meanings which Hegel and Sartre had already bestowed on these terms. To appreciate the way the distinction features in de Beauvoir, and the extent to which her use of it is indebted to Hegel and Sartre, I shall first of all itemize the meanings it has for these two philosophers, and particularly the meanings it has for Sartre. Then I shall document the meanings these terms are given in *The Second Sex*, and then I shall make some concluding comments.

My focus shall be on the concept of the Other as it functions in these philosophers, for it is here that the greatest diversity of meaning is to be found. But first a word about the concept of the Subject. As we encounter this concept in *The Second Sex*, the Subject is variously the self, consciousness, the Absolute, the essential, the sovereign, and a transcendence. Male human beings are assigned to this category, and it is to be contrasted with the category of the Other, to which female human beings are assigned. As I read it, de Beauvoir's argument will be that these categories are philosophical (or logical), but that assignation of human beings to either category is an historical undertaking which is not binding on later generations.

In Hegel, as de Beauvoir reads him, the Other is any subject or consciousness besides oneself; it is, furthermore, the inessential, the object, and all other consciousnesses, to which one is opposed.[3] The reasons for such hostility are explored by Sartre in his *Being and Nothingness*, to which I shall now turn.

For Sartre, the Other is all of the following:

– My fellow man.[4]
– Any other person.[5]
– Someone whose existence 'brings a factual limit to my freedom'.[6]
– Someone to whom I am an object, by whom I am perceived as an object.[7]
– Someone who makes an object of my situation, and thereby puts limits to it.[8]
– Someone whose freedom limits my freedom.
– Someone who makes me appear to myself in certain ways, thereby provoking certain affective and moral responses in me, such as shame and guilt.
– Someone who establishes me in a new kind of being which can support new qualifications.[9]
– Someone who *steals* the world from me.[10]
– Someone who, in turn, is an object for me, whom I identify as an object.[11]
– Someone who cannot be an object for me so long as I am an object for him.
– Someone whose existence as an independent subject or self furnishes proof of my existence as an independent subject or self.[12]
– A transcendence transcended, that is, someone who achieves his goals, and advances beyond these goals to further goals.

For de Beauvoir, the Other is, first of all, Hegel's other: 'Things become clear, on the contrary, if, following Hegel, we find in consciousness itself a fundamental hostility towards every other consciousness; the subject can be posed only in being opposed – he sets himself up as the essential, as opposed to the other, the inessential, the object.'[13] Following Hegel, but not slavishly so, the Other is variously associated by de Beauvoir with the inessential, the submissive,[14] the subordinate and the dependent.[15] To be the Other is to be doomed to immanence;[16] it is to be someone who is forever transcended by another ego,[17] and, finally, it is to have a limited liberty.[18]

Earlier I have said that de Beauvoir's concept of the Other owes something, but by no means everything, to her awareness of the meaning which this term had for Hegel and Sartre. I now want to emphasize that there is a considerable divergence between her concept and that of Sartre. Sartre's concept of the Other has epistemological and phenomenological emphases in which de Beauvoir has no interest. The Other also appears in Sartre's presentation as an enemy, a powerful foe, a threat, and a spectral presence. In de Beauvoir, on the other hand, the Other is associated with submissiveness, dependence, immanence, limitation and subordination. Thus while the language is the same, the meanings, associations and emphases are quite different.

(2)   Transcendence and Immanence

De Beauvoir contrasts transcendence with immanence, thereby marking a contrast or polarity which is intended as a *logical* contrast, and not, as some critics have supposed, a gender-based one. *Immanence* refers to a sphere or mode of existence characterized by passivity, submission to biological fate, and confinement or restriction to a narrow round of uncreative and repetitive chores. Thus defined, immanence is to be contrasted with *transcendence*, which refers to a sphere or mode of existence characterized by activity, by freedom from biological fate, by the freedom to burst out of the present and into the future, by a capacity to transform the world so that it accommodates itself to one's intentions. *Historically*, women have occupied the category of immanence (but this does not imply that they are doomed to immanence for eternity). The following passage concerning *nomadic woman* conveys the meaning of immanence quite fully:

> The woman who gave birth, therefore, did not know the pride of creation; she felt herself the plaything of obscure forces, and the painful ordeal of childbirth seemed a useless or even troublesome accident... The domestic labours that fell to her lot because they

were reconcilable with the cares of maternity imprisoned her in repetition and immanence; they were repeated from day to day in an identical form, which was perpetuated almost without change from century to century: they produced nothing new.[19]

Historically, according to de Beauvoir, nomadic man was a very different kind of creature, one which, as she describes him, illustrates equally effectively the concept of transcendence:

> [The nomadic male] furnished support for the group, not in the manner of worker bees by a simple vital process, through biological behaviour, but by means of acts that transcended his animal nature... He did not limit himself to bringing home the fish he caught in the sea: first he had to conquer the watery realm by means of the dugout canoe fashioned from a tree-trunk; to get at the riches of the world he annexed the world itself. In this activity he put his power to the test: he set up goals and opened up roads towards them; in brief, he found self-realization as an existent. To maintain, he created; he burst out of the present, he opened the future.[20]

(3)   Actions and Functions

The distinction between actions and functions is very closely related to that between transcendence and immanence, and is, indeed, pre-supposed by the latter distinction. *Functions* belong to, and define the realm of immanence; *actions* belong to, and define the realm of transcendence. We are given at least four ways of identifying functions. In the human context, functions are (1) simple, vital processes, that is, instinctual forms of behaviour; (2) labours which produce nothing new; (3) cares which confine one to the present; and (4) chores or tasks which are endlessly repeated. Actions, by contrast, are (1) the means whereby one sets up goals; (2) the means by which one annexes the world; (3) the means whereby one achieves self-realization; (4) the means by which one creates; and (5) the means whereby one lays the foundation for a new future. The distinction between functions and actions is to be understood, once again, as a logical or philosophical one; it marks off two dramatically different realms of behaviour, and ways of existing as a human being, from each other. The fact that women have, historically, been forced to perform functions does not entail that the category of function is a female category, so that women's liberation would necessitate a transcendence of the feminine.[21] Women's liberation is not a transcendence of the feminine; it is a transcendence of immanence, it is securing for women a freedom from immanence, from having endlessly to perform functions, from having to perform chores which confine one to the present.

(4) A Philosophical Anthropology

By philosophical anthropology is meant here an elaborated concept of human nature, a stated and defended view of the kind of being a human being is.[22] De Beauvoir's philosophical anthropology, thus understood, is to be found mainly in the very early sections of *The Second Sex*.[23] There are four, more or less interconnecting parts to her concept of human nature. They are as follows. (1) A human being is a subject who achieves liberty only by continuously reaching out towards additional liberties, towards an indefinitely open future. (2) Every human subject is a 'free and autonomous being',[24] one capable of self-originating actions without being dependent on other human beings for the realization of this capacity. (3) A human being is a historical reality, one not given but existing to be made; one best perceived not in terms of what it is, but in terms of its *possibilities*, in terms of what it is capable of becoming. There are many echoes here of Sartre's *Existentialism and Humanism*, but, interestingly, it is with Merleau-Ponty that de Beauvoir herself associates this idea:

> man is defined as a being who is not fixed, who makes himself what he is. As Merleau-Ponty very justly puts it, man is not a natural species: he is an historical idea. Woman is not a completed reality, but rather a becoming, and it is in her becoming that she should be compared with man: that is to say, her *possibilities* should be defined . . . when we have to do with a being whose nature is transcendent action, we can never close the books.[25]

(4) Each human being is the possessor of a body, which is both the means by which we negotiate the world and a brake on our projects. The original authors of this idea are said to be Heidegger, Sartre and Merleau-Ponty: 'Nevertheless it will be said that if the body is not a *thing*, it is a situation, as viewed in the perspective I am adopting – that of Heidegger, Sartre and Merleau-Ponty: it is the instrument of our grasp upon the world, a limiting factor for our projects.'[26] It has been held against de Beauvoir that she has a very negative attitude

towards the human body in general, and towards the female body in particular,[27] so it is worth exploring further what she has to say about the body *both* as our means of contact with the world, *and* by that very fact a limitation of our ability to negotiate with the world. De Beauvoir is careful to stress both sides of this paradoxical drama of the body. It is both liberating and constricting. Without it we could not be inserted into the world at all, yet because of it, because of a myriad of biological features and afflictions, our point of view on the world will always be affected.[28] Biological facts are a key to understanding woman; but they are insufficient as an account of what any woman can be, and *a fortiori*, they are insufficient for the purpose of setting up a hierarchy of the sexes.

Biologically speaking, woman is at a disadvantage to man. De Beauvoir spells out this disadvantage, as she sees it, in no uncertain terms:

> Woman is weaker than man, she has less muscular strength, fewer red blood corpuscles, less lung capacity, she runs more slowly, can lift less heavy weights, can compete with man in hardly any sport; she cannot stand up to him in a fight. To all this weakness must be added the instability, the lack of control, and the fragility already discussed: these are facts.[29]

Yet having drawn up this doleful list of 'weaknesses', de Beauvoir immediately proceeds to assure us that from the perspective of what she variously calls 'existentialist ethics' and 'the human perspective', they count for nothing. As she explains, once we adopt the perspective of existentialist ethics, interpreting the body on the basis of *existence*, then biology becomes 'an abstract science'. The reason it becomes an abstract science is that physiological facts depend for their meaning on the *context* in which they present themselves, and in these contexts their meaning depends on factors which are not biological at all. Thus in a social context in which physical strength has become very largely redundant, 'differences in strength are annulled'.[30]

Superficially, therefore, bodily weakness may be seen as a relational concept whereby women, on average, are not capable of matching men. But at a more profound level it is a concept grounded in the ends that humans set themselves, and the conflicts they then find themselves caught up in. In a context where there is no question of *physically* matching, or pitting humans against one another, and/or against the physical environment, the concept of physical weakness or frailty loses much of its interest.

CONCLUSION

In his Translator's Preface, H. M. Parshley ventures the opinion that 'Whatever the fate of existentialism as a philosophical and literary movement may be, the chief concepts used by Mlle Beauvoir in the present work and referred to above have general validity, and therefore they could be – and doubtless most of them have been – expressed more or less adequately in quite other terms.'[31] Here Parshley wants to say, both that *The Second Sex* has a basis in existentialism, and that a prior understanding of existentialism will not confer any particular advantage on the reader. It will not surprise anyone at this stage when I say that I should want to agree with the first half of Parshley's thesis, and reject the second. *The Second Sex* has a philosophical structure which can be identified, whose constituents are a number of philosophical distinctions and a philosophical anthropology, itself comprising several further philosophical distinctions such as that between History and Nature. Much, though by no means all, of this philosophical structure had been constructed in de Beauvoir's earlier writings of the 1940s; it reappears in *The Second Sex* with its meaning unaltered, but sometimes cloaked in a new language.

A good example of this continuity of meaning, but change of language, is provided by the distinction between immanence and transcendence. In her *The Ethics of Ambiguity* de Beauvoir speaks of two kinds of existence which are available to humans, which she describes as perpetuating life and surpassing it. If living is nothing more than the maintenance of life, she contends, then living is only not dying, and human existence is indistinguishable from an absurd vegetation. The awfulness of oppression, she goes on to advise, is that it divides the human world into two camps: those who enlighten mankind by showing it the future, and those who are condemned to mark time hopelessly in order merely to support the collectivity; 'their life is a pure repetition of mechanical gestures; their leisure is just about sufficient for them to regain their strength'.[32] In *The Second Sex* these same endlessly repeated mechanical gestures are called *functions*, and they are contrasted with *actions*. Those who are confined to the realm of functions (women) are said to be doomed to immanence, whereas in the earlier work they are said to perpetuate life and not to surpass it. So I would venture to say that *The Second Sex* has technical refinements of a linguistic kind which are absent from the earlier writings, but the ideas and distinctions remain, for the most part, the same.

The distinction between the Subject and the Other marks the clearest new departure in the philosophical thinking contained in *The Second Sex*. De Beauvoir had already done much of the groundwork for this distinction, particularly in *The Ethics of Ambiguity*, where she discusses at length the relationship between oppressor and oppressed, between children and adults, between blacks, white women and adult males, between colonist and native, between those who shape the future and those who merely mark time, between those who consent to a condition and those who have it imposed on them. Each of these distinctions or dichotomies, as the case may be, marks out a relationship of subordination or control, and this division, in turn, brings into play further cognate ideas such as the inessential, the submissive, the dependent, the incidental, and so on. Taking its *language* from various philosophical sources, but especially from Hegel, Sartre, Merleau-Ponty, Lévi-Strauss and Lévinas,[33] and its *meanings* both from these same authors and from her own earlier philosophical works, Simone de Beauvoir formally constructs the division into Subject and Other for the purpose of providing a secure philosophical foundation for the central thesis of *The Second Sex*. Thus the philosophy of *The Second Sex* is both her own creation, and rooted in the Western philosophical tradition. This philosophy must be studied to be understood; its insights cannot be made instantly available to the casual reader, no matter how accomplished at his work the translator happens to be.

11 *The Second Sex*: Woman as the Other

At an early stage in the Introduction to *The Second Sex* Simone de Beauvoir quotes, with approval, the following passage from Claude Lévi-Strauss's *Les Structures élémentaires de la parenté*: 'Passage from the state of Nature to the state of Culture is marked by man's ability to view biological relations as a series of contrasts; duality, alternation, opposition, and symmetry, whether under definite or vague forms, constitute not so much phenomena to be explained as fundamental and immediately given data of social reality.'[1] As de Beauvoir sees it there are two such dualities, or contrasts, to be noted in social reality as we know it. First, there is the duality of the *Subject* and the *Other*; second, there is the duality of *Man* and *Woman*. These pairs of opposites are not unrelated, moreover: Man always appears as the Subject, while Woman always appears as the Other.

The Other, as we first encounter this concept in *The Second Sex*, has three defining characteristics: it is a separate existence, it is hostile, and it is 'the inessential'. The major acknowledged influence here is Hegel:

> These phenomena would be incomprehensible if in fact human society were simply a *Mitsein* or fellowship based on solidarity and friendliness. Things become clear, on the contrary, if, following Hegel, we find in consciousness itself a fundamental hostility towards every other consciousness; the subject can be posed only in being opposed – he sets himself up as the essential, as opposed to the other, the inessential, the object.[2]

Throughout the history of Western thought from Aristotle to such contemporaries as Lévinas and Mauriac, woman, says de Beauvoir, has consistently been consigned to the category of the Other:[3] 'She is defined and differentiated with reference to man and not he with reference to her; she is the incidental, the inessential as opposed to the essential. He is the Subject, he is the Absolute – she is the Other.'[4]

It wasn't until the 18th century that some attempt was made to challenge this depreciation of woman: 'Diderot, among others, strove to show that woman is, like man, a human being. Later John Stuart Mill came fervently to her defence.'[5] But these philosophers, says de

114

Beauvoir, showed unusual impartiality. With the intensification of the Industrial Revolution the denigration of woman resumed with added ferocity: 'Even within the working class the men endeavoured to restrain women's liberation, because they began to see the women as dangerous competitors – the more so because they were accustomed to work for lower wages.'[6]

The situation of woman, says de Beauvoir, as she concludes the Introduction to Book I,[7] is that she,

a free and autonomous being like all human creatures, nevertheless finds herself living in a world where men compel her to assume the status of the Other. They propose to stabilize her as object and to doom her to immanence since her transcendence is to be over-shadowed and forever transcended by another ego (*conscience*) which is essential and sovereign.[8]

The drama of woman lies in this conflict between, on the one hand, the fundamental aspirations of every subject, always regarding itself as the essential, and, on the other, the compulsions of a situation in which she is the inessential. Having identified this drama, de Beauvoir says that she will address the following questions:

How can a human being in woman's situation attain fulfilment? What roads are open to her? Which are blocked? How can inde-pendence be recovered in a state of dependency? What circum-stances limit woman's liberty and how can they be overcome? These are the fundamental questions on which I would fain throw some light.[9]

BIOLOGY AND WOMAN

The Second Sex is divided into two volumes: Book I, entitled 'Facts and Myths', and Book II, called 'Woman's Life Today'. Book I is divided into three parts, called 'Destiny', 'History' and 'Myths'. Part 1, Book I is itself divided into three sections, called 'The Data of Biology', 'The Psychoanalytic Point of View' and 'The Point of View of Historical Materialism'.

The chapter on biology begins with a rehearsal of well-established biological facts and, by degrees, proceeds to more controversial and original material. De Beauvoir presents this material as follows: (a) Males and females, she stresses, are two types of individuals which are differentiated within a species for the purpose of reproduction. (b) They are defined primarily as male and female by the gametes which they produce – sperm and eggs respectively. (c) In the higher forms of life reproduction has a dual function: maintenance of the species and the creation of new individuals. (d) In mammals the division of the two vital components – maintenance of the species and creation of new individuals – is realized definitively in the separation of the sexes: 'It is in this group that the mother sustains the closest relations – among vertebrates – with her offspring, and the father shows less interest in them. The female organism is wholly adapted for and subservient to maternity, while sexual initiative is the prerogative of the male.'[10]

(e) 'The female is the victim of the species.'[11] De Beauvoir develops this crucial point as follows: 'During periods of the year, fixed in each species, her whole inner life is under the regulation of a sexual cycle (the oestrus cycle), of which the duration as well as the rhythmic sequence of events, varies from one species to another.'[12] She is the victim in the further sense that in sexual activity

> she is *taken*. Often the word applies literally, for whether by means of special organs or through superior strength, the male seizes her and holds her in place; he performs the copulatory movements; and, among insects, birds, and mammals, he penetrates her. In this penetration her inwardness is violated, she is like an enclosure that is broken into.[13]

(f) But the fundamental difference between male and female mammals lies in this: the sperm 'through which the life of the male is transcended in another, at the same instant becomes a stranger to him and separates from his body; so that the male recovers his individuality intact at the moment when he transcends it'.[14] The egg, on the other hand, begins to separate from the female body when, fully matured, it emerges from the follicle and falls into the oviduct; but if fertilized by a gamete from outside, it becomes attached again, through implantation, in the uterus. So, 'First violated, the female is then alienated – she becomes, in part, another than herself. She carries the foetus inside her abdomen until it reaches a stage of development that varies according to the species.'[15]

(g) In spite of an optimistic view having all too obvious social utility, *gestation*, says de Beauvoir, is a fatiguing task of no individual benefit to the woman but, on the contrary, demanding huge sacrifices of her. It is often associated in the first months with loss of appetite and vomiting, which are not observed in any female domesticated animal, and which signal 'the revolt of the organism against the invading species'.[16] De Beauvoir emphasizes in a footnote that she is making a purely *physiological* point at this juncture, adding 'It is evident that maternity can be advantageous psychologically for a woman, just as it can also be a disaster.'[17]

(h) In the end, says de Beauvoir, woman escapes the iron grasp of the species by way of the menopause, when she is

> now delivered from the servitude imposed by her female nature... And what is more, she is no longer the prey of overwhelming forces; she is herself, she and her body are one. It is sometimes said that women of a certain age constitute 'a third sex'; and, in truth, while they are not males, they are no longer females. Often, indeed, this release from female physiology is expressed in a health, a balance, a vigour that they lacked before.[18]

These biological considerations are an essential element in a woman's situation. 'But I deny', says de Beauvoir in a crucial, but often overlooked passage, 'that they establish for her a fixed and inevitable destiny. They are insufficient for setting up a hierarchy of the sexes; they fail to explain why woman is the Other; they do not condemn her to remain in this subordinate role for ever.'[19]

In a more philosophical vein de Beauvoir concludes the section on biology by arguing that woman should be understood on the basis of her *possibilities* rather than on the basis of her limitations. The philosophy here is heavily influenced by Merleau-Ponty's postwar defences of existentialism in *Les Temps Modernes*:

> It is only in a human perspective that we can compare the female and the male of the species. But man is defined as a being who is not fixed, who makes himself what he is. As Merleau-Ponty very justly puts it, man is not a natural species: he is a historical idea. Woman is not a completed reality, but rather a becoming, and it is in her becoming that she should be compared with man; that is to say, her *possibilities* should be defined. What gives rise to much of the debate is the tendency to reduce her to what she has been, to what she is today, in raising the question of her capabilities; for the fact is that capabilities are clearly manifested only when they have been realized – but the fact is also that when we have to do with a being whose nature is transcendent action, we can never close the books.[20]

PSYCHOANALYSIS AND WOMAN

What specifically interests de Beauvoir about psychoanalysis is its contribution to the study of woman. But a study of its contribution, she declares, soon reveals its gender bias: 'Freud never showed much concern with the destiny of woman; it is clear that he simply adapted his account from that of the destiny of man, with slight modifications.'[21] So far as the specifically *sexual* nature of a woman is concerned, Freud, says de Beauvoir, admits that woman's sexuality is as fully evolved as that of a man;

> but he hardly studies it in particular. He writes: 'The libido is constantly and regularly male in essence, whether it appears in man or woman.' He declines to regard the feminine libido as having its own original nature, and therefore it will necessarily seem to him like a complex deviation from the human libido in general.[22]

Thus having described the sexual development of the boy, who is mother-fixated (the Oedipus complex), and dreads mutilation at the hands of his father (the castration complex), Freud, says de Beauvoir, 'at first described the little girl's history in a completely corresponding fashion, later calling the feminine form of the process the Electra complex; but it is clear that he defined it less in itself than upon the basis of his masculine pattern'.[23]

De Beauvoir presents Freud's account of the Electra complex as follows:

> the little girl has at first a mother fixation, but the boy is at no time sexually attracted to the father. This fixation of the girl represents a survival of the oral phase. Then the child identifies herself with the father; but towards the age of five she discovers the anatomical difference between the sexes, and she reacts to the absence of the penis by acquiring a castration complex – she imagines that she has been mutilated and is pained at the thought. Having then to renounce her virile pretensions, she identifies herself with her mother and seeks to seduce the father. The castration complex and the Electra complex thus reinforce each other... The little girl entertains a feeling of rivalry and hostility towards her mother. Then the super-ego is built up also in her, and the incestuous tendencies are repressed; but her super-ego is not so strong, for the Electra complex is less sharply defined than the Oedipus because the first fixation was upon the mother, and since the father himself is

the object of the love that he condemns, his prohibitions are weaker than in the case of his son-rival. It can be seen that like her genital development the whole sexual drama is more complex for the girl than for her brothers.[24]

De Beauvoir addresses 'two essential objections' to the Freudian theory of female sexual development: (i) Freud assumes that woman feels that she is a mutilated man. But, retorts de Beauvoir, this feeling is not experienced at all in many cases, while the lack of male sexual attributes occasions, not so much regret as indifference, or even disgust. (ii) The concept of the Electra complex is still very vague 'because it is not supported by a basic description of the feminine libido'.[25] Specifically, if the sexual response evoked by fathers in daughters is supposed to be highly localized, then the theory in most cases is nonsense. If, on the other hand, it is admitted that the Electra complex has only a very diffuse emotional character, then the whole question of *emotion* is raised, 'and Freudianism does not help us in defining emotion as distinct from sexuality'.[26]

De Beauvoir concludes her critique of psychoanalysis as follows. The very language of psychoanalysis ('drives', 'tendencies', 'complexes', and so on) suggests that the drama of the individual unfolds within that individual. But a life is a relation to the world, and the individual defines himself by making his own choices in and through the world around him:

We must therefore turn toward the world to find answers for the questions we are concerned with. In particular psychoanalysis fails to explain why woman is *the Other*. For Freud himself admits that the prestige of the penis is explained by the sovereignty of the father, and, as we have seen, he confesses that he is ignorant regarding the origin of male supremacy.[27]

HISTORICAL MATERIALISM AND WOMAN

While psychoanalysis marked an advance over basic biology in the study of woman, historical materialism, says de Beauvoir, marks an advance over both. First, it recognizes that human beings are not merely members of the animal kingdom, and that therefore woman is not simply to be understood as a mammalian organism. Second, it refuses to see woman *exclusively* in terms of her sexual nature: 'Woman's awareness of herself is not defined exclusively by her sexuality: it reflects a situation that depends upon the economic organization of society, which in turn indicates what stage of technical evolution mankind has attained.'[28]   P ɤ ʋ

This economic and social context can either favour or burden the female members of the population. The burdens of maternity, for instance, assume widely varying importance according to the customs of the country: 'they are crushing if the woman is obliged to undergo frequent pregnancies and if she is compelled to nurse and raise the children without assistance; but if she procreates voluntarily and if society comes to her aid during pregnancy and is concerned with child welfare, the burdens of maternity are light and can be easily offset by suitable adjustments in working conditions'.[29]

As de Beauvoir sees it, this is the perspective from which Engels approaches the history of woman in *The Origin of the Family, Private Property and the State*. In this work, as she reads it, the status of woman is seen to be uniquely dependent on the social division of labour. Where there is common ownership of land, and the methods of agriculture are rudimentary, 'woman's strength was adequate for gardening... the two sexes constituted in a way two classes, and there was equality between these classes'.[30] This equality persists during the more active, hunting phase: 'While man hunts and fishes, woman remains in the home; but the tasks of domesticity include productive labour – making pottery, weaving, gardening – and in consequence woman plays a large part in economic life.'[31]

The major change in the status of woman comes about with the invention of sophisticated machinery for working land. Through the discovery of copper, tin, bronze, and iron, and with the appearance of the plough, agriculture enlarges its scope, and intensive labour is called for in clearing woodland and cultivating the fields. Then man has recourse to the labour of other men, whom he reduces to slavery. Private property appears: master of slaves and of the earth, man becomes the proprietor also of woman: 'This was "the great historical defeat of the feminine sex."'[32] It is to be explained, continues de Beauvoir's paraphrase, by the upsetting of the old division of labour which occurred in consequence of the invention of new tools. She then quotes Engels again: '"The same cause which had assured to woman the prime authority in the house – namely, her restriction to domestic duties – this same cause now assured the domination there of the man; for woman's housework henceforth sank into insignificance in comparison with man's productive labour – the latter was everything, the former a trifling auxiliary."'[33] Then maternal authority gave way to paternal authority, property being inherited from father to son and no longer from woman to her clan. 'Here we see the emergence of the patriarchal family founded upon private property.'[34]

According to Engels, she says, equality cannot be re-established until the two sexes enjoy equal rights in law; but this enfranchisement requires participation in general industry by the whole female sex: ' "Woman can be emancipated only when she can take part on a large social scale in production and is engaged in domestic work only to an insignificant degree. And this has become possible only in the big industry of modern times, which not only admits of female labour on a grand scale but even formally demands it." '[35]

Thus the fate of woman and of socialism are bound up together. Both are to be set free through the economic development consequent on the social upheaval brought about by machinery. The problem of woman is in this way reduced to the problem of her capacity for labour:

Puissant at the time when techniques were suited to her capabilities, dethroned when she was no longer in a position to exploit them, woman regains in the modern world her equality with man. It is the resistance of the ancient capitalistic paternalism that in most countries prevents the concrete realization of this equality; it will be realized on the day when this resistance is broken, as is the fact already in the Soviet Union, according to Soviet propaganda. And when the socialist society is established throughout the world, there will no longer be men and women, but only workers on a footing of equality.[36]

But de Beauvoir remains hugely unimpressed by the classical Marxist account of female history, and she launches attack after attack against it. Against Engels she points out that:

(1) The turning-point of all history is said to be the passage from the regime of community ownership to that of private property, but no explanation is provided as to how this could have come about.
(2) Neither is it clear that the institution of private property necessitated the enslavement of women.
(3) If human consciousness had not included the original category of the Other, and an original aspiration to dominate the Other, 'the invention of the bronze tool could not have caused the oppression of woman'.[37]

De Beauvoir further argues that the attempt by Engels, Bebel, and later Marxists to subsume the oppression of women under class oppression, and to reduce the antagonism of the sexes to class antagonism, is fundamentally misconceived. For one thing, she says, there is no biological basis for class division. In the second place, woman cannot simply be regarded as a worker; this is because her reproductive function is as important as her productive capacity, no less in the social economy as in individual life. Engels 'slighted' the issue of reproduction by promising the abolition of the family when socialism arrived. But, retorts de Beauvoir, 'We know how often and how radically Soviet Russia has had to change its policy on the family according to the varying relation between the immediate needs of production and those of re-production.'[38] What is more, she says, to abolish the family is not necessarily to emancipate woman: 'Such examples as Sparta and the Nazi regime prove that she can be none the less oppressed by the males, for all her direct attachment to the state.'[39]

Sex and reproduction, she contends, involve a passion, a fury, and even a revolt which defy all attempts at being policed. This is an intensely personal drama incapable of being reduced to the level of a *service*, or a task, and it resists all attempts at supervising it by way of a code of regulations. As de Beauvoir herself phrases it,

> It is impossible simply to equate gestation with a *task*, a piece of work, or with a *service*, such as military service. Woman's life is more seriously broken in upon by a demand for children than by regulation of the citizen's employment – no state has ever ventured to establish obligatory copulation. In the sexual act and in maternity not only time and strength but also essential values are involved for woman. Rationalist materialism tries in vain to disregard this dramatic aspect of sexuality; for it is impossible to bring the sexual instinct under a code of regulations.[40]

12 Existentialism and the Origins of Male Supremacy

Part II, Book 1 of *The Second Sex* is entitled 'History', and it is divided into the following five chapters: (1) 'The Nomads'; (2) 'Early Tillers of the Soil'; (3) 'Patriarchal Times and Classical Antiquity'; (4) 'Through the Middle Ages to Eighteenth-Century France'; (5) 'Since the French Revolution: the Job and the Vote'. Chapter 1 offers an account, from 'an existentialist'[1] perspective, of the early origins of woman's relegation to the category of the Other, and for this reason I shall concentrate on it.

De Beauvoir opens her explanation of male supremacy with the following challenging sentences:

> This has always been a man's world; and none of the reasons hitherto brought forward in explanation of this fact has seemed adequate. But we shall be able to understand how the hierarchy of the sexes was established by reviewing the data of prehistoric research and ethnography in the light of existentialist philosophy.[2]

She gives the following three reasons for male supremacy in prehistory: (1) Women had to carry the burden of reproduction, and this made them heavily dependent on men for protection and food. (2) Domestic labours are merely *functions*, not activities; such functions – traditionally and still largely carried out by women – imprisoned women in the sphere of repetition and immanence. (3) Early man's activity was often dangerous; it was concerned, not with giving life but with *risking* life, and it was this feature which gave it 'supreme dignity'.

De Beauvoir describes the *burden of reproduction* as follows:

> Pregnancy, childbirth and menstruation reduced their capacity for work and made them at times wholly dependent upon the men for protection and food. As there was obviously no birth control, and as nature failed to provide women with sterile periods like other mammalian females, closely spaced maternities must have absorbed most of their strength and their time, so that they were incapable of providing for the children they brought into the world.[3]

Besides the burden of reproduction there was also the burden of domesticity; what is more, these two burdens combined to imprison 'woman' in a realm of repetition and immanence. As de Beauvoir herself puts it,

> The domestic labours that fell to her lot because they were reconcilable with the cares of maternity imprisoned her in repetition and immanence; they were repeated from day to day in an identical form, which was perpetuated almost without change from century to century; they produced nothing new.[4]

It was very different for the adult male, says de Beauvoir; he furnished support for the group, not in the manner of worker bees by a simple vital process, through biological behaviour, in other words, but by means of acts that transcended his animal nature. She develops this idea of distinctively human, and, historically speaking, distinctively male, activity as follows:

> He did not limit himself to bringing home the fish he caught in the sea: first he had to conquer the watery realm by means of the dugout canoe fashioned from a tree-trunk; to get at the riches of the world he annexed the world itself; he set up goals and opened up roads towards them; in brief, he found self-realization as an existent. To maintain, he created; he burst out of the present, he opened the future. This is the reason why fishing and hunting expeditions had a sacred character. Their successes were celebrated with festivals and triumphs, and therein man gave recognition to his human estate.[5]

The final reason advanced from this existentialist perspective for male supremacy in prehistoric times was the *danger* inherent in the activities just described. De Beauvoir explains this point as follows:

> If blood were but a nourishing fluid, it would be valued no higher than milk; but the hunter was no butcher, for in the struggle against wild animals he ran grave risks. The warrior put his life in jeopardy to elevate the prestige of the horde, the clan to which he belonged. And in this he proved dramatically that life is not the supreme value for man, but on the contrary that it should be made to serve ends more important than itself... For it was not in giving life but in risking life that man is raised above the animal; that is why superiority has been accorded in humanity not to the sex that brings forth but to that which kills.[6]

Here, says de Beauvoir, we have the key to the whole mystery. On the biological level a species is maintained only by creating life anew, yet this creation succeeds only in repeating the same life in further individuals. Like the animal, the human male contributes to the perpetuation of the species by way of the reproductive process; but unlike the animal, the human male also 'remodels the face of the earth, he creates new instruments, he invents, he shapes the future'.[7] What is more, it is the peculiar misfortune of woman to be an active accomplice of man in those very activities which ensure his elevation: 'She joins the men in the festivals that celebrate the successes and the victories of the males.'[8]

Historically, then, the specific difference between men and women has been that the female has been the victim, or prey, of the species, destined to reproduce but not to create, to repeat but not to invent, to suffer and not to subdue. And it is because humanity values creation and invention far more than reproduction and suffering that men have been able to assume mastery.

Following a historical study of the status of woman from the nomads to the 1940s,[9] de Beauvoir draws the following series of conclusions. First, the whole of female history has been, literally, man-made. Essentially this means that women have done what men have either permitted or compelled them to do. She develops this point as follows. Just as in America there is no Negro problem but rather a white problem; just as anti-Semitism is not a Jewish problem, but rather a problem of the views and attitudes of non-Jews, so, too, the woman problem has always been a man's problem, that is, it arises out of men's treatment of women. Men have always held the lot of women in their hands,

> and they have determined what it should be, not according to her interest, but rather with regard to their own projects, their fears, and their needs. When they revered the Goddess Mother, it was because they feared Nature; when the bronze tool allowed them to face Nature boldly, they instituted the patriarchate.[10]

Second, women who have achieved pre-eminence, according to de Beauvoir, have done so at the expense of losing their sexual identity. More technically, the women who have accomplished works comparable to those of men are those who have been exalted by the power of social institutions above all sexual differentiation. For example, 'Queen Isabella, Queen Elizabeth, Catherine the Great were neither male nor female – they were sovereigns.'[11]

Third, notwithstanding their having achieved pre-eminence, most female legendary figures, says de Beauvoir, are oddities; they are 'adventuresses and originals', notable less for the importance of their actions than for the singularity of their fates: 'Thus if we compare Joan of Arc, Mme Roland, Flora Tristan, with Richelieu, Danton, Lenin, we see that their greatness is primarily subjective; they are exemplary figures rather than historical agents.'[12]

According to de Beauvoir the great man springs from the masses and is propelled onward by circumstances; the masses of women, on the other hand, are on the margin of history, and circumstances are an obstacle for each individual, not a springboard. In order to change the face of the world it is first of all necessary to be firmly anchored in it; unfortunately the women who are firmly rooted in society are precisely those who are subjugated by it. The consequence, says de Beauvoir, is that

> unless designated for action by divine authority... the ambitious woman and the heroine are strange monsters. It is only since women have begun to feel themselves at home on earth that we have seen a Rosa Luxemburg, a Mme Curie appear. They brilliantly demonstrate that it is not the inferiority of women that caused their historical insignificance: it is rather their historical insignificance that has doomed them to inferiority.[13]

Anti-feminists, says de Beauvoir, have obtained two contradictory conclusions from the study of female history: (1) Women have never created anything great. (2) The situation of woman has never prevented the emergence of great female leaders. De Beauvoir replies that the successes of a privileged few do not outweigh, or excuse, the systematic demotion of the mass of women; moreover, the very fact that such successes have been so rare constitutes decisive proof that circumstances are indeed heavily weighed against them. She then continues:

> As has been maintained by Christine de Pisan, Poulain de la Barre, Condorcet, John Stuart Mill, and Stendhal, in no domain has woman ever really had her chance. That is why a great many women today demand a new status; and once again their demand is not that they be exalted in their femininity; they wish to be accorded at last the abstract rights and concrete possibilities without the concurrence of which liberty is only a mockery.[14]

However, says de Beauvoir, while women demand a new status, they are far from having achieved it and the institutions of patriarchy are still largely intact. Not only have 'abstract rights' not been granted to women everywhere; abstract rights themselves have never sufficed to assure women a definite hold on the world. True equality, she adds, simply does not exist.

Inequality persists for the following three reasons: (i) The burdens of *marriage* weigh much more heavily upon woman than upon man. This is because the burden of maternity has still not been sufficiently alleviated, and because the care of children and the upkeep of the home is still undertaken almost exclusively by women. The result, says de Beauvoir, is that 'it is more difficult for woman than for man to reconcile her family life with her role as worker. Whenever society demands this effort, her life is much harder than her husband's.'[15]

(ii) The woman who seeks independence through work has to do so under far less favourable circumstances than her male competitors. To begin with, her wages in most jobs are lower than those of men. Second, because she is a newcomer in the world of males, she has fewer opportunities for success than they have. Men and women alike 'hate to be under the orders of a woman; they always show more confidence in a man'.[16] Because of this circumstance, de Beauvoir advises that in order to 'make it', a woman is well advised to secure masculine backing.

(iii) Society continues to be deeply ambivalent in its expectations of women. On the one hand, the work-world of factories, offices and educational establishments is opened up to her; but, on the other, marriage is still considered to be her appropriate destiny. These values are then transmitted from one generation to another. Parents, observes de Beauvoir,

> still bring up their daughters with a view to marriage rather than to furthering her personal development; she sees so many advantages in it that she herself wishes for it; the result is that she is often less deeply involved in her profession. In this way she dooms herself to remain in its lower levels, to be inferior; and the vicious circle is formed: this professional inferiority reinforces her desire to find a husband.[17]

De Beauvoir concludes that it is natural enough for many women workers and employees to perceive the right to work as merely an obligation from which marriage will deliver them. At the same time, because of the self-awareness which the working woman has achieved, and because she can, in addition, free herself from marriage by means of a job, 'a woman no longer accepts domestic subjection with docility. What she would hope is that the reconciliation of family life with a job should not require of her an exhausting, difficult performance.'[18]

13 The Married Woman

As de Beauvoir herself never opted for marriage it has, on occasion, been suggested that she was less than qualified to write about it.[1] But de Beauvoir and Sartre did seriously, if briefly, consider marriage in 1929,[2] and her reasons for rejecting Sartre's proposal of marriage in the early 1930s were never less than plausible.[3] Besides, she had witnessed her parents' marriage at close quarters, she had observed the behaviour of her married relations at Merignac, and whatever remaining illusions she had about the role of women evaporated when she went to the United States in 1947. As she put it to Deirdre Bair,

> because I had never felt discrimination among men in my life, I refused to believe that discrimination existed for other women. That view began to change, to crumble, when I was in New York and I saw how intelligent women were embarrassed or ignored when they tried to contribute to a conversation men were having. Really, American women had a very low status then. Men wanted them for sex and babies and to clean house and that's very much what they wanted for themselves, too.[4]

Finally, de Beauvoir consulted a wide variety of literature in preparing the material on marriage: not just some of the major novelists (Zola, Tolstoy, Mansfield, Woolf), as some critics would have us believe, but also St Paul, Rousseau, Proudhon, Comte, Freud, Hegel, Saint-Simon, Fourier, Montaigne, Havelock Ellis, a study of matrimonial choice among the Belgian middle class by Claire Leplae (*Les Fiançailles*), a study of female orgasm by a Dr Gremillon, Balzac's *Physiologie du Mariage*, Hélène Deutsch's *Psychology of Women*, Léon Blum's *Du Mariage*, Kierkegaard's *In Vino Veritas* and *Propos sur le mariage*, and the *Kinsey Report*.[5] Let us now see what she herself made of all these literary, anecdotal and scientific materials.

De Beauvoir's general view of marriage is unremittingly bleak: it is an institution the aim of which is to make the economic and sexual union of man and woman serve the interests of society, not to assure their mutual happiness; it is 'obscene in principle in so far as it transforms into rights and duties those mutual relations which should be founded on a spontaneous urge';[6] it confines the wife to the home, which (quoting Bachelard) is seen as ' "a kind of counter-universe or universe in opposition" ';[7] it dooms her to housework, and 'Few tasks are more like the torture of Sisyphus than housework, with its endless repetition';[8] by contrast, it provides the husband with an anchorage in immanence, but does not confine him therein; finally, it imposes the obligation of conjugal love, but this leads, in turn, to all kinds of repression and lies.

But the full version of her disquisition on marriage, and in particular on the fate of the married woman, is far bleaker still. I shall summarize it under the following headings: (a) Marriage as woman's destiny; (b) Sex and Marriage; (c) The Home; (d) Conflicts within Marriage; (e) Conclusion.

MARRIAGE AS WOMAN'S DESTINY

Marriage, she begins, is the destiny traditionally offered to women by society. Marriage, she continues, has always been a very different thing for each of the sexes, a fact which reflects the unequal status of men and women. The male world allows its members to find self-fulfilment as husband and as father; women, by contrast, are absorbed into families dominated by fathers and brothers, and woman 'has always been given in marriage by certain males to other males'.[9]

Marriage is enjoined upon woman for two reasons: (i) she must provide society with children; (ii) she is needed 'to satisfy a male's sexual needs and to take care of his household'.[10] Marriage is therefore a kind of trade-off: in carrying out the above duties the married woman renders a *service* to her spouse; in return

> he is supposed to give her presents, or a marriage settlement, and to support her. Through him as intermediary, society discharges its debt to the woman it turns over to him. The rights obtained by the wife in fulfilling her duties are represented in obligations that the male must assume.[11]

While marriage is a burden and a benefit for both partners, there is little symmetry in their respective positions. For young women it is the only means of integration into the community, and 'if they remain unwanted they are, socially viewed, so much wastage'.[12] The young woman is *given* in marriage, whereas young men *get* married, they *take* a wife. In their case 'They look to marriage for an enlargement, a confirmation of their existence, but not the mere right to exist... They have a perfect right to prefer celibate solitude; some marry late, or not at all.'[13]

In marrying, a woman acquires an appendant status; as de Beauvoir explains, she becomes an appendage of her husband:

> She takes his name; she belongs to his religion, his class, his circle; she joins his family, she becomes his 'half'. She follows wherever his work calls him and determines their place of residence; she breaks more or less decisively with her past, becoming attached to her husband's universe...[14]

Marriage, observes de Beauvoir, represents for the man a happy synthesis of immanence and transcendence: in his occupation and his political life he encounters change and progress, but when he returns home he restores his soul, he finds his anchorage once again in the world. The married woman, by contrast, is doomed to the continuation of the species and the care of the home, and 'she reaches out beyond herself towards the social group only through her husband as intermediary'.[15]

For a woman, says de Beauvoir, marriage is a more advantageous career than many others, but only because the remaining career options are so dismal. To her, her husband represents capital which she is entitled to exploit. In return for keeping house and rearing children she has the right to accept support 'and is even urged to do so by traditional morality. She is naturally tempted by this relatively easy way, the more so because occupations open to women are often disagreeable and poorly paid.'[16]

Because marriage represents such an attractive career option, because sexual freedom remains socially constrained for the unmarried woman, and because maternity, in particular, 'is respectable only for a married woman', a great many adolescent girls, says de Beauvoir, when asked about their plans for the future, reply that they want to get married. But young men do not have the same outlook on marriage; at any rate, they do not regard it as their fundamental project. There is, moreover, no major advantage for a young man in getting married, since board and lodgings are readily available, as indeed is sexual gratification. De Beauvoir concludes that 'the girl in search of a husband is not responding to a masculine demand, she is trying to create one'.[17]

While the young woman is more eager for marriage than the man, and while marriage is of greater benefit to her than to the man, none the less she frequently fears it. In general, this is because it entails greater sacrifices for her, and in particular because it implies a more drastic rupture with the past. Many adolescent girls, says de Beauvoir, 'feel anguish at the thought of leaving the paternal home; this anxiety increases as the event draws near. Here is the moment when many neuroses originate.'[18]

Since satisfying the sexual needs of her husband, notes de Beauvoir, is essentially a *service* which his wife provides, it is logical to ignore her personal preferences in the matter of a spouse. A service is provided for anyone willing and able to afford it; in the case of sex within marriage, it is provided for *whoever* is prepared to assume the role and responsibilities of husband. Therefore the prospective wife must be prepared to renounce loving a specific individual in order to assure herself the lifelong protection of an eligible male. In naive form, says de Beauvoir, 'this is the very doctrine enunciated by Hegel when he maintains that woman's relations as mother and wife are basically general and not individual. He maintains, therefore, that for her it is not a question of *this* husband but of *a husband* in general, of children in general.'[19]

SEX AND MARRIAGE

Because marriage is the means whereby woman perpetuates female functions in their universal form, there are two consequences attendant on what de Beauvoir calls her erotic fate: (i) she has no right to sex outside marriage; (ii) in her case, sexual pleasure and reproduction will not necessarily go hand in hand. In performing *his* reproductive tasks the husband is guaranteed at least some sexual gratification, but the same does not hold true for his wife, in whom the reproductive function is very often dissociated from erotic pleasure. What de Beauvoir seems to have in mind is that sexual and reproductive functions occur *simultaneously* in the male, thus guaranteeing him sexual pleasure in his performance of both functions; in the female, however, sexual union is *followed* by pregnancy, 'that heavy payment exacted from woman in exchange for a brief and uncertain pleasure'.[20] Because sex for a married woman has pregnancy as its consequence, she cannot experience any complete pleasure in the performance of sexual and reproductive functions.

The rise of 19th-century individualism gave birth to the concept of *conjugal love*, but de Beauvoir is no more impressed with the notion of a perfect concord of souls than she is with American attempts at marriage counselling. Sexual pleasure, she advises, is not merely a matter of technique, and 'traditional marriage', she continues, 'is far from creating the most favourable conditions for the awakening and developing of feminine eroticism'.[21]

The difficulties and dangers attendant on sexual initiation and sexual exploration can readily be overcome, says de Beauvoir, if both partners freely give themselves to each other, if they give and take on the basis of 'willing generosity'. However, marriage transforms into rights and duties 'those mutual relations which should be founded on a spontaneous urge; it gives an instrumental and therefore degrading character to the two bodies in dooming them to know each other in their general aspect *as* bodies, not as persons'.[22] Because of this suppression of passion under the dead weight of rights and duties, de Beauvoir, in unusually strong language, describes marriage as 'obscene'. She mitigates this criticism of marriage only by allowing that the early years of marriage can be rewarding, not least for the woman. In a passage more than reminiscent of her description of the early years of her parents' marriage, she writes:

> Marriage promotes a carefree abandon in woman by eliminating the notion of sin still commonly associated with the flesh; regular and frequent intercourse engenders a carnal intimacy that favours sexual maturation. For these reasons there are wives who find full gratification during the first years of marriage.[23]

Yet despite the possibility of ease and happiness during the early years of marriage, the woman runs a great risk when she undertakes to sleep all her life, and exclusively, 'with a man with whom she is sexually unacquainted, since her erotic fate depends essentially on her partner's personality'.[24]

A union based on convenience, argues de Beauvoir, has little prospect of inducing love, and it is a pure 'absurdity', she continues, to suppose that two married persons, bound by ties of practical, social and moral interest, will provide each other with sexual satisfaction for the duration of their married life. De Beauvoir then follows up this socio-sexual observation with a highly abstract, philosophical argument designed to demonstrate that a married couple cannot, logically, experience sexual love. Sexual love is essentially a sexual exchange between two consenting *individuals*. But a husband and a wife lose their individuality in becoming a *couple*; they become the same, and cannot therefore give themselves to each other as individuals. As a consequence, sexual union for the married couple becomes a kind of 'joint masturbation'.[25]

THE HOME

Having discussed the difficulty of achieving sexual love within marriage, de Beauvoir next turns her attention to the 'specifically feminine' domain of the home. Whereas the husband can and does find self-expression in projects outside the home, his wife, by contrast, is confined 'within the conjugal sphere'. As de Beauvoir sees it,

> it is for her to change that prison into a realm. Her attitude towards her home is dictated by the same dialectic that defines her situation in general: she takes by becoming prey, she finds freedom by giving it up: by renouncing the world she aims to conquer a world.[26]

For the married woman the home becomes the centre of the world; indeed it becomes the only world. It becomes, in de Beauvoir's words, 'refuge, retreat, grotto, womb, it gives shelter from outside dangers; it is this confused outer world that becomes unreal'.[27] The home becomes a fortress especially at night-time when, with the shutters closed, she creates her own light, one that illuminates her dwelling exclusively. In this way 'Reality is concentrated inside the house, while outer space seems to collapse.'[28]

The activity of *furnishing* her home has two major compensating benefits for the housewife: (i) it enables her, to some extent, to fill the void in her erotic life through contact with soft velvety materials; (ii) it enables her to express her individuality. The reason in the latter case is that 'she is the one who has chosen, made, hunted out furnishings and knick-knacks, who has arranged them in accordance with an aesthetic principle'.[29]

Housework, on the other hand, does not lend itself to self-realization. On the contrary, it is a kind of Sisyphean torture, a relentlessly negative exercise of eliminating disorder, a grinding routine providing no escape from immanence and little affirmation of individuality. De Beauvoir gives the following memorable description of housework:

> The maniac housekeeper wages her furious war against dirt, blaming life itself for the rubbish all living growth entails. When any living being enters her house, her eye gleams with a wicked light: 'Wipe your feet, don't tear the place apart, leave that alone!' She wishes those of her household would hardly breathe; everything means more thankless work for her. Severe, preoccupied, always on the watch, she loses *joie de vivre*, she becomes overprudent and

avaricious. She shuts out the sunlight, for along with that come insects, germs, and dust, and besides, the sun ruins silk hangings and fades upholstery; she scatters napthalene, which scents the air. She becomes bitter and disagreeable and hostile to all that lives; the end is sometimes murder.[30]

But housework has many sides to it, and some are more satisfying than others. Cooking, for instance, is more agreeable than cleaning, not least because it involves shopping and affords an opportunity for gossip. Shopping presents a constant challenge, from which the housewife can emerge triumphant:

> a solid cabbage, a ripe Camembert, are treasures that must be cleverly won from the unwilling storekeeper; the game is to get the best for the least money ... She is pleased with her passing triumph as she contemplates her well-filled larder.[31]

Cooking, too, has its rewards; it is 'revolution and creation; and the woman can find a special satisfaction in a successful cake or a flaky pastry, for not anyone can do it: one must have the gift'.[32] Unfortunately, as with other housework, repetition soon spoils these pleasures: 'The magic of the oven can hardly appeal to Mexican Indian women who spend half their lives preparing tortillas, identical from day to day, from century to century.'[33]

The worst thing about domestic labour is that its products lack permanence. No matter how good the newly-baked cake looks and smells, it must be eaten or else it will go mouldy. There is also the constant danger of mishaps, and the inevitable results of wear-and-tear:

> linen is scorched, the roast burns, chinaware gets broken; these are absolute disasters, for when things are destroyed, they are gone forever. Permanence and security cannot possibly be obtained through them.[34]

Some parts of housekeeping bring negligible psychological reward: since much of it is dedicated to keeping the domestic *status quo* 'the husband, coming into the house, may notice disorder or negligence, but it seems to him that order and neatness come of their own accord'.[35] For this reason, there is more to be gained from cooking and serving what one has cooked: 'The cook's moment of triumph arrives when she gets a successful dish on the table: husband and children receive it with warm approval, not only in words, but by consuming it gleefully.'[36] Yet even here success and approbation are at best contingent: 'she is upset if they are not hungry, to the point that one wonders whether the fried potatoes are for her husband or her husband for the fried potatoes'.[37]

CONFLICTS WITHIN MARRIAGE

Even where there is a negligible age difference between the spouses, there is an incongruity built permanently into marriage, says de Beauvoir. It arises from the fact that the young man and the young woman have been brought up quite differently: 'she comes out of a feminine world in which she has been taught feminine good deportment and a respect for feminine values, whereas he has been trained in the principles of male ethics'.[38] The inevitable consequence, thinks de Beauvoir, will be frequent minunderstandings and conflict, not least at the sexual level. He is the custodian of values, a demigod endowed with virile prestige, and a male with whom 'she must share an experience that is often shameful, grotesque, objectionable or upsetting, in any case incidental'.[39]

Marriage is tailor-made to bring out the worst in a man, particularly the tendency to dominate and tyrannize his dependants:

> All the resentments accumulated during his childhood and his later life...all this is purged from him at home as he lets loose his authority upon his wife. He enacts violence, power, unyielding resolution; he issues commands in tones of severity; he shouts and pounds the table: this farce is a daily reality for his wife.[40]

But he will never completely subdue his wife, who always retains her own view of things brought with her from childhood and religion, either making her incapable of understanding a husband more intelligent than she is, or, 'on the contrary, it may elevate her above dull masculine sobriety, as sometimes happens with the heroines of Stendhal, Ibsen, and Shaw. Sometimes out of hostility...she will assume complete moral authority.'[41]

In addition to all these difficulties and tribulations the married woman must become adept at the 'job' of 'holding on' to her husband, for what is at stake is extremely serious: material and moral security, a home of one's own, the dignity of wifehood, 'a more or less satisfactory substitute for love and happiness'. A married woman soon learns that her 'erotic attractiveness' quickly palls with familiarity, and, unfortunately, that there are other desirable women all about. She retaliates by attempting to make herself seductive, by endeavouring to please, and 'in so far as she can, she will make herself indispensable to his social success and to his work'.[42]

But above all a married woman has to master the art of 'managing' a husband, not denying him a sufficiency of freedom, and not permitting him an excess. What de Beauvoir calls 'this melancholy science' takes great skill; thus

> If she is too obliging, a wife finds her husband escaping her; whatever money and passion he devotes to other women is taken from her; and she runs the risk of having a mistress get enough power over him to make him divorce her or at least to take first place in her life. But if she denies him any adventure whatever, if she annoys him with her watchfulness, her scenes, her demands, she is likely to turn him against her.[43]

Speaking as if with the voice of experience, de Beauvoir reckons that the most advisable course of action is that of making concessions in a calculated fashion. The justification for all such subterfuges is that the married woman has been required to immerse herself *totally* in the marriage. As de Beauvoir reminds us, 'She has no gainful occupation, no legal capacities, no personal relations, even her name is hers no longer... If he leaves her, she can usually count on help neither from her own inner resources nor from without.'[44]

De Beauvoir allows that there are many marriages that go well, in the sense that husband and wife reach a compromise within, and about, the relationship. But, she quickly adds, there is one 'curse' which even successful marriages rarely escape, namely, *boredom*, described as 'A thousand evenings of vague small talk, blank silences, yawning over the newspaper, retiring at bedtime!'[45] The ideal, according to de Beauvoir, 'would be for entirely self-sufficient human beings to form unions one with another only in accordance with the untrammelled dictates of their mutual love'.[46] Marriage, however, makes such a union impossible. The reason is that love is an outgoing movement, an impulse towards another person; marriage, on the other hand, involves accepting a burden, it 'involves not love but repulsion'.[47] De Beauvoir concedes that on occasion a *true* collaboration exists between a married couple, and gives as an example the Joliot-Curies. 'But then', she quickly points out, 'the woman, as competent as the man, steps out of her role as wife; their relation is no longer of the conjugal type'.[48]

Certain escape routes from the tyranny of marriage are available to married women, observes de Beauvoir, but she concludes that all such escapes lead to ruination. So, some women turn into shrewish matrons, some become complaisant, masochistic victims and slaves of their families, some revert to childhood narcissism, seeking refuge in romantic dreams, pretences, invalidism, scenes, imaginary dramas, flowers and clothes. But, she cautions, 'This symbolic behaviour through which women seek escape can lead to mental decay, obsessions, even crimes. An odious husband may finally be murdered as the only way out of an intolerable situation.'[49]

CONCLUSION

Marriage, de Beauvoir concludes, is a disaster for the woman, not because it fails to guarantee her happiness – for happiness cannot be guaranteed – but because 'it mutilates her', because 'it dooms her to repetition and routine'.[50] A woman, then, enjoys a relatively brief happiness for about the first twenty years of her life, and then, following marriage, her life, in a sense, comes to an end: 'Mistress of a home, bound permanently to a man, a child in her arms, she stands with her life virtually finished for ever.'[51]

14 The Mother

In her personal life Simone de Beauvoir not only rejected marriage but children as well. Her rejection of motherhood and children was, if anything, the more emphatic of the two. She explained her position as follows to Deirdre Bair:

> He asked me if I would feel deprived in later years if I did not have a child. I didn't tell him everything I felt, I just said no. But I wrote in my memoirs about how children never held any attraction for me. Babies filled me with horror. The sight of a mother with a child sucking the life from her breast, or women changing soiled diapers – it all filled me with disgust. I had no desire to be drained, to be the slave to such a creature. No, all I said to Sartre was that I had no desire to recreate myself and since I had him I had no need of a miniature or substitute.[1]

De Beauvoir's discussion of motherhood in *The Second Sex* is far more wide-ranging, and at times more sympathetic to maternity and motherhood, than the above reply would lead us to expect. It is, in fact, extremely comprehensive, moving from the situation of women with unwanted pregnancies to the various stages of gestation, giving birth, infancy, raising boys, raising girls, and the whole impact of all these circumstances and developments on the marriage. I shall summarize the main features of her discussion under the following headings: (a) abortion; (b) pregnancy; (c) childbirth; (d) mother and child; (e) child-rearing.

ABORTION

While traditionally it was believed that in maternity woman fulfils her biological destiny, the reproductive function in human beings, says de Beauvoir, has increasingly come under voluntary control. Even in countries where the Catholic Church has an oppressive influence on legislation affecting women's reproduction, contraception is practised in a clandestine manner: 'either the man uses *coitus interruptus* or the woman rids her body of the sperm after intercourse'.[2]

But despite such precautions some women get 'caught', and this unwelcome development leads de Beauvoir immediately to a discussion of abortion. De Beauvoir's general position on abortion is as follows: (i) Repressive legislation against abortion is hypocritical, dangerous to women, and incapable of preventing women terminating their pregnancies. (ii) Men tend to take abortion lightly, and are also hypocritical about it: universally men condemn abortion, but individually they accept it as a conventional solution to a problem. (iii) Even when a woman does procure an abortion, 'even desires it, woman feels it as a sacrifice of her femininity: she is compelled to see in her sex a curse, a kind of infirmity, and a danger. Carrying this denial to one extreme, some women become homosexual after the trauma of an abortion.'[3]

Contraception and abortion would ensure that all pregnancies were *wanted* pregnancies, but as things stand, says de Beauvoir, 'woman's fecundity is decided in part voluntarily, in part by chance'.[4] De Beauvoir's most general, and pervasive point about pregnancy and motherhood is now introduced: how pregnancy and motherhood are experienced by a woman will depend on whether her attitude is one of revolt, resignation, satisfaction or enthusiasm. While her husband's attitude will be a contributing factor, pregnancy remains 'above all a drama that is acted out within the woman herself' for the simple, overwhelming reason that 'the foetus is a part of her body, and it is a parasite that feeds on it; she possesses it, and she is possessed by it'.[5]

PREGNANCY

In gestation, life appears as a kind of creation, while to all appearances at least the pregnant woman acquires a completeness of identity otherwise denied her. As de Beauvoir explains:

> The fusion sought in masculine arms... is realized by the mother when she feels her child heavy within her or when she clasps it to her swelling breasts. She is no longer an object subservient to a subject; she is no longer a subject afflicted with the anxiety that accompanies liberty, she is one with that equivocal reality: life. Her body is at last her own, since it exists for the child who belongs to her. Society recognises her right of possession and invests it, moreover, with a sacred character.[6]

However, adds de Beauvoir, this completeness which the pregnant woman *thinks* she has achieved is illusory. In the first place, *she* does not really make the baby; it makes itself within her. In the second place, her flesh engenders flesh only, not a free creation, for what she brings forth is just 'a gratuitous cellular growth, a brute fact of nature as contingent on circumstances as death and corresponding philosophically with it'.[7] In the third place, while a woman can have her own reasons for wanting a child, she cannot also have the child's reasons for existing; she cannot give to *this* independent person his own reasons for existing. In a sense, then, observes de Beauvoir, the mystery of the Incarnation repeats itself in each mother:

> every child born is a god who is made man: he cannot find self-realization as a being with consciousness and freedom unless he first comes into the world; the mother lends herself to this mystery, but she does not control it; it is beyond her power to influence what in the end will be the true nature of this being who is developing in her womb.[8]

As the pregnancy advances, the relationship between mother and foetus changes. The foetus is firmly settled in the mother's womb, the two organisms are mutually adapted, and between them biological exchanges take place that enable the woman to regain her balance. In particular, says de Beauvoir, she no longer feels herself *the prey of the species*; on the contrary, 'it is she who possesses the fruit of her body'. Moreover, as she recognizably becomes a mother-to-be, her infirmities begin to work to her advantage:

> As her weakness becomes more pronounced, it excuses everything. Many women find in their later pregnancy a marvellous peace: they feel justified. Previously they had always felt a desire to observe themselves, to scrutinize their bodies; but they had not dared to indulge this interest too freely, from a sense of social propriety. Now it is their right; everything they do for their own benefit they are also doing for the child.[9]

During this mellow period the pregnant woman's *raison d'être* resides literally in her body, a circumstance that gives her a rich sense of abundance. Moreover, while she is thus fulfilled the woman has the additional satisfaction of feeling she is *interesting*, something, says de Beauvoir, that has been her deepest wish since adolescence:

> as wife she suffered from her dependency with regard to man; now she is no longer in service as a sensual object, but she is the incarnation of the species, she represents the promise of life, of eternity. Her entourage respects her; her caprices become sacred,

and this, as we have seen, is what encourages her to have 'longings'.[10]

De Beauvoir is also quick to remark that this experience of fecundity, uniting the woman with the species, does not replicate itself in all women. For instance, women who see themselves 'essentially as erotic objects, who are in love with their own bodily beauty, are distressed to see themselves deformed, disfigured, incapable of arousing desire. Pregnancy seems to them no holiday, no enrichment at all, but rather a diminution of ego.'[11]

CHILDBIRTH

With the onset of childbirth, the union of foetus and mother is once more disturbed. Once again the woman does not possess herself, but is possessed, not on this occasion by the species, but by the infant about to be born. Moreover, while every transition is fraught with anxiety,

childbirth seems especially terrifying. When the woman approaches her term, all her childish terrors come to life again.[12]

It frequently happens, says de Beauvoir, that the woman is of two minds in her approach to the agonizing ordeal: 'she means to prove to herself and to her entourage – to her mother, to her husband – that she can weather the storm without assistance; but at the same time she bears a grudge against the world, against life, and in protest she remains passive'.[13] In fact, she says, the attitude of the woman towards her maternity will reflect her attitude towards the world in general, which may be stoical, resigned, demanding, domineering, rebellious, passive or terse. These 'psychological bents' will have an enormous bearing on the difficulty and duration of childbirth ('which is also affected, of course, by purely organic factors').

Because the duration of labour (the translation says 'delivery') can vary so much, it is unwise, says de Beauvoir, to generalize about it. Instead of offering a generalization about it, then, she describes the following *range* of attitudes and responses towards it:

For some women childbirth is a martyrdom. Some women, on the contrary, consider the ordeal a relatively easy one to bear. A few find sensual pleasure in it. There are some women who say that childbirth gives them a sense of creative power; they have really accomplished a voluntary and productive task. Many, at the other extreme, have felt themselves passive – suffering and tortured instruments.[14]

MOTHER AND CHILD

The first relations of the mother with the newborn infant are equally variable: from a feeling of complete emptiness on the one hand, to an amazed curiosity on the other. De Beauvoir describes this latter response as follows:

> It is strangely miraculous to see and hold a living being formed within oneself and issued forth from oneself... The newborn would not exist had it not been for her, and yet he leaves her. There is an astonished melancholy in seeing him outside, cut off from her.[15]

But overall, claims de Beauvoir, the main reaction is one of disappointment:

> The woman would like to feel the new being as surely hers as is her own hand; but everything he experiences is shut up inside him; he is opaque, impenetrable, apart; she does not even recognize him because she does not know him. She has experienced her pregnancy without him: she has no past in common with this little stranger.[16]

The bond between mother and child is, in many women, regained 'through nursing an intimate animal relationship with their infants, after the birth-separation has occurred: it is more tiring than pregnancy, but it enables the nursing mother to prolong the state of being on vacation in peace and plenitude, enjoyed in pregnancy'.[17] But the response in other women is not so tranquil, says de Beauvoir, because in general the new infant presents itself as a series of demands which simply have to be met. So in their case

> Even nursing affords... no pleasure; on the contrary, she is apprehensive of ruining her bosom; she resents feeling her nipples cracked, the glands painful; suckling the baby hurts; the infant seems to be sucking out her strength, her life, her happiness. It inflicts a harsh slavery upon her and it is no longer a part of her: it seems to be a tyrant; she feels hostile to this little stranger, this individual who menaces her flesh, her freedom, her whole ego.[18]

According to de Beauvoir many other factors help determine the new mother's attitude to her child, not least the attitudes adopted by her own mother in turn, and the response of her husband. Another unique feature of this relationship, she observes, is the fact that it is at first completely one-sided. The baby takes no part in it:

> its smiles, its babble, have no sense other than what the mother gives them; whether it seems charming and unique, or tiresome, commonplace, and hateful, depends upon her, not upon the baby. This is the reason why cold, unsatisfied, melancholy women who expect to find a companionship, a warmth, a stimulation in the infant which will draw them out of themselves are always deeply disappointed.[19]

Arising out of all these observations on pregnancy, childbirth and suckling, de Beauvoir concludes that 'no maternal "instinct" exists'.[20] In any event, she continues, the word scarcely has any application to the human species, since 'The mother's attitude depends on her total situation and her reaction to it. As we have just seen, this is highly variable.'[21]

At the same time de Beauvoir is quick to allow that 'Unless the circumstances are positively unfavourable the mother will find her life enriched by her child.'[22] She also distinguishes at this stage between women who are *motherly* and women who are *fecund*. The latter lose interest in their offspring at birth or at weaning, and desire only a new pregnancy; women in the former cohort, on the other hand, feel that it is the separation that provides them with the child: 'it is no longer an indistinguishable part of themselves but a portion of the outer world; it no longer vaguely haunts their bodies, but can be seen and touched'.[23]

CHILD-REARING

There remains a fatal flaw in our culture, claims de Beauvoir, namely, that the woman to whom the helpless infant is entrusted is almost always a discontented woman: 'sexually she is frigid or unsatisfied; socially she feels herself inferior to the man; she has no independent grasp on the world or on the future. She will seek to compensate for all these frustrations through her child.'[24] For this reason, says de Beauvoir, the mother's relationship with the child will always have two dimensions to it: it will *literally* be a relation with the child, but it will also be a *symbolic* relation with male-dominated society:

Just as when she coddled and tortured her dolls by turns, her behaviour is symbolic; but symbols become grim reality for her child. A mother who punishes her child is not beating the child alone; in a sense she is not beating it at all: she is taking her vengeance on a man, on the world, or on herself.[25]

What de Beauvoir calls 'this cruel aspect of maternity' takes, she says, diverse forms. Thus along with mothers

who are frankly sadistic, there are many who are especially capricious and domineering; now they treat the child as a doll, now as an obedient little slave; if vain, they show it off; if jealous, they hide it away. Frequently they expect too much in the way of gratitude for their care.[26]

Child-rearing places the married woman in a particularly awkward situation. She is caught between the demands and expectations of society on the one hand, not least those of her husband (who is 'irritated by the child's faults as he is by a spoiled dinner') and, on the other, by the brute fact that the existence for which she is made responsible is as mysterious as an animal, as turbulent as a natural force, but for all that is quintessentially human. As de Beauvoir observes,

One can neither train a child without talking, as one trains a dog, nor make him listen to reason through the use of adult words; and he takes advantage of this situation by answering words with animal-like sobs or tantrums and by opposing restraints with impertinent words.[27]

The woman who has time for what de Beauvoir calls 'her educational function' can enjoy it, much as she has already been at ease with her pregnancy. But when she is struggling with domestic chores, and, in particular, when she is occupied with her husband, then the child is 'merely harassing and bothersome'. In that event the main thing is to prevent him getting into trouble. But because the child's interests and those of his parents do not mesh, he has to be restrained and this results in friction. The consequences for both mother and child are not exactly enviable:

Forever burdened with him, his parents constantly impose sacrifices he does not understand: he is sacrificed to their peace and quiet and also to his own future. Quite naturally he rebels. He does not comprehend the explanations his mother tries to give him, for she cannot penetrate into his consciousness; his dreams, his fears, his obsessions, his desires, make up a world into which she cannot see: the mother can only control, blindly and from without, a being who finds her irrelevant rules an absurd imposition.[28]

This mutual incomprehension persists throughout childhood, according to de Beauvoir, though the situation varies according to the sex of the child. While it is more difficult to raise a boy, she claims, the mother normally adjusts better to it. There is more at stake as well:

A son will be a leader of men, a soldier, a creator; he will bend the world to his will, and his mother will share his immortal fame; he will give her the houses she has not constructed, the lands she has not explored, the books she has not read. Through him she will possess the world – but only on condition that she possesses her son.[29]

So far as her daughter is concerned, however, the mother does not hail a member 'of the superior caste'; rather she hails, and seeks, a double. Moreover, the tensions between mother and child become particularly aggravated in the relationship between mother and daughter. On the one hand, says de Beauvoir, she will want to give her daughter both the opportunities she herself had, as well as those she herself missed. But because of her ambivalent attitude towards her own sex, she will also seek to impose her own fate on her daughter as well. Real conflicts develop as the girl grows older. Her tendency to establish her independence from her mother will be received with ingratitude, leading to a two-sided jealousy: 'She is doubly jealous; of the world, which takes her daughter from her, and of her daughter, who in conquering part of the world robs her of it.'[30]

The most serious deterioration in the mother–child relationship is likely to occur in the case of an elder daughter, says de Beauvoir, as she introduces a further series of heavily autobiographical paragraphs on this topic. Not only will the elder daughter be loaded with disagreeable tasks, she will also be treated as an adult and burdened with all the cares of an adult: 'she, too, will have to learn that "life is no novel, no bed of roses"'. The precocious talents of an eleven- or twelve-year-old girl also show up painfully the cruel limitations of the woman's world: if the daughter falters in carrying out her domestic duties she is scolded and chastised, whereas if she carries them out to perfection – something which is well within her compass – she demonstrates the fact that housework is *something which any eleven-year-old can do*. The child's dexterity also has the effect of making her mother feel redundant: 'she is filled with anger and fear if she finds that the life of the family goes on perfectly well without her. She cannot bear to have her daughter become really her double, a substitute for herself.'[31]

As de Beauvoir sees it, the most distressing feature of the mother–daughter relationship is the tendency of the mother to see in her daughter's maturation the evidence of her own decline. She gives the following graphic account of this most poignant aspect of this relationship:

> each year brings her nearer her decline, but from year to year the young body develops and flourishes; it seems to the mother that she is robbed of this future which opens before her daughter. Here is the source of the irritation some women feel when their daughters first menstruate: they begrudge them their being henceforth real women. In contrast with the repetition and routine that are the lot of the older woman, this newcomer is offered possibilities that are still unlimited: it is these opportunities that the mother envies and hates; being unable to obtain them for herself, she often tries to decrease or abolish them.[32]

CONCLUSION

De Beauvoir begins to wind up her account of motherhood with an attack on 'two currently accepted preconceptions' about it. They are (i) that maternity is sufficient to give every woman as much as she needs out of life; (ii) the child is sure of being happy in its mother's arms. Against the first preconception she points out that there are a great many mothers who are unhappy, embittered and dissatisfied. Against the second preconception she observes that as parents themselves are deeply scarred by their own early home life, 'their approach to their own children is through complexes and frustrations; and this chain of misery lengthens indefinitely. In particular, maternal sado-masochism creates in the daughter guilt feelings that will be expressed in sado-masochistic behaviour towards her children, and so on without end.'[33]

Neither does de Beauvoir mince her words when it comes to describing the grotesque contradiction in society's attitude towards women and children: constantly put down, put upon, and excluded from the various spheres of public life, it is precisely this same female person who is entrusted with

> the most serious undertaking of all: the moulding of a human being. There are many women whom custom and tradition still deny the education, the culture, the responsibilities and activities that are the privilege of men, and in whose arms, nevertheless, babies are put without scruple, as earlier in life dolls were given to them to compensate for their inferiority to little boys. They are permitted to play with toys of flesh and blood.[34]

De Beauvoir concludes her section on 'The Mother' with a number of practical suggestions. They are as follows. (1) It would be in the interests of the child if its mother were 'a complete, unmutilated person, a woman finding in her work and in her relation to society a self-realization that she would not seek to attain tyrannically through her offspring'.[35] (2) It would be desirable for the child to be left to its parents 'infinitely less than at present, and for his studies and his diversions to be carried on among other children, under the direction of adults whose bonds with him would be impersonal and pure'.[36]

15 The Independent Woman

Book II of *The Second Sex* is called 'Woman's Life Today', and it is, basically, a 400-page proof of the opening sentence 'One is not born, but rather becomes, a woman'.[1] It is civilization as a whole, says de Beauvoir, which produces 'this creature, intermediate between male and eunuch, which is described as feminine'.[2] By means of a copious documentation of the events of childhood, adolescence, sexual initiation, marriage, motherhood, lesbianism, prostitution, middle age and old age, de Beauvoir ventures to demonstrate exactly how society has constructed this Other known as woman.

Part VII, Book II, is called 'Towards Liberation', and it contains two relatively short chapters, one on 'The Independent Woman', and a conclusion. The *independent woman* is the woman who is capable of finding in her profession a means of economic and social autonomy. Such women are worthy of study in their own right, says de Beauvoir, because (i) they are the subject of intense debate between feminists and anti-feminists, and (ii) 'The woman who is economically emancipated from man is not for all that in a moral, social, and psychological situation identical with that of man.'[3] The difficulty she faces is that of asserting herself *both* as female *and* as a self-determining, or sovereign, subject. And de Beauvoir continues:

> She refuses to confine herself to her role as female, because she will not escape mutilation; but it would also be a mutilation to repudiate her sex. Man is a human being with sexuality; woman is a complete individual, equal to the male, only if she too is a human being with sexuality. To renounce her femininity is to renounce a part of her humanity.[4]

In any event, it is precisely because the marks of femininity are socially shaped and imposed that they cannot be renounced or discarded at will. The woman who dresses 'to suit herself' will inescapably appear 'outlandish'. Inversely, the woman who conforms has to 'insinuate herself into a world that has doomed her to passivity'.[5] This immersion in passivity is all the more burdensome because women who are confined to the feminine sphere have grossly magnified its importance: 'they have made dressing and housekeeping difficult arts'.[6] Men's attire, by contrast, is basically functional; what

149

is more, 'nobody expects him to take care of himself; some kindly disposed or hired female relieves him of this bother'.[7]

In addition, says de Beauvoir, the woman wants to retain her womanliness for her own satisfaction; she can regard herself with approval to the extent that she is capable of combining the life she has made for herself with the destiny which her mother, her childhood games and her adolescent fantasies have prepared for her. She has, in addition, entertained narcissistic dreams and expectations:

> to the male's phallic pride she still opposes her cult of self; she wants to be seen, to be attractive... Obedient to the feminine tradition, she will wax her floors, and she will do her own cooking instead of going to eat at a restaurant as a man would do in her place. She wants to live at once like a man and like a woman, and in that way she multiplies her tasks and adds to her fatigue.[8]

The independent woman will encounter her most difficult problems, says de Beauvoir, in the field of sex. *To begin with*, she will suffer from an inferiority complex, born of the fact that 'she lacks leisure for such minute beauty care as that of the coquette whose sole aim in life is to be seductive; follow the specialist's advice as she may, she will never be more than an amateur in the domain of elegance'.[9] The second difficulty, says de Beauvoir, for the independent woman is that she will never be able completely to switch off mentally so as to be in a position to offer herself 'spontaneously' as 'prey', as 'a subtle quivering of the flesh'. The difference in her case is that she *knows* she is offering herself; she *knows* that she is a conscious agent, a subject.

Neither, says de Beauvoir, is an independent woman granted the same sexual latitude as her male counterpart. If she exercises her sexual freedom she risks compromising her reputation and her career. At the very least a burdensome hypocrisy is demanded of her. Thus the more solidly she establishes her reputation in society, the more ready people will be to close their eyes; 'but in provincial districts especially she is watched, as a rule, with narrow severity. Even under the most favourable circumstances – where fear of public opinion is negligible – her situation in this respect is not equivalent to man's. The differences depend both on traditional attitudes and on the special nature of feminine eroticism.'[10]

One possible avenue which is open to her is to engage in 'one-night stands'. But the risks for her are far greater than for a man. For one thing, the risk of venereal disease is greater 'because it is the man who is responsible for taking precautions against infection'; in the second place, no matter how careful she may be, a woman is continuously exposed to the danger of conception. Above all, there is the difference in physical strength between men and women, which always leaves women vulnerable to male violence.

A second alternative, says de Beauvoir, is to take a permanent lover, as a man often takes a mistress, and to support or help him financially. But this is possible only for women who are financially well off and who are capable of a crude dissociation of sex and sentiment. There is also a fraudulence in such a relationship to which women are more sensitive than men, 'for the paying client is also an instrument herself, since her partner uses her as a means of subsistence'.[11]

It is extremely difficult, says de Beauvoir, for a woman *both* to satisfy her erotic desires *and* at the same time maintain her dignity while obtaining satisfaction. If she takes the initiative the man may recoil, 'for most men are very jealous of their role'.[12] She concludes that a woman can only take when she makes herself prey, when she becomes 'a passive thing, a promise of submission'.[13] The result is that if and when she succeeds she will think that 'she has performed this magic conjuration intentionally, she will be subject again'.[14] On the other hand, she risks 'remaining in the status of unnecessary object if the male disdains her. That is why she is deeply humiliated when he rejects her advances.'[15] Rejection is far less costly for the man, since he has merely failed in an enterprise, nothing more. The woman, on the other hand, 'has consented to make herself flesh in her agitation, her waiting and her promises; she could win only in losing herself: she remains lost. One would have to be very blind or exceptionally clear-sighted to reconcile oneself to such a defeat.'[16]

A further fundamental difference, says de Beauvoir, between loving a woman and loving a man is the fact that a man must be loved for what he is, for what he has made of himself, whereas a woman can be loved for her possibilities, her shortcomings, her very lack of accomplishments. She develops this point as follows:

if she is not very intelligent, clear-sighted, or courageous, a man does not hold her responsible: she is the victim, he thinks, and often with reason, of her situation. He dreams of what she might have been, of what she perhaps will be: she can be credited with any possibilities, because she *is* nothing in particular. This vacancy is what makes the lover weary of her quickly; but it is the source of the mystery, the charm, that seduces him and makes him inclined to feel an easy affection in the first place.[17]

The unusual nature of her eroticism, coupled with the difficulties which beset a life of freedom 'urge' a woman towards monogamy. But it is far more difficult for a woman, says de Beauvoir, to reconcile marriage with a career than it is for a man. To begin with, it seems natural to a man that housework and child-rearing are the proper province of his wife. In addition, the independent woman *herself* takes the view that in marrying she has assumed duties from which her personal life does not exempt her. Thus she wants to be presentable, to be a good housekeeper, a devoted mother, such as wives traditionally have been. But this is a weight of obligation which can easily become unbearable. She assumes it, says de Beauvoir, through regard for her partner

> and out of fidelity to herself also, for she intends ... to be in no way unfaithful to her destiny as a woman ... Brought up in an atmosphere of respect for male superiority, she may still feel that it is for man to occupy the first place ...[18]

De Beauvoir concludes her mammoth study of woman by asking whether there is an original curse that condemns men and women 'to rend each other or whether the conflicts in which they are opposed merely mark a transitional moment in human history'.[19] She believes that no biological or physiological structures impose an eternal hostility upon male and female as such. For one thing, it is to the species that all individuals, male and female, are subordinated; for another, 'humanity is more than a mere species: it is an historical development; it is to be defined by the manner in which it deals with its natural, fixed characteristics, its *facticité*'.[20]

De Beauvoir identifies two stages in the battle between the sexes, one in which women are on the defensive, the other in which they are bent on transcendence. During the defensive stage woman seeks to destroy the inferior status which has been socially imposed on her. During this phase, therefore, 'She sets about mutilating, dominating man, she contradicts him, she denies his truth and his values.'[21] But in doing so she is merely defending herself. Both her immanence and her inferiority were socially imposed and must, therefore, be socially contested: 'The existent who is regarded as inessential cannot fail to demand the re-establishment of her sovereignty.'[22]

During the second, contemporary phase woman seeks to leave the realm of immanence for the realm of transcendence. The difficulty now is getting the male to accept her in this new role. He is, of course, very well pleased to remain the sovereign subject, the absolute superior, the essential being. He therefore resists her emergence as a subject. Inevitably, this triggers off a further aggressive response from the woman. What is more, 'It is no longer a question of a war between individuals each shut up in his or her sphere: a caste claiming its rights attacks and is resisted by the privileged caste. Here two transcendences are face to face; instead of displaying mutual recognition, each free being wishes to dominate the other.'[23]

The quarrel will continue, says de Beauvoir, as long as men and women fail to recognize each others as equals, 'that is to say, as long as femininity is perpetuated as such'.[24] The trouble is that both sexes, for different reasons, want to perpetuate femininity as such: 'Woman, who is being emancipated from it, wishes none the less to retain its privileges; and man, in that case, wants her to assume its limitations.'[25]

A world where men and women would be equal is easy to *visualize*, says de Beauvoir, who then proceeds to sketch it for us as follows:

> for that precisely is what the Soviet Union promised: women reared and trained exactly like men were to work under the same conditions and for the same wages. Erotic liberty was to be recognized by custom, but the sexual act was not to be considered a 'service' to be paid for; woman was to be *obliged* to provide herself with other ways of earning a living; marriage was to be based on a free agreement that the contracting parties could break at will; maternity was to be voluntary, which meant that contraception and abortion were to be authorised and that, on the other hand, all mothers and their children were to have exactly the same rights, in or out of marriage; pregnancy leaves were to be paid for by the state, which would assume charge of the children, signifying not that they would be *taken away* from the parents, but that they would not be *abandoned* to them.[26]

It is idle, she concedes, to suppose that *by themselves* economic and social changes will bring forth the new woman; but until such changes do occur 'the new woman cannot appear'.[27] Essentially what the little girl needs to experience around her is an androgynous and not a masculine world. This whole new androgynous experience is described as follows by de Beauvoir:

> If the little girl were brought up from the first with the same demands and rewards, the same severity and the same freedom, as her brothers, taking part in the same studies, the same games,

promised the same future, surrounded with women and men who seemed to her undoubted equals, the meaning of the castration complex and of the Oedipus complex would be profoundly modified. Assuming on the same basis as the father the material and moral responsibility of the couple, the mother would enjoy the same lasting prestige; the child would perceive around her an androgynous world and not a masculine world. Were she emotionally attracted to her father – which is not even sure – her love for him would be tinged with a will to emulation and not a feeling of powerlessness; she would not be oriented towards passivity. Authorised to test her powers in work and sports, competing actively with the boys, she would not find the absence of the penis – compensated by the promise of a child – enough to give rise to an inferiority complex; correlatively the boy would not have a superiority complex if it were not instilled into him and if he looked up to women with as much respect as to men. The little girl would not seek sterile compensation in narcissism and dreaming, she would not take her fate for granted; she would be interested in what she was *doing*, she would throw herself without reserve into undertakings.[28]

The result would not, insists de Beauvoir, be a boring, uniform world since, to begin with, there will always be certain differences between man and woman, not least on the bodily level:

her eroticism, and therefore her sexual world, have a special form of their own and therefore cannot fail to engender a sensuality, a sensitivity, of a special nature. This means that her relations to her own body, to that of the male, to the child, will never be identical with those the male bears to his own body, to that of the female, and to the child; those who make much of 'equality in difference' could not with good grace refuse to grant me the possible existence of differences in equality.[29]

16 Responses to *The Second Sex*: 1962–79

There is an extensive literature on *The Second Sex*, enough now to justify a book in its own right. I propose to devote three chapters of the present work to summarizing this secondary literature; then I shall offer a further, final chapter in which I propose to reply to the main criticisms of *The Second Sex* and defend de Beauvoir against these criticisms. The present chapter concentrates on the responses contained in the following works: M. Cranston, 'Simone de Beauvoir', in J. Cruickshank (ed.), *The Novelist as Philosopher* (1962); R. Cottrell, *Simone de Beauvoir* (1975); J. Leighton, *Simone de Beauvoir on Woman* (1975); and K. Bieber, *Simone de Beauvoir* (1979).

Maurice Cranston appears to be in two minds about *The Second Sex*. On the negative side, he feels that it has been 'in a way impoverished by the author's repudiation of motherhood and family life'.[1] He is not unwilling to see it as 'a brilliant and belligerent book';[2] but 'precisely because it goes on and on about women being like men, and thus fails to explore the *uniqueness* of woman, it is something of a disappointment as a study of its subject'.[3] Cranston is not even sure she is particularly well qualified to write such a book; as he puts it himself, 'Unmarried, and uninterested in motherhood, living, in fact, to all intents and purposes just like a man, Simone de Beauvoir is not ideally qualified by experience to write the kind of book she hoped to write.'[4] At the same time he is prepared to acknowledge that, 'read as a corrective to the old-fashioned patriarchal ethos which still prevails in Latin societies, *Le Deuxième Sexe* must at least be acknowledged as a forceful and opportune polemic'.[5]

On the fully positive side, Cranston acknowledges it as 'another long book, fortified by a great wealth of psychological, sociological and other empirical material'.[6] But its central argument, he observes, is a simple one: once again in de Beauvoir's writing, freedom is posited as the supreme ideal, 'and the author claims that in past and present societies women as a sex have been and still are being denied freedom'.[7]

155

The past, as de Beauvoir represents it, belongs to the male sex,

but she wants the future to be shared equally between the sexes. Equality would not worsen the position of men; on the contrary, it would 'free men from those shameless acts of cruelty to which women have hitherto had to resort to defend themselves in a man's world'. Women are at best educated for submission; the spirit of revolt is crushed in them. Simone de Beauvoir believes that they should be educated just as boys are and, as she puts it, 'educated for liberty'.[8]

In sum, *The Second Sex* is a forceful and timely polemic against old-fashioned patriarchal value systems, written by a woman who was not ideally qualified to write such a book.

Robert Cottrell, likewise, is divided in his opinions about *The Second Sex*, but he supplies a much fuller discussion of it than Cranston. His most interesting point about it has to do with the role he assigns to it in relation to de Beauvoir's later writings. *The Second Sex*, he advises, should be seen as a long preamble to the four volumes of the autobiography which she would later write. In other words, 'while analyzing the situation of women in general, Beauvoir was preparing the way for a study of a particular woman – herself'.[9]

Cottrell goes on to describe *The Second Sex* as

a mammoth edifice that rests on two slender postulates: first, that man, conceiving of himself as the essential being, the subject, has made woman into the inessential being, the object, the Other; second, that there is no such thing as feminine nature and that all notions of femininity are therefore artificial.[10]

Both postulates, he declares, are enunciated in the Introduction, 'and are derived from concepts elaborated by Sartre in *L'Être et le Néant*, a book to which Beauvoir frequently refers as if to a sacred text whose validity and authority no right thinking person could question'.[11]

The second postulate – that there is no feminine nature – is derived, he says, from one of the most fundamental of existentialist principles, namely, that there is no human nature:

If there is no archetypal human nature, there obviously can be no feminine or masculine nature. As Beauvoir expresses it in one of the most telling aphorisms in *Le Deuxième Sexe*: 'One is not born a woman; rather one becomes a woman.'[12]

De Beauvoir's position on woman's biological make-up and its implications is given both a strong, and a somewhat weaker statement, he argues. Strongly, she argues that a woman's situation is naturally determined in part by the biological factors associated with menstruation and childbearing, and that 'She can only become human by transcending, which usually means reacting against, these factors.'[13] The logic of her argument, says Cottrell, leads her to affirm that humanity is not an animal species, and that a woman becomes human to the extent that she reacts against her nature, 'the word nature here meaning those biological factors that help determine her situation'.[14] But de Beauvoir also adopts a less extreme view to the effect that if one 'assumes' rather than 'accepts' one's situation, then one transcends it. Cottrell comments that

> The nicety of this distinction – a crucial one in her ethics because the former term implies choice, the latter, submission – may escape many women. However, it permits Beauvoir to assert, quite correctly, that she has never opposed maternity and homemaking as long as they are 'assumed', although she declares that 'at the present time it is almost impossible to assume maternity in complete freedom'.[15]

In his less sympathetic remarks Cottrell says that 'Beauvoir's views on the couple, on fidelity, on the second sex, and old age are at times too personally oriented to be completely valid. Too often she looks in her mirror and thinks she sees humanity.'[16] On the other hand, he allows, 'it must also be said that in defending her freedom and her right to "contingent love affairs" she was demanding for women privileges which, she felt, had been reserved for men'.[17]

The book, he continues, 'no doubt fails to come to grips with maternity and family life. She no doubt advocates a kind of "virile independence" that is better suited to a woman who is unmarried, childless, exceptionally intelligent, violently ambitious, and relatively well-off (in short, like Beauvoir) than to the majority of women'.[18] A more serious criticism from Cottrell is that 'the existentialist suppositions on which the study rests are debatable, and that the book's philosophical bases are too heavily reliant on the works of Sartre'.[19] He notes that de Beauvoir herself said, in 1963, that were she to rewrite the book, she would give far greater importance to economic factors, 'and far less to philosophical speculation about the nature of consciousness. More specifically, she says that she would base the notion of the Other, together with the Manicheism it entails, not on an idealistic, *a priori* struggle pitting each consciousness against every other consciousness, but on the economic reality of supply and demand.'[20]

But Cottrell concludes his analysis on the following positive note:

> Despite all the criticisms that have been levelled at *Le Deuxième Sexe*, the fact remains that it is the most important, the most forceful vindication of women's rights to have appeared in the twentieth century. In this book more than in any of her others, Beauvoir has realized her wish to leave a mark on the world.[21]

Jean Leighton devotes Chapter 1 of her book *Simone de Beauvoir on Woman* to a study of *The Second Sex*, and the remaining chapters to a study of the novels and the manner in which they exemplify the central tenets of *The Second Sex*. She concludes that 'The somber thesis of *The Second Sex* that it is a malediction to be a woman finds substantial support in the novels inasmuch as the feminine characters are preponderantly unhappy, divided and neurotic creatures.'[22] It is this 'pessimistic element of woman's malediction and inferiority to man' that dominates the work as far as Leighton is concerned, leading her to accuse de Beauvoir of an attenuated misogyny.[23]

Leighton identifies two main apparent contradictions in de Beauvoir's writing. One is the oscillation from extreme pessimism to extreme optimism. Thus on the one hand de Beauvoir's view of human beings

> is a dark one indeed. People are frightful to one another – mothers to their children, men to women, husbands to wives and vice versa. The great majority seem bent on domination, vengeance and a will to power, and are consumed with dissatisfaction and resentment. Loyalty and fidelity are in short supply. The negative emotions dominate this book, and the final note, after it has been granted that some admirable women exist or that in principle generous human feelings are possible, is that such cases are rare, almost miraculous exceptions.[24]

But, on the other hand, there is an opposing current of uplift, what Leighton calls a

> naive optimism which rhapsodizes about unshackled human love, sexual passion and especially man's creative achievement... The main theme itself is the apotheosis of optimism since it really denies all cultural and biological determinism. The existentialist doctrine

of absolute freedom is no doubt reflected here. If the cultural situation alone is entirely responsible for woman's immanence, dependence, and inferiority, then to change it would mean deliverance. How it is to be changed is slighted, but the utopian hope clashes with the predominating pessimistic one.[25]

The second major difficulty with *The Second Sex*, as Leighton sees it, is that the standards by which women are judged are essentially masculine standards. This, inevitably, leads de Beauvoir to paint a very unflattering portrait of her own sex.[26] Undoubtedly, Leighton concedes,

she always stoutly attributes all the hypochondriacal wailing, the stupidity, laziness, self-pity, narcissism, ineffectual flopping around the house, preying like vampires on men, and the general paltriness of spirit to woman's 'situation'. But this cannot explain the curious fact that in a book ardently *for* woman and her liberation and happiness the author does not appear to admire women very much, at least in their present 'enslaved' condition.[27]

Another problem raised by the apotheosis of masculine values is that it is accompanied by 'an impassioned indictment of the injustice, cruelty and egotism of the male in his historical and present treatment of half of the human race'.[28] But that serves merely to raise the question: 'are these masculine values so splendid after all? Why should women therefore necessarily want to emulate them?'[29]

The 'current feminist movement' writes Leighton in a Postscript, refuses to concur in the adulation of masculine virtues. On the contrary, it exalts femininity 'and the gentle, maternal, sensitive traits that are encouraged in women. It holds, sensibly, that these qualities should be encouraged in everyone.'[30] Simone de Beauvoir's 'misogyny' disturbs her, she says, 'because twenty centuries of misogyny is enough... Feminist critics should not add fuel to the ancient, irrational and unjust claims of male chauvinists about women's inferiority.'[31]

Finally, Konrad Bieber's *Simone de Beauvoir* gives *The Second Sex* a very sympathetic hearing. Basically, Bieber sees de Beauvoir's work as a relentless homage to the truth about woman's subjugation by man, and he wonders why the book should ever have been the subject of controversy. As he says,

What is amazing is not the relatively mild passion Beauvoir displays in proffering her accusations against male supremacy. It is the

curious fact that, at its appearance, this essay should have stirred
critics to rare extremes of passion and partisanship. Loath to grant
her even partial accuracy in her presentation, most critics at that
time harped on minor details.[32]

Bieber shows no such aggression in his presentation of *The Second
Sex*, repeatedly extolling its philosophical, sociological and political
merits. On the political side he makes the point that 'by explaining
historically, biologically, psychologically, sociologically, and philosophically what woman's condition has been through the ages, she
has eventually equipped the combative champions of women's rights
in our day with the weapons to be used in the continued fight for
equality and justice, as it turned out not only for women but for all
human beings treated unfairly'.[33] The book itself he describes as 'an
honest attempt by a thinker of high integrity at recording why women
had to struggle so long and hard to gain even the limited recognition
of their place in society that has been achieved to date'.[34] Bieber
expresses open disagreement with de Beauvoir on one point only,
namely, her claim that there is no maternal instinct. He thinks this
claim 'excessive', but doesn't labour the point. He concludes his
remarkably courteous treatment of *The Second Sex* with the following
hymn of praise:

> *The Second Sex* stands as a solid achievement in its earnest treat-
> ment of one of the major problems of all times... Here is the finest
> contribution to the effective freeing of woman. Now the road to
> even more progress is open, thanks to her pioneering effort, her
> measured advocacy of reason and good sense. *The Second Sex*
> remains one of her best books, the least likely to become obsolete,
> despite the rapid pace of scientific discovery and the immense
> amount of publications on the question of women.[35]

17 Responses to *The Second Sex*: 1981–85

In this chapter I shall look at the responses to *The Second Sex* which are contained in the following works: A. Whitmarsh, *Simone de Beauvoir and the Limits of Commitment* (1981); J. B. Elshtain, *Public Man, Private Woman* (1981); C. McMillan, *Women, Reason and Nature* (1982); T. Keefe, *Simone de Beauvoir: A Study of her Writings* (1983); G. Lloyd, *The Man of Reason* (1984); and, finally, M. Evans, *Simone de Beauvoir, A Feminist Mandarin* (1985). While several of these contributions belong to the heavyweight philosophical division, I shall give special attention to McMillan's critique, which is both highly sophisticated and extremely conservative,[1] a not unexpected combination, perhaps, from an author who is heavily influenced by the neo-Wittgensteinian school of philosophy.[2]

Anne Whitmarsh examines *The Second Sex* in Chapter 6 of her book *Simone de Beauvoir and the Limits of Commitment*. Both *The Second Sex* and the later work *Old Age* are, she writes, *par excellence* essays in demystification for a social purpose: 'In these works Simone de Beauvoir attempts to expose the myths and prejudices surrounding two categories of persons, women and old people.'[3] The methodology, says Whitmarsh, is the same in each case: it is that of presenting with meticulous care the evidence accumulated from immensely detailed research. Moreover, 'by describing the reality in this way, she hoped to improve the situation'.[4] Her mission, says Whitmarsh, was all the more pressing 'because she was involved by her own experience of being a woman and of growing old in a society that treats these two groups unjustly or with indifference'.[5]

According to Whitmarsh, existentialism supplies the ethical basis of *The Second Sex*, a claim which she then explains as follows:

Just as Simone de Beauvoir refuses to accept the idea of human nature, so she insists that there is no such thing as feminine nature: 'One is not born, but rather becomes, a woman.' Individuals are

161

born human beings, not women or men, and they all have the same right to freedom and the same duty to use it.[6]

Whitmarsh sees de Beauvoir as extremely hostile both to marriage and to motherhood, 'two interrelated conditions that are particularly responsible for limiting women's potential'.[7] The institution of marriage receives from de Beauvoir 'unqualified condemnation'.[8] Maternity, for its part, is dismissed as repetition, as perpetuation of the species, and as stagnation. In fact, ventures Whitmarsh,

> her existentialist argument appears to be a rationalisation of a deeply felt disgust (the equivalent of Sartre's *nausée*) at the thought of pregnancy, the foetus, childbirth. She describes the female body as 'an obscure, alien thing,' and the foetus as a 'quivering jelly which is elaborated in the womb' which itself evokes an image of 'the soft viscosity of carrion.' Even if a woman deeply desires to have a child, her body revolts against the process. This disgust, shared with Sartre, of the flesh and of biological functions, could have its origins in the puritanical attitudes fostered by their upbringing.[9]

In her concluding remarks on *The Second Sex*, Whitmarsh observes that de Beauvoir herself later rejected its existentialist foundation for a more Marxist one.[10] And there are, she continues, other criticisms which can be made of it. One of these is the use of a tedious amount of material to demonstrate a reasonably obvious thesis. Moreover, her sources are predominantly literary rather than scientific. They paint 'a very black picture of the condition of women – too black, it might be said ... Are there *no* happy and fulfilled women in this world?'[11] In her effort to prove her point, says Whitmarsh, 'she seems to blame some women for succumbing so easily, claiming that although their situation is partly imposed on them from outside it is also partly of their own making. Seen in this existentialist light, it is their right to lead full, free and autonomous lives, but it is also their duty to do so.'[12]

Yet for all that *The Second Sex* remains 'a remarkable book for the time at which it was written'.[13] De Beauvoir, says Whitmarsh,

> was one of the first in France to challenge the Freudian explanation of the psychology and behaviour of women and to see the import-ance right through history of social role-conditioning in the exploita-tion of women and the way they are persuaded of their own

inferiority. Because of her conviction that most of the differences between the sexes were created by society, she understood that behaviour patterns would not necessarily be altered by laws but only by a completely new approach, like bringing up boys and girls in exactly the same way. Her originality in so many aspects of this whole question – take for example her passionate defence of children's rights – explains the initial reaction to a book that has now become a classic of feminist literature.[14]

In a footnote to an analysis of Shulamith Firestone's *The Dialectic of Sex*, Jean Bethke Elshtain reminds her readers that Firestone traces her intellectual origins to Simone de Beauvoir's *The Second Sex*, and that de Beauvoir, in turn, had praised Firestone's book. This reciprocation Elshtain considers most unfortunate, in view of Firestone's 'celebration of terrible forms of male-dominated scientism and technological authoritarianism'.[15] Elshtain announces in the same footnote that she will discuss what to her are the most salient features of de Beauvoir's book in Chapter 6; she adds that *The Second Sex* 'defies easy categorization', explaining that 'Much of de Beauvoir's discussion, for an American woman, seemed strained when it first appeared in translation in 1953, particularly the sections on sexuality.'[16]

At first glance, says Elshtain in Chapter 6, her project and that of de Beauvoir are identical, namely, to have it come about that the modern 'woman-in-society' alters her inherited and, 'in some ways, restricting or damaging views of herself; both of us want change in a direction that would transform her world for the better'.[17] But de Beauvoir, she quickly adds, never quite mastered the distinction between political inquiry *for* women and abstract theorizing *about* women, a failure which was in no small measure due to her appropriation of 'Sartrean categories which have no meaning in ordinary discourse, terms that are unavailable to social participants themselves'.[18]

De Beauvoir takes as her starting-point, not the self-understanding of female subjects, but the Sartrean distinction between immanence and transcendence. Immanence in de Beauvoir is 'a variant of Sartre's Being-in-itself';[19] with Sartre, 'she identifies woman with nature, the practico-inert, the sphere of immanence. This world of everyday life is first treated as an abstraction and then condemned as a morass, a bog, non-civilization.'[20] immanence is contrasted with transcendence, and this, says Elshtain, is Sartre's Being-for-itself in a different linguistic guise. Elshtain objects to this ontology on three grounds: (a) it is pathologically dependent on Sartre's ontology; (b) it is not derived from women's self-understanding; (c) it leads de Beauvoir to contradict herself: 'Although de Beauvoir declares women free and autonomous a priori ... she consigns them to a region declared to be one of determination, totally lacking in autonomy.'[21]

The denigration of women in de Beauvoir is not just inspired by a Sartrean ontology, it is guided by Sartre's own put-downs of women as a class. Thus, following Sartre's reference to woman's 'unfortunate anatomy', de Beauvoir hurries to depict the female body as a body that ' "seems wanting in significance by itself" '.[22] Elshtain comments that 'This narcissistic male view, reminiscent of the Greek misogynists who saw women as misbegotten men and not fully human, is repeated by de Beauvoir as a serious piece of wisdom rather than probed as the male's ' "advertisement for myself" '.[23]

The only hope for women on this narcissistic Sartrean view is to 'shuck off their female identities'; de Beauvoir declares civilization to be male and men its essential parts; 'women, the flip side of the coin, lie outside civilization and are inessential'.[24] These terms of analysis place women in an impossible situation: either they can speak 'the language of Immanence, in which case they remain outside civilization babbling, as it were, from the bog, or they can begin to speak in the voice of civilization which is a *male* voice, framed by, for, and about males'.[25] In short, women have a grotesque choice between remaining primitive inhabitants of the swamp, or becoming men.

Carol McMillan devotes Chapter 6 of her book *Women, Reason and Nature* to a sustained critique of radical feminism, and in particular to a critique of the contributions to radical feminism made by Shulamith Firestone and Simone de Beauvoir. What is striking about Firestone's argument in *The Dialectic of Sex*, observes McMillan, is the view, standing in marked contrast to the orthodox feminist position, that 'the *biological* facts of womanhood form the axis around which the whole feminist debate must ultimately revolve'.[26] Biology, on this view, is central because in pregnancy women are unable to pursue their interests as singlemindedly as before because of 'the discomfort they experience. With the birth of children they are confined to the home, they inevitably lack the power and control over their lives that are necessary if they are to resist economic dependence on men and the supposedly inevitable oppression that goes with it.'[27] It follows logically that, as Firestone herself puts it, ' "The heart of woman's oppression is her child-bearing and child-rearing role." '[28]

Firestone, says McMillan,

is, in fact, following Simone de Beauvoir here and developing a thought that is central to Beauvoir's account of the relation of woman to her biology... The idea of biology as a mighty tyrant against whom woman is continually struggling recurs with persistence throughout Beauvoir's book; every physical phenomenon she discusses is seen to vindicate the thesis of her basic schema.[29]

As McMillan sees it, then, it follows from de Beauvoir's account of such experiences as pregnancy and the enslavement to the species which it imposes that 'woman's struggle is against nature and not against convention if her true individuality is to be manifested in being liberated from the bonds of biology'.[30]

A central assumption of all such radical feminism, says McMillan, is that the notion of *oppression* can play an intelligible role in any discussion of a woman's procreative role. The kinds of use that commonly give the term 'oppression' its sense occur in situations in which power or force is cruelly and despotically exerted by someone or by a group of people over others. Hence to talk of oppression intelligibly 'we need two forces: one enslaving and the other enslaved. We need human subjects who are involved in a drama in which one group of agents is enslaved or rendered passive by another. In other words, the notions of agency and action must be applicable to both parties if the notion of oppression is to be appropriate.'[31] But given that these are the logical conditions for the correct application of the terms 'oppression' and 'oppressive', it is difficult to see, says McMillan, how it can be argued that a woman's *biology* oppresses her:

> Beauvoir, for instance, talks of woman as being 'in the iron grip of the species'... and argues that her body 'is something other than herself', that her 'individuality is the prey of outside forces'... Yet unless one is prepared to assume some kind of Cartesian dualism here, it is hard to see why there should be, and how there can be, this supposed conflict between body and mind, between biology and the individual. Such an assertion is all the more curious when Beauvoir herself claims to be following Merleau-Ponty and Sartre – two philosophers both strenuously opposed to any form of Cartesian dualism – by stating that 'woman, like man, *is* her body'.[32]

A woman cannot, then, be oppressed by her body since that presupposes a distinction between a woman and her body, a Cartesian-like dualism, where none exists. Moreover, even if such a dualism could be philosophically sustained, there is yet a further difficulty with the view proposed by de Beauvoir. This is the idea that the individuality of woman is oppressed and made passive by something we would not normally think of as being autonomous and active, namely, mere given, natural biological facts. McMillan develops this point as follows:

> Beauvoir makes it look as though woman were struggling with an active force by making precisely what Hannah Arendt observed to be an unfounded assumption in feminist argument: she invents a fictional 'subject', the human species – in Sartre's terms, a 'demiurge' – to give her argument the plausibility it so desperately needs. And without this fiction, the argument has, of course, to fall flat. Other feminists, like Firestone, do not use this fiction, but only because they fail to see that without it their arguments have no starting-point.[33]

McMillan agrees that feminists might still argue that even if it does not make sense to talk of biology as an *oppressive* fact in the lives of women, nevertheless biology does constrain them, and they could, and should, be freed from such constraint. She quotes at length here from Rudolph Schaffer's *Mothering*, focussing on such statements as

> There is... no reason why the mothering role should not be filled as competently by males as by females... technological progress, in this respect as in so many others, can free mankind from biological constraints and make possible new patterns of social living. Technology has perfected milk formulas and the feeding bottle so that anyone, of either sex, can satisfy a baby's hunger... Thus all the original reasons for confining childcare to women are disappearing: *mother* need not be a woman.[34]

As McMillan sees it, Schaffer's aim of liberating women from motherhood has, as its logical foundation, a certain view of the relationship between freedom, action, morality and human nature. On this view, to be free is to have technological control over natural circumstances. Furthermore, where such control has been achieved it becomes morally correct to use it, since any enlargement of the realm of freedom is a good thing. Finally, it is precisely in those activities for which there is no parallel in the animal world that human distinctiveness comes to manifest itself. McMillan will now argue that this whole line of thought, whose intellectual antecedents she traces back to *The Second Sex*, is profoundly mistaken.

De Beauvoir, she says, 'happily endorses the view that men are infinitely more human than women precisely because they have transcended nature'.[35] Because the notion of the transcendence of nature is made central to this concept of human distinctiveness, 'it becomes imperative, feminists argue, to see that women can become authentic agents only by transcending, so to speak, their reproductive functions'.[36] Reproductive control thus becomes the litmus test of women's liberation, and of the extent of their assimilation into the human family. Moreover, as contraception and abortion are the means whereby reproductive control is achieved, these forms of birth control should be promoted. De Beauvoir supports abortion on precisely such grounds, says McMillan, that is, on the grounds that it facilitates the transcendence of nature and, therefore, the expression by women of their human distinctiveness: 'She asserts that through abortion and contraception female human society rises above animal life and shows that it is "never abandoned wholly to nature".'[37] McMillan allows that de Beauvoir describes abortion as one of the cruellest experiences a woman will ever have, but she holds that de Beauvoir is driven into this contradictory position because she hangs her whole discussion of the humanity of woman on the degree of control woman has over her reproductive functions. 'And so', says McMillan, 'Rousseau's contention ... that women should accept their constraints, and that society should be structured in such a way that it helps rather than hinders them in doing this, would, according to Beauvoir's account, be tantamount to the assertion that mankind should never have striven to rise beyond the animal kingdom.'[38]

De Beauvoir's argument is based on, and flawed by, an imbalanced concept of agency, says McMillan. What transforms behaviour into agency, she contends, depends neither on the degree of control the agent's actions have over nature, nor on the fact that a particular action bears absolutely no resemblance to anything that an animal has ever done, 'but on the fact that it is committed against a background of thoughts and intentions ... Hence someone may still be an agent and capable of action even if his or her life is characterized by powerlessness to effect productive change or to gain control over events. An outstanding example of this is afforded by the patience with which a person can suffer affliction (cf. *The Book of Job*).'[39]

Everything hinges, then, on whether the behaviour or experience can be subsumed under the aspect of intentionality. In this context, the contrast between two women in labour, one of whom accepts an anaesthetic, the other of whom doesn't, turns out to be the very opposite to what one has been led to expect by the radical feminist camp. On this feminist view, the first woman raises herself beyond a merely animal level through the technological control exercised over her pains, while the second woman fails precisely because she submits to the forces of nature. But according to McMillan 'this actually contradicts what we would normally say in the situations in question'.[40] The reason is that the woman who readily accepts an anaesthetic 'by that very act relinquishes her capacity for action and reduces herself to a passive thing'.[41] We cannot, precisely *because* we are embodied, blot out physical sensations without also blotting out consciousness of, and perhaps control over, the events we are experiencing. 'In short', she concludes, 'loss of control and consciousness is not just a possible side-effect of pain relief; it is inevitable. Hence the incoherence of Beauvoir's claim that anaesthetization of birth necessarily makes a woman an active agent, even where the sense of agency is limited to control over natural events.'[42]

Terry Keefe devotes the whole of Chapter 5 of his book *Simone de Beauvoir: A Study of her Writings* to an examination of *The Second Sex*. For the most part his study provides a summary (16 pp.) of her book, but this summary is full of passing critical comments, and is followed by a sequence of detailed criticisms as well as by a number of favourable remarks. Overall he finds much to admire, and much also to criticize in *The Second Sex*, a reaction which is not untypical of his response to her other writings.

On the positive side, Keefe finds that the chapters on sexual initiation and lesbianism 'offer an extremely thoughtful examination of female sexuality that is much wider than the titles suggest'.[43] On the other hand, he considers the chapter on marriage 'a great disappointment'. He regards it as methodologically weak and uneven, despite its containing 'truly brilliant sequences on housework and cooking in particular'.[44] But, he contends, de Beauvoir's attack on the institution of marriage carries no weight. In the end the chapter amounts to no more than 'a description of the very worst forms that marriage *can* take'.[45] Even de Beauvoir herself admits, he says, that she is attacking *traditional* marriage, whereas modern marriage is becoming ' "une union librement consentie par deux individualités autonomes" '. Her remarks on passionate love, he continues, and on love itself 'suggest that her general grasp of what is common or even possible in marriage is exceedingly poor'.[46] She seems confused, he argues, on the whole question of the relationship between individuals and social institutions: there need not be any paradox in marriage having *both* an erotic *and* a social function. Keefe's final criticism of the chapter on marriage is that it makes little sense, in the context of de Beauvoir's existentialist philosophy, to lay the blame for marriage failure on the institution of marriage rather than on those individuals who contract into it. All in all, he concludes, 'Perhaps the most charitable point to make is that her view on marriage has to be seen in conjunction with her beliefs that work is the key to women's liberation, and that the having of children is the "meaning" or "goal" of the institution itself.'[47]

De Beauvoir's account of motherhood is 'even less satisfactory', says Keefe. The liberal views expressed in the section on abortion would be endorsed by most feminists, 'but shed little light on motherhood as such'. So far as pregnancy is concerned, 'she is concerned to structure her remarks around the trite point that different women react in different ways according to the circumstances'.[48] Perhaps, he adds, 'these "facts" are intended to provide some kind of justification for her controversial claim that the "maternal instinct" does not exist... but such an assertion obviously requires a much more systematic and detailed defence than it finds here'.[49] De Beauvoir's study of the mother–child relationship in terms of the child's Otherness is, says Keefe, 'badly lacking in plausibility, and her affirmation that maternal devotion is only rarely authentic seems singularly arbitrary'.[50]

De Beauvoir's central thesis, according to Keefe, is that womanhood or femininity is a cultural rather than a natural construct. This is not simply the plausible, but lightweight, argument that the *idea* of femininity is a cultural construct, for what idea isn't? 'She must, therefore, be taken to mean that women themselves are as they are now because of the kind of culture or civilisation to which they belong, rather than by virtue of the natural differences between themselves and men.'[51] But as Keefe sees it, de Beauvoir never argues convincingly for her central, structuring thesis. She wants to argue for the negative thesis that biological or genetic factors do not causally determine female nature, but she fails strikingly to make a case for the alternative thesis that *culture* carries out the function assigned in other theories to biology. In fact, Keefe argues, de Beauvoir cannot *coherently* argue that culture is determining, since existentialism repudiates *all* determinism in human behaviour.

Genevieve Lloyd identifies the philosophical origins of *The Second Sex* in the very opening sentence of her commentary on it: 'De Beauvoir's idea of woman as other', she says, 'is articulated in terms drawn from the Sartrean struggle for dominance between looker and looked-at.'[52] At the same time, she observes, de Beauvoir introduces two variations to the meaning that Sartre assigns to this distinction: (a) only one sex, the male sex, is in the privileged role of looker; (b) the female sex connives in its role of looked-at: 'Women are engaged in the struggle, but they are somehow not serious antagonists. Unlike the original master–slave struggle from which it all derives, the outcome here is not really a "subjugation". Women have themselves submitted to constitute a permanent Other.'[53]

There is, Lloyd allows, a positive side to de Beauvoir's use of the original Hegelian framework as mediated by Sartre. Hegel did not regard women as lacking the status of spiritual subjects, though he did see them as closer to Nature than men. Yet woman does share in the more advanced stages of spirit, albeit vicariously, through her relations to man. But, advises Lloyd, 'For de Beauvoir, as for Sartre, the conditions of selfhood are, in contrast, quite uncompromising. Nothing short of actual engagements in "projects" and "exploits" will do. In the lack of that, human subjects are forced back into mere immanence.'[54] Unfortunately, de Beauvoir's account of female biology makes it difficult to see how women can accomplish to the full the repudiation of the Hegelian nether world of immanence. The reason is that de Beauvoir presents the female body, and the uniquely female bodily functions, as an intrinsic *obstacle* to transcendence, making women a '"prey of the species"'. At this point, comments Lloyd,

> the notion of woman as other may well seem to have overreached itself... Why should a woman's direct experience of her own body be an experience of lack of transcendence, of immersion in life?... Here it may well seem that de Beauvoir has appropriated, along with the Sartrean idea of transcendence, his notorious treatment of the female body as the epitome of immanence.[55]

One reason women experience their own bodies as immersed in life, rather than transcending it, is that this is the way they have been socialized into perceiving their bodies; and Lloyd is prepared to concede to de Beauvoir that 'there is certainly something correct about the suggestion that women experience their own bodies in ways that reflect the conditioning effects of a male objectifying look'.[56] But she thinks there is more to de Beauvoir's depiction of women as doomed to immanence than the pervasiveness of sexist cultural conditioning, or the fact that 'woman's primary responsibility for child care or domestic labour sets limits to her involvement in "projects" and "exploits" '.[57] There seem to be *conceptual* reasons as well, in particular the idea, emanating from Hegel and Sartre, that transcendence is a transcendence of life, and therefore *of* the feminine. On this view, the female of the species is more closely tied to life than the male. The female is absorbed in living, bound to her body like an animal, whereas the male investigates and establishes the *reasons* for living, calling the very matter of living into question. It follows that transcendence is essentially a *masculine* activity, and that to be capable of transcendence women must cease to be female. In Lloyd's words, it is 'as if they can achieve transcendence only at the expense of alienation from their bodily being'.[58]

It is, concludes Lloyd, not just outrageous and repugnant that women should be expected to struggle with their own bodies in order to achieve transcendence, something which is never required of men. What this elevation of male activity also signifies, more ominously, is that the core concepts of the existentialist odyssey are *male concepts* through and through. If transcendence is possible only for men, and cannot be achieved by women without repudiating their own bodies, then 'the ideal of transcendence is, in a more fundamental way than de Beauvoir allows, a male ideal... it feeds on the exclusion of the feminine. This is what makes the ideal of a feminine attainment of transcendence paradoxical.'[59]

Mary Evans devotes Chapter 3 of her book *Simone de Beauvoir, A Feminist Mandarin* to a discussion of *The Second Sex*, but de Beauvoir's feminist classic also features in the challenging Introduction to Evans's book. There she advises her readers of her intention to argue that there is little to suggest 'that the novels were written by a feminist or even by a woman. One might discern, in de Beauvoir's fiction, that the author is French, a socialist, and a philosopher, but there is little to identify the author as a feminist.'[60] Indeed, she continues, were it not for the fact that de Beauvoir had written *The Second Sex*

> it is not inconceivable that she would never have been identified with feminism at all. It is true that she may well have given her support to causes such as the liberalization of the French abortion laws, but then so did many other women, and men, who had no significant or specific commitment to or identification with feminism.[61]

In Chapter 3 Evans writes that '*The Second Sex* has been a major landmark in discussions of relations between the sexes',[62] and that

'Prior to the publication of *The Second Sex* in 1949 de Beauvoir wrote nothing explicitly about the condition of women, although the three novels which she had published by that date ... all contain strong, central female characters.'[63] Evans is highly critical of the section on biology in *The Second Sex*, launching a series of criticisms against it, but chiefly the following: (a) De Beauvoir is mistaken in taking gestation and childbirth to be 'essentially a passive act'. It is true that 'Women may be the carriers of unborn children but the acts of birth and lactation would be interpreted as involving more active participation on the part of the mother than de Beauvoir allows.'[64]

(b) There is a tradition in contemporary feminism which regards maternity (Evans says 'motherhood') 'as fundamentally active and normal, while any attempt to detract from these qualities is seen as a feature of the patriarchal debasement of women's activities'.[65] (c) De Beauvoir accepts, implicitly and without reservation, the Darwinian orthodoxy of a progression from the simplest to the most complex organisms. As a result, she is led to accept 'the concept of general and extensive difference between male and female, man and woman, which now seems at least questionable'.[66] (d) Another problem underlying de Beauvoir's discussion of sexual difference is her uncritical assumption 'that it is possible to make generalizations about human beings from a study of animal behaviour – a view repeated uncritically in her later work'.[67] (e) Thus when de Beauvoir comes to discuss human biology specifically, 'it is no surprise that men and women appear as very different creatures'. It is fully to de Beauvoir's credit that she raises the issue of human biology, even if, says Evans,

> in doing so she herself reflects many contemporary attitudes and misconceptions about women's biology, and too rapidly assumes that male biology is some sort of norm, from which women deviate. Indeed, a considerable amount of recent feminist polemic has been concerned to demonstrate that women's biology is only problematic to men, and in male terms. The argument has then been developed into the view that menstruation and pregnancy are physical attributes with positive features – a case totally different from de Beauvoir's in which these aspects of female biology are only ever conceived of in negative terms.[68]

Evans writes that while the suspicion with which de Beauvoir views maternity and marriage might appear exaggerated several decades later, there yet remains much in her discussion 'that remains pertinent'. Specifically, 'her discussion of maternity rightly raises crucial questions about the reasons for women's desire for children and the complex of male/female relations in which a desire for a child becomes paramount'.[69] At the same time, says Evans, 'curious contradictions remain a puzzling part of *The Second Sex* and its part in feminist history'.[70] For instance, de Beauvoir is strongly anti-Freud, yet 'does not question the "normality" of sexual desire being heterosexual (some passages in the section on lesbianism contain crudely stereotypical portraits of lesbians)'.[71]

But for Evans, perhaps the major difficulty lies with the book's 'political implication' that women must assert their independence from the state of 'otherness' traditionally assigned to them. They must become free women: doing, acting and choosing on the same terms as men. Unfortunately, she says, it is not obviously part of de Beauvoir's programme that there occur any changes in the male cohort 'except in so far as changes are forced upon them by the new woman's greater inclination to argue and reject the more extreme instances of male control'.[72] De Beauvoir does not extend her call for change to the need for systematic social changes; she does not, for example, advocate, as have later feminists, the reorganization of the social world so that, for example, men take an equal share in child care, 'nor does she ask exactly what will constitute equality between the sexes'. The consequence of this one-sided approach, says Evans, is that 'women of the new era have to carry what might almost be described as a double burden in that they have to relinquish the safety of the position of the dependent other, but it is not expected that the world of men into which they move will have radically altered'.[73]

Approaching the end of her chapter on *The Second Sex*, Evans locates the book firmly in the tradition of liberalism and liberal feminism extending from Mary Wollstonecraft to Betty Friedan. Liberal feminists are united in their belief in the ameliorative and redemptive power of education. Notwithstanding their existentialist underpinning, de Beauvoir's final conclusions are essentially liberal: educate women differently and female subordination will cease. Evans comments favourably: 'And in so far as this case goes, their strength and its value are undeniable: much in the past and present education and socialization of girls has been negative and dismissive of their talents. So to restructure the nature of their education would be no mean service.'[74] The trouble is that these better educated women then enter the same old world, as did the generation that emerged from the colleges of North America in the 1950s; a world, says Evans, 'in which the sexual division of labour between adults remains unaltered, class divisions remain intact, and hierarchical structures of social and political control are the norm rather than the exception of social organization'.[75] The same holds true for liberal feminist demands in the 1970s and 1980s, she says, such as demands for reorganization of the school curriculum, the abolition of coeducation, and policies of positive discrimination towards women in education. All these changes would contribute towards the goal of a more sexually egalitarian society. Unfortunately, says Evans, 'these changes could only *contribute* towards this new world. The liberal solution of more, and different, education has at some point to confront the problem of the social structure of the world outside the classroom and the lecture hall.'[76]

18 Responses to *The Second Sex*: 1986–94

In this chapter I complete my survey of critical responses to *The Second Sex*. This survey is intended to be comprehensive, and at the same time it has no pretensions to being exhaustive. To complete it, I propose to document the responses contained in the following works: J. Okely, *Simone de Beauvoir: A Re-Reading*; K. Soper, 'The Qualities of Simone de Beauvoir', *New Left Review*, March–April 1986; M. Gatens, *Feminism and Philosophy*; M. Le Doeuff, *Hipparchia's Choice*, and T. Moi, *Simone de Beauvoir: The Making of an Intellectual Woman*.

Judith Okely devotes Chapters 3 and 4 of her book *Simone de Beauvoir: A Re-Reading* to a consideration of *The Second Sex*. Chapter 3 is called 'The Impact of *The Second Sex*', while Chapter 4 is called 'Re-reading *The Second Sex*'. Chapter 3 is devoted in large part to a reconstruction of the argument of *The Second Sex*, but it also contains some prefatory remarks written from the vantage point of the mid-1980s. Here Okely claims that

> A subsequent generation of feminists and male sympathisers have found the book, just from the measure of their own contrasting experience, both false and depressing. They cannot recognise any authenticity because the historical conditions have changed. Women from other races and cultures have not, in any case, necessarily recognised their own experience in the text at any time.[1]

The book has serious political weaknesses, she further claims, in that the cause of women's liberation is only very loosely aligned to a socialist agenda, and that agenda itself is merely introduced as an afterthought. Because de Beauvoir's socialism is embraced merely as an afterthought, and because *The Second Sex*'s hope for transformation seems to rest partly on women's recognition of their own complicity in their subordination, 'It seems', says Okely, 'that women must wait for their male socialist liberator.'[2]

A further problem with *The Second Sex* in the years immediately following its publication was that its existentialist foundations remained very largely hidden from view. De Beauvoir never explains the specific development which her theory makes in terms of Sartre's work: 'Consequently there is little evidence that the thousands of women readers of *The Second Sex* interpreted it in relation to Sartre's early philosophical work, let alone that of Hegel. The detailed existentialist implications were ignored, or only half understood.'[3] Okely adds that the general invisibility of existentialist theory was facilitated by the work of zoologist translator Howard Parshley 'who sanitised and mistranslated a great deal of the existentialist terminology'.[4]

Referring to the impact of *The Second Sex* on women readers specifically, Okely remarks that it encouraged some women, herself included, to reject marriage, and that many of her generation either delayed or rejected maternity as well. Commenting on de Beauvoir's depiction of the institution of marriage, she offers the following words of praise:

> Insofar as de Beauvoir gives a description of the bourgeois institution of marriage which presupposes the woman's position as that of economic dependant who offers unpaid services such as housework, sex, emotional support and major childcare, the text stands the test of time. The passages on this subject which I once underlined are, for the most part, still relevant. There have been some changes for middle-class western women. The married 'career' woman has avoided problems of an earlier generation by employing a working-class 'nanny' for childcare and domestic labour. Her economic dependence has thus been eased by the labour of other women... The situation for the working-class woman with outside work, and that of the single mother, requires more concrete analysis than that offered by de Beauvoir. Nevertheless, despite changes in sexual attitudes, birth control, legal reforms and divorce, marriage remains a dominant institution with continuing implications for the subordination of women. De Beauvoir's words retain their power.[5]

In Chapter 4 of her book Okely offers a 're-reading' of *The Second Sex* which is at once more critical, and better informed, than her (reported) response two decades earlier. Here she argues that de Beauvoir never convincingly explains why woman fails to become the Subject. This is all the more surprising in view of the fact that her text makes oblique references to Hegel's master–slave dialectic, wherein the slave succeeds in seeing himself as 'essential'. But as far as de Beauvoir is concerned, woman cannot reach the necessary consciousness for emancipation. The depressing conclusion to be drawn, says Okely, is 'that woman can never win freedom for herself, except perhaps by some independent change in society and the "master" male'.[6]

In her search for the basis of patriarchal ideas and myths about woman, de Beauvoir seizes upon the female capacity to gestate, but her depiction of female reproductive parts, especially the womb, bears all the marks of Sartre's extensive discussion of viscous substance in *Nausea* and in *Being and Nothingness*, as well as some of his own personal disgust with aspects of the sexual body. Okely concludes that 'In aiming to deconstruct the myth of the feminine, de Beauvoir thus naively reproduces her male partner's and lover's ideas about the female body, while possibly deceiving herself that these are objective and fixed philosophical truths.'[7]

Third, de Beauvoir is widely considered to have rejected *biological* factors as the basis of women's oppression, but as she *also* rejects economic and psychoanalytic explanations of female subordination it is not clear, says Okely, that de Beauvoir has completely abandoned biological determinism. What *is* clear is that she never regards biological data as irrelevant to her argument. On the contrary, says Okely, 'Again and again she slips into biological reductionism to explain the primary cause of women's subordination.'[8]

In addition, says Okely, she is guilty of anthropomorphism when she introduces 'experiences of violation and "interiorities" when commenting on non-human animals. She makes no distinction between a human who reflects on his or her experience of sexual intercourse and an animal which does not.'[9] Moreover, de Beauvoir's refusal to consider *male* sexuality and masculinity as problematic 'occurs', says Okely, 'throughout her work'.

In *The Second Sex*, finally, the focus is on woman as victim. Thus, for example, breastfeeding is depicted primarily as tiring and detrimental to the mother. There is, says Okely, 'no discussion of any sensual pleasure, nor of the contraction of the womb during breastfeeding'.[10]

In her review article on the Evans and Okely books, Kate Soper looks first at their treatment of the question of de Beauvoir's feminism. What is curiously absent from Evans's discussion, she says, is any reference to de Beauvoir's own rather straightforward definition of 'feminism' as ' "fighting on specifically feminist issues independently of the class struggle" ', adding that 'Consistently with that definition de Beauvoir has argued that she has not been a "feminist" for most of her life, and only became one through her association with the MLF in 1971.'[11] While Okely, in contrast to Evans, assumes de Beauvoir's entitlement to the feminist label from the start, she does not sufficiently stress a basic flaw in de Beauvoir's existentialist alternative to the Hobson's choice between domestic conformity on the one hand, and derided and ostracized spinsterhood on the other:

> Women, her example seemed to suggest, could lead diverse and autonomous lives freed of the normal constraints of marriage and motherhood, without being doomed to loneliness or celibacy. What Okely does not sufficiently stress perhaps is the extent to which it was no more than appearance... The most – possibly the only really – infuriating aspect of de Beauvoir's writing is the way she manages to combine the most correct and upright socialist sentiment with almost total impercipience about the economic, moral and sexual pressures that make escape from conventional relations with men well-nigh impossible for the majority of women at the present time.[12]

In defence of de Beauvoir Soper writes that her feminist 'individualist' ethics did have positive political *implications* which have not been sufficiently acknowledged by her critics. She explains her argument as follows: 'For even though the "model" of emancipation de Beauvoir provided was either inappropriate or unrealizable for the majority of women (and even for a majority of her readers), the fact that it was provided did help to focus many of the demands on such key issues as abortion, birth control and civil rights, that were to provide the initial platforms for a specifically feminist politics.'[13]

Soper further argues that while the Enlightenment conception of Nature as a woman to be variously seduced, violated, mastered, cultivated or transcended by a 'masculine' Reason played an important role in de Beauvoir's intellectual formation, this formation was more acutely influenced by 'the particular processing of Enlightenment ideology to be found in Hegelian-Sartrean ontology'.[14] But the truly decisive influence here, continues Soper, was not Hegel, but Sartre:

> What is curiously missing here, however, is any recognition that it is not so much the influence of Hegel (who is acknowledged to allow the 'Slave' to triumph in the end) but rather Sartre's re-interpretation

of the Master–Slave dialectic which is in conflict with the explicit commitment to female emancipation and sexual reciprocity.[15]

Hegel's mistake, according to Sartre, was to suppose that a consciousness could remain a subject while it simultaneously presented itself to the Other as an object. Since, for Sartre, 'slave' consciousness is inescapably objectified in the Other's look, it is rendered incapable, as a consequence, of transcending its immersion in life. Given, then, de Beauvoir's acceptance of this Sartrean metaphysics, it is, says Soper, 'difficult to see how *The Second Sex* can simultaneously demand any genuine reciprocity between the sexes. For even if women were able to abandon their complicity with their "objectification", it is not clear how the parity of status they would thereby attain could be anything other than parity in the eternal struggle for subjecthood.'[16]

But the crucial flaw, she thinks, lies not in the book's adherence to a suspect Sartrean metaphysics, but in its failure to be true to its own central insight:

the central, and basically correct thesis that women are 'made' not 'born' could have been so much more profoundly pressed home had de Beauvoir spent less time describing the symptoms of 'otherness' in the 'product' and more on the analysis of the fundamental economic and social structures that have gone into its 'making'.[17]

In the Introduction to her book *Feminism and Philosophy*, Moira Gatens advises her readers of the dangers connected with the tendency to import into feminist theory philosophical beliefs and distinctions which are supposedly neutral in character. Neither de Beauvoir nor Firestone was sufficiently alert to these dangers, she says, for

both entertain a philosophical dualism of the most orthodox kind, that predisposes their work toward locating the source of women's inferior status in female biology. They both accept the mind/body and nature/culture distinctions, treating them as given rather than as social constructions that embody historical and cultural values. To fail to take note of the value-laden character of any particular theory is implicitly to perpetuate the values that have been constructed by a culture that devalues women and those aspects of life with which they have been especially associated, for example, nature and reproduction.[18]

Gatens devotes Chapter 3 of her book to a quite sympathetic consideration of *The Second Sex*. Yet she repeats the accusation that 'the particular form of existentialism employed by de Beauvoir is that developed by Jean-Paul Sartre in *Being and Nothingness*',[19] and she remarks, in the second next paragraph, that

existentialism also harbours its biases against women. The values that existentialism espouses turn out to be no less antagonistic to women's possibilities than other theories we have considered. Its presuppositions, it will be argued, are such that women, their traditional activities, their bodies, and their subjectivities are rendered problematical relative to men, their pursuits, and their bodies.[20]

It is undeniable, says Gatens, towards the end of her largely expository chapter on *The Second Sex*, that de Beauvoir was one of the first, 'if not the first', to draw a coherent distinction between women's biological sex and the way that sex is lived in culture. This distinction, she says, is

invaluable in terms of separating woman's *social* or *historical* existence from her *possibilities*. The existentialist perspective, it seems to me, was a crucial factor in the successful completion of this task. However, this distinction can be made without assuming the masculine perspective along with its denigration of the female body and femininity.[21]

There is, as I outlined in the Preface to this book, a long-standing orthodoxy to the effect that de Beauvoir's existentialism is derivative, that it is at best a second-hand and much-diluted version of Sartre's existentialism, and that therefore the philosophical foundation of *The Second Sex*, such as it is, is Sartrean through and through. So I have to confess that when I first read Michèle Le Doeuff's brilliant, but merciless, critique of *Being and Nothingness* I fully expected that *The Second Sex* would quickly follow it to the guillotine. To my amazement (truly) this did not happen: on the contrary, Le Doeuff is very tender with de Beauvoir and goes to considerable pains to distance de Beauvoir's existentialism from that of Sartre.

Le Doeuff's general thesis is that in de Beauvoir's hands existentialism changes 'from the phallocentric discourse that it was into a proper tool for a feminist inquiry'.[22] She hastens to add that these transformations were not consciously thought–out by de Beauvoir; indeed, as she observes, 'nowhere does Beauvoir give a critique of Sartre's categories, nowhere does she state her intention to displace or modify them'.[23]

The novelty of de Beauvoir's approach to the existentialist formulation of problems 'could well be this', says Le Doeuff: 'she explicitly approaches her investigation from the perspective of existentialist morality'.[24] There are, in fact, two differences to be noted here; the first consists of the fact that de Beauvoir has a *perspective*, not a system, and the second is her stated intention of conducting her inquiry from the point of view of existentialist *morality*. So, as Le Doeuff reads her, 'What she takes from existentialism is thus not a collection of "theoretical positions" which have been gathered together in a dogmatic approach, but values. Authenticity and freedom form the ethical background to her work, and there is nothing ordinary about this.'[25] There is nothing ordinary about it both because facts will be read in the light of values, and because the values which will shape and colour the descriptions will be those of *existentialist* ethics, not utilitarianism or any other normative ethical theory.

Another profound contrast between Sartre's and de Beauvoir's existentialism, says Le Doeuff, can be found in the fact that the concept of *bad faith* is central to Sartre's system, whereas it merely hovers on the horizon of de Beauvoir's thought 'as a kind of hollow mould of oppression, and it is noticeable that the category of "the bad faith of the other" is never used, even when the context invites it'.[26] De Beauvoir is loath to chastise; she has an innate respect for other people, even for people, such as men, whom she has every reason not to respect. By contrast, Sartre is like Camus' magistrate, one for whom the ethic of mercy must always yield to the ideal of justice; in Le Doeuff's words, 'With the concept of bad faith Sartre claimed to have access to the other's inner consciousness; Simone de Beauvoir is decent enough to examine only what people say. To speak of someone's "bad faith" is to put that person's intentions on trial, since what is accused is an inner attitude.'[27]

This psychological and moral distance which thus exists between Sartre and de Beauvoir is fascinating at the biographical level, but it also has knock-on effects at the *philosophical* level. Since no one is in the dock in *The Second Sex*, no one is found guilty and sentenced. Yet women everywhere are the second sex, and as systematic oppression on this scale does not happen accidentally responsibility must be apportioned somewhere. As Le Doeuff perceives it, de Beauvoir shifts the blame from individuals on to the socio-historical situation: 'all the evil is blamed on the situation, the set of harmful traditions and perverse ideologies, a nasty history without a Subject, formed of codes and oppressive institutions'.[28] From this impersonal, sociological perspective a lie is never a lie to oneself; rather lies are 'the "lying ideals" of the language promoting untoward and unfortunate institutions'.[29] Le Doeuff explains that for de Beauvoir 'the kind of lie which must be fought is the social lie, such as the bourgeois optimism which sets an ideal of happiness sparkling in the young wife's eyes that is utterly unrelated to the reality she will encounter'.[30]

Le Doeuff is anxious to emphasize that de Beauvoir doesn't merely amputate Sartrean masculinist prose from her writing, nor does she merely jettison 'the imaginary productions (the little stories assuming a superiority, presumed guaranteed, over others)' from her inquiry. She also, very crucially, shifts the emphasis from a sovereign subject to a subject who finds herself constantly confronted by obstacles not of her own making. So it is not that she is not free (something a true existentialist could never claim), but that she is hemmed in, deprived of many of the instruments of self-assertion. As de Beauvoir herself said, women lack the abstract rights, and even if they had them that still would not be enough.

So, does Le Doeuff have anything bad to say about *The Second Sex*? Very little, really. She writes that anyone who turns to *The Second Sex* looking for positive role models will be disappointed; nor will they find there any references to the idea of a collective women's movement. The latter should not surprise us, she says, for existentialism is a philosophy for free *individuals*, and de Beauvoir had the pardonable prejudice that no one was free before her. The difference between de Beauvoir's and Le Doeuff's generations, 'including those who paid great tribute to her, is that each of us took the view that "fortunately, I am not the only one, not the first here; but I am certainly here, all the same"'.[31]

Le Doeuff also identifies for her readers what might be called the paradox of *The Second Sex*, namely, that its very success derives from its theoretical failure. Its theoretical failure consists of the fact that it seeks an explanation of women's subjugation and fails to find it. We are left, then, with an explanatory vacuum, 'an oppression without a fundamental cause'. But if nothing causes women's oppression, then it has to be created and maintained 'by countless mechanisms or institutional buttresses', and it was from this insight that the second, sociological volume of *The Second Sex* emerged.

Toril Moi sees much to admire in *The Second Sex*, not least the fact that it fashioned the *political* agenda for feminism in the decades following its publication, including the 1990s. The master-narrative of *The Second Sex*, as Moi reads it, is a narrative of liberation, and contemporary feminist debates are all, ultimately, debates between contending feminist visions of liberation. The basic political split is that between those 'who accept the strategic use of intellectual and political separatism in order to achieve a new, truly egalitarian society, and those who are convinced that women's interests are best served by the establishment of an enduring regime of sexual difference in every social and cultural field'.[32] To represent current feminist debates in these terms, Moi argues, is to acknowledge the singular impact of *The Second Sex*.

At the same time, Moi does not hesitate to underline the defects, as she sees them, of *The Second Sex* considered as a political text. Its deepest political deficiency, she contends, is its naive optimism in the emancipatory powers of socialism, in its capacity, that is, to liberate us not just from capitalism but from patriarchy as well. Putting the point with a different emphasis, Moi also writes that

> In the end, then, the deepest political flaw of *The Second Sex* consists in Beauvoir's failure to grasp the progressive potential of 'femininity' as a political discourse. More than forty years after the publication of her epochal essay, it is easy to see that she vastly underestimated the potential political impact of an independent women's movement, just as she failed to provide an adequate analysis of female sexuality.[33]

In Chapter 6 of her book *Simone de Beauvoir: The Making of an Intellectual Woman*, Moi looks at *The Second Sex* considered, not as a political text, but as a *sociological* one; for it is, she contends, one of the fundamental moves that de Beauvoir makes that she shifts the focus of her study from Sartrean ontology, from the claim that bad faith is *self-inflicted* by free agents, to the claim that 'women's social, political and historical circumstances are responsible for most – if not all – of their shortcomings'.[34] 'Without this shift from Sartrean ontology to sociology and politics', she says, '*The Second Sex* could not have been written.'[35]

Yet what is distinctive about the prose style of Sartre and de Beauvoir alike is their insistence 'on a rather repetitive set of phallic metaphors to illustrate their theory of freedom and transcendence'. The question then is whether existentialism *logically* requires phallic symbolism for its articulation. Moi holds that the central existentialist claim that consciousness is free and transcendent does *not* logically entail that consciousness 'is an erection', while wanting also to claim that de Beauvoir *in practice* genders freedom and consciousness in a phallocentric fashion, thus producing 'a contradiction within existentialist theory that a gender-neutral reading of the terms would avoid'.[36] Such a contradiction is said to occur when, in the context of human beings having been metonymized as consciousness, 'childbirth, for instance, regardless of its actual metaphorical similarities to the phallic projection of a thing into the world, would seem to be considered too biological, too bound up with facticity, to be valorized as transcendent'.[37]

If the imagery of the project, and of transcendence, inescapably *limits* the field of application of these concepts, and in particular limits them so as to exclude the bodily, the natural and the feminine, then contrariwise, the imagery of immanence, with its obsessional association with 'darkness, night, passivity, stasis, abandonment, slavery, confinement, imprisonment, decomposition, degradation and destruction', *expands* the meaning of this concept beyond rational limits. This may be seen as a major philosophical weakness, thinks Moi, for 'short of death, we always retain a glimmer of consciousness, however alienated, misguided and sunk in bad faith we may be: if human beings suffer from it, one might say, immanence cannot possibly be the same thing as death'.[38] She adds that 'The very power of Beauvoir's obsessional imagery of womb-like darkness and destruction ... has less to do with the requirements of her argument than with the intensity of her own personal obsession with annihilation, emptiness and death.'[39]

As yet, no theory of *sexual difference* is implied by the foregoing; to quote Moi, 'So far, everything Beauvoir has said is true for men as well as women.'[40] But de Beauvoir does, of course, posit a theory of sexual difference, for 'While we are all split and ambiguous, she argues, women are *more* split and ambiguous than men.'[41] Women are more split and ambiguous because of the kind of alienation they undergo in childhood. Unlike little boys, who quickly find in the penis an object in which to alienate themselves, little girls, deprived of an obvious object of alienation, end up alienating themselves in themselves, that is, in their own bodies. At the same time, says Moi, de Beauvoir insists that hers is 'a theory of the *social* construction of femininity and masculinity, and, moreover, categorically refuses the idea of a biological or anatomical "destiny" of any kind'.[42] The difficulty, then, that Moi has with de Beauvoir's theory is that 'when it comes to explaining exactly *how* we are to understand the relationship between the anatomical and the social, her discourse becomes curiously slippery'.[43] Why, for instance, should (anatomical) difference be construed as *inferiority*? Moi herself believes that had de Beauvoir availed herself of the Lacanian theory of the alienation of the child in the gaze of the other, she could have found 'a way of linking an anatomical and psychological argument with a sociological one... The gaze of the other... would necessarily see – and, in most cases, instantly ideologize – anatomical differences, and therefore proceed to invest girls and boys with different psychosexual values.'[44]

Moi turns next to de Beauvoir's analysis of the female body in its sexual and reproductive aspects, but devotes vastly more space to its analysis of sexual desire and coupling than she does to reproduction and the reproductive burden. De Beauvoir's representation of sexual desire, she says, (a) reproduces the contrast between male simplicity and female complexity; (b) is entirely ruled by her own metaphors ('If transcendence is like an erection, erections must be transcendent'); (c) verges on the delirious, in her account of female sexual arousal, as in her association of female sexual desire with the soft throbbing of a mollusc, and points to 'strong unconscious obsessions'.[45] Finally, Moi suspects that, in her account of female sexual arousal and female orgasm, 'the intensity, hostility and rawness of Beauvoir's prose spring from the same source: a deeply ambivalent relationship to the mother'.[46]

19 Simone de Beauvoir's Existentialist Feminism: A Defence

In the first half of this book I set out to prove (a) that Simone de Beauvoir made, and was therefore capable of making, her own distinctive contribution to existentialism; (b) that she began to do so in the early 1940s; (c) that her most distinctive and characteristic contribution to existentialism was to have developed an *existentialist ethics*; and (d) that this ethics has interesting affinities with some of the views expressed by Merleau-Ponty during the mid-1940s, and that it diverges from just about everything that Sartre said to a degree that I called oceanic.

There are two things that I want to take from this sequence of argument. The first is that by early 1947 de Beauvoir has completed her own version of existentialism: this existentialism, I want to stress, is hers and hers alone. Second, I see her, as she approaches the writing of *The Second Sex*, as a considerable philosopher in her own right. The fact that she did not hold such a high opinion of herself does not particularly bother me; on this issue, as on various others, I am happy to follow Marx's advice that we should not judge an individual according to the opinion she has of herself. The fact that others, including many of my own contemporaries, have a low opinion of de Beauvoir, at any rate as a philosopher, is, I think, a sad reflection on teaching practices in philosophy. I am reminded of the ruthless exclusion of Marx from otherwise reputable histories of philosophy, a signal case of politics imposing on our subject. The equally ruthless exclusion of de Beauvoir from anthologies of existentialist prose, and from collections of critical essays on existentialism, was no less political: the enemy within needed to be silenced as much as the enemy outside. It is time to end this shameful episode in the history of philosophy, and if this book makes even the smallest contribution to the achievement of that goal, I for one shall be delighted.

The Second Sex sets out to answer one question: Why are women consigned to the category of the Other? De Beauvoir gives two quite different answers to this question. (1) Women are consigned to the category of the Other because they are the *females* of the species. (2) Women are consigned to the category of the Other because, having been *raised to become women*, there is no other category they could possibly occupy. Michelle Le Doeuff is certain, or at any rate convinced enough to be willing to bet money on it, that de Beauvoir herself did not have much time for the first of these two answers, and that to fill the explanatory vacuum it leaves in its wake, she had to write a second volume. But if de Beauvoir was that unhappy with Volume 1, why did she publish it? The conclusion that I have drawn is that de Beauvoir sees merit in *both* answers, and that therefore she regards neither answer as conclusive.

It is tempting to read *The Second Sex* as two completely separate volumes, the first written by an epigone who had overdosed on Sartrean masculinism (Cottrell, Elshtain, Lloyd, Okely, Soper, Gatens, Moi), the second by a sociologist who has turned her back on Sartrean ontology, or at the very least on the pathological misanthropy of Sartrean ethics (Le Doeuff mainly, also Moi). But I am inclined to resist this temptation, accepting neither the 'decent woman' hypothesis, that of the paragon who was always prepared to listen to people and, in marked contrast to Sartre, never descends to concocting nasty little stories about them, nor the orthodoxy that de Beauvoir was incapable of developing a philosophy of her own, needing constantly to draw inspiration from Sartre's writings. If, as I have argued during the first half of this book, de Beauvoir produced her own existentialist philosophy from the early 1940s, then she followed her own philosophical lights, not Sartre's, from the outset. The core of her existentialism is her ethical theory (not, *pace* Le Doeuff, her moral intuitions and common decency). Her ethical theory is located in her writings from 1943 to 1947, where she alerts us to the tragic ambiguity of human existence, where she identifies an absolute evil (*un mal absolu*) and reintroduces into moral philosophy an interest in the everyday virtues and vices. (There is a tragic ambiguity, for instance, in the fact that society relegates women to the role of domestic and reproductive slaves, and yet it is precisely these same women who are entrusted with the function of rearing children.) The scope of the theory is augmented in various ways in *The Second Sex*, for example, in her meditations on 'a truly socialist ethics' which will be 'concerned to uphold justice without suppressing liberty, and to impose duties upon individuals without abolishing individuality'.[1] This is the philosopher who sets about writing, and who completes the writing of *The Second Sex*. The fact that she draws obsessively on the same few philosophical distinctions, such as that between transcendence and immanence, throughout both volumes, only adds substance to my opinion.

It was not just that two volumes were written, I now want to add, but that two volumes were needed to do justice to the two-sided nature of woman as de Beauvoir saw it, namely, to the female/feminine duality. It is worth noting that in the famous sentence introducing the second volume, de Beauvoir writes 'One is not born, but rather becomes, a woman.' She does not write 'One is not born, but rather becomes, a female.' I read her as saying that you are born a female, but become a woman. De Beauvoir saw that both dimensions, that of femaleness and that of womanliness, needed emphasizing: hence two volumes, the first of which deals extensively with the concept of femaleness. In the later section on the independent woman, de Beauvoir refers to her as 'a human being with sexuality', and she adds, in the same crucial passage, that 'She refuses to confine herself to her role as female, because she will not accept mutilation; but it would also be a mutilation to repudiate her sex.'[2] There can, I think, be no mistaking her meaning: to emphasize the sex (or femaleness) but not the humanity (or womanliness), or the humanity but not the sex, of woman is 'mutilating'; it is deliberately and erroneously to suppress a chunk of the relevant evidence.

The Second Sex, as I have said, consists of two distinct but connected volumes, the first devoted to exploring the claim that women are consigned to the category of the Other because they are the females of the species, the second exploring the claim that women are relegated to the category of the Other because, having been brought up to become women, there is no other category they could possibly occupy. The claim that women are the females of the species transmutes, following research, into the claim that women are the *victims* of the species, that they are required to perform reproductive tasks for the species which men are not required to perform, and that these reproductive tasks jeopardize women's health and severely limit their prospects of self-development. In short, women are oppressed by their biology.

Carol McMillan attacks the thesis that biology oppresses women on the grounds that oppressors, by definition, are human beings or groups of human beings, and that biology fits into neither category. This is true, but trivial. Biology, understood as biological make-up, is not *per se* human, but if it has the same or similar consequences for human beings as does oppression, then there can be no real objection to extending the term 'oppressor' to it as well.

McMillan advances a more sophisticated objection to the claim that biology oppresses women when she says that such a claim can have no legitimate place in a feminist philosophy which consciously associates itself with the writings of Merleau-Ponty and Sartre. For such an oppression to be possible we must suppose a metaphysical distinction between a woman and her body. But de Beauvoir, following Merleau-Ponty and Sartre, actively repudiates such a Cartesian-like dualism, asserting that a woman *is* her body, that there is no Cartesian gulf between them.

This criticism seriously misrepresents both de Beauvoir and Merleau-Ponty.[3] At this early stage of her argument de Beauvoir is intent on developing the general claim that from puberty to the menopause woman is 'the theatre of a play that unfolds within her and in which she is not personally concerned'.[4] This is followed by two pages concerning the menstrual cycle, culminating with the philosophical declaration 'Woman, like man, *is* her body; but her body is something other than herself.'[5] The superscript refers us to the following quotation from Merleau-Ponty's *Phénomenologie de la perception*: 'So I am my body, in so far, at least, as my experience goes, and conversely my body is like a life-model, or like a preliminary sketch, for my total being.' It is very clear from this cautiously worded sentence that Merleau-Ponty does not intend a metaphysical equation of self and body. From one perspective the body, and bodily experiences, offer but 'a preliminary sketch' for the full philosophical story of the human being; from the other, as so much human experience is channelled through the human body, it becomes appropriate to identify bodily experience and experience as such.

Not only does Simone de Beauvoir not inherit a philosophical materialism from Merleau-Ponty, neither does she propose any such philosophical thesis herself. Wishing us to take full cognizance of what Merleau-Ponty has written, she rephrases his sentence as follows: 'Woman, like man, *is* her body; but her body is something other than herself.' She explains comprehensively what she means in the accompanying pages. She means all of the following: (a) a woman experiences her body as a theatre whose productions she does not personally direct; (b) 'it is during her periods that she feels her body most painfully as an obscure, alien thing';[6] (c) she experiences a more profound alienation when pregnancy occurs; (d) she does not succeed in escaping the constraints of the body until she experiences the menopause; (e) *despite* the constraints imposed by the body, it is none the less our point of access to the world, what makes possible different kinds of encounter with that same world ('For, the body, being the instrument of our grasp upon the world, the world is bound to seem a very different thing when apprehended in one manner or another');[7] (f) the limitations imposed on woman by her bodily make-up are not yet as onerous as they seem, and should not be used to justify the imposition of further constraints, especially those of an institutional character: 'But I deny that they establish for her a fixed and inevitable destiny. They are insufficient for setting up a hierarchy of the sexes; they fail to explain why woman is the Other; they do not condemn her to remain in this subordinate role for ever';[8] (g) woman should be understood on the basis of her *possibilities*, for woman is not 'a completed reality, but rather a becoming and it is in her becoming that she should be compared with man'; (h) when we are dealing with a being 'whose nature is transcendent action, we can never close the books'.

I tend to side with de Beauvoir on the issue of sex and destiny. On this view there are two sexes, a differentiation which refers to the distinctive contribution to human reproduction which is made by these two very broad groups of human beings. While that is not all that sexual difference amounts to, as we shall see, it is its most conspicuous characteristic and it neither entails nor justifies relegation of females to a subordinate status. Assigning a subordinate status to females is, in the end, a political decision and, needless to say, a deplorable one.

In her attack on androgynism Jean Bethke Elshtain claims that 'Important distinctions, like male and female, are not only embedded in language, they are constitutive of a way of life.'[9] In other words, sex differentiation is not merely sex differentiation. But what exactly does Elshtain mean? Either she means that the distinction between female and male, and such-like, *reflects* a way of life, or that collectively such distinctions *mark out* a way of life. The former tells us very little, other than that individuals are differentiated within a species for the purposes of reproduction. If we add in *further* distinctions, then the first interpretation transmutes into the second. In that event, the distinctions between male and female, masculine and feminine, boy and girl, mother and father, aunt and uncle, bride and groom, and so on, do indeed collectively mark out and constitute a way of life. But it is a way of life which is, in large part, *rejected* by androgynists, because they believe that a far superior way of life, one which opens up opportunities for self-development rather than one which closes them off, is possible for these same human beings. Sexist language and distinctions, such as some of those cited above, are designed to confine people to certain categories, roles, functions, accomplishments, and so on, and this happens from the day you are born ('Pink for a girl, blue for a boy'). We can distinguish, then, between the biologically constructed body and the socially (or politically) constructed one. This is but another way of expressing the distinction between sex and gender, a distinction which, following de Beauvoir, I accept, but Elshtain appears to reject.

I do not agree with everything de Beauvoir says, and in particular I disagree with her account of sexual activity, with her stance on the menopause, and with her views on Engels.[10] But first I want to point out a *logical* difficulty which is posed by her argument. If, as she holds, the female body is 'wholly adapted for and subservient to maternity',[11] then how can she further hold that biological considerations 'do not establish for woman a fixed and inevitable destiny'? A body which is wholly adapted for maternity need not necessarily be in a maternal condition, no more than a knife – an instrument wholly adapted for cutting – need be in continual use, or has always to be used for this precise purpose. But a body which is *wholly subservient* to maternity does not seem to be favoured with the same freedom. How, then, do we square this implication with de Beauvoir's further, emphasized, claim that woman is a historical being and, by implication, that her destiny is not just a biological one?

With the menopause, writes de Beauvoir, woman finally escapes the iron grip of the species. This was very true of Irish women of my mother's generation, and even later generations of Irish women who, thanks largely to the menopause, could then get on with their lives, free of the burden, and sometimes the nightmare of serial pregnancy. In truth, it wasn't so much the iron grip of the *species* from which they escaped as the primal chant of a baby-culture, and a culturally-bound ethic which decreed, ironically very de Beauvoir-like, that the married woman's body was 'wholly adapted for and subservient to maternity'.

With the winning of reproductive choice for women, even for Irish women, the reproductive choice to complete one's family will normally have been made far in advance of the menopause; in other words, it is not now the menopause which liberates women from the iron grip of the species, but family planning. The tendency now is to see the menopause as part of the ageing process, to be negotiated with the same set of attitudes and beliefs that one uses in addressing other features of that same process. The *third age* rather than the third sex is, in my opinion, a more appropriate expression for this phase of a woman's life. It describes the phase that follows reproduction and retirement, and precedes the *fourth age*, when one sinks into sickness and dependency.[12]

De Beauvoir's claim that women of a certain age are no longer females understandably upsets and angers some of her readers. Here is what one of her readers, an evening student, wrote in her term essay on de Beauvoir:

> However, there is more to being female than [being] just a reproductive organism. If there was not, then regimes such as that of Ceausescu would not have stirred such an outcry. Also, my mother to me will always embody the very essence of femininity. The scented soaps and perfumes, the love of floral patterned dresses and hair enhanced with combs and slides all connote the female. This is the gentler side of woman, and one which turns us from the very sterile notion of simple reproduction to the totality of woman, and femininity.[13]

If we read de Beauvoir as saying that women of a certain age are no longer *women*, then this student's reply is fully justified; if, on the other hand, we read her as saying that women of a certain age are no longer *female* (which, in fact, is what she does say), then the statement is not as provocative as it seems. In a sense, all that de Beauvoir is saying is that women who no longer have a reproductive capacity are no longer reproductive beings. Looked at from this perspective, what is *prima facie* a gratuitously cruel remark about older women turns out, on inspection, to be a merely worthless, careless tautology.

De Beauvoir's presentation of the two-sex body sees sexual intercourse as a penetration and a violation of the female, and therefore as a further victimization of the female. This is a view of sex, that is, of sexual activity, which has, in more recent times, been given its most strident and uncompromising expression in Andrea Dworkin's *Intercourse*, whose polemic culminates with the declaration that 'Inferiority, sex-based or race-based or both, seems to be the requisite context for fucking.'[14] It is interesting to note that John Stoltenberg, a self-confessed admirer of Dworkin's writing, does not take this view, implying as it does that sexual activity premised on mutuality and justice is, or at least seems to be, a logical impossibility. Stoltenberg holds that sex premised on mutuality and justice *is* something which can be achieved by human beings, though sex does not necessarily have to be penetrative sex.[15] I, too, am convinced that this is possible, and would like to think that sexual union, rather than sexual possession and usurpation, will become the socialized norm.

I want to comment, next, on de Beauvoir's critique of Engels. The general point I wish to make is that Engels, in his *Origin of the Family*, does not subsume the oppression of women under class oppression, nor does he reduce antagonism between the sexes to class antagonism, nor does he believe that human relationships can be reduced to relationships within the production process. The truth of the matter is that, as Engels sees it, women's oppression has an economic *dimension* to it. This consists in the fact that housework – the labour contribution of women – is seen as a purely *private service* which the married woman performs for her husband and children, and as such one which is not remunerated. It is not seen as a form of social production, or as contributing to social production.

This leaves two alternatives: (a) *recognize* housework as a contribution to social production, or (b) encourage *all* women to participate in the paid labour force. With the Industrial Revolution, says Engels, option (b) opened for women, if at a price, namely, that 'if she carries out her duties in the private service of her family, she remains excluded from public production and unable to earn; and, if she wants to take part in public production and earn independently, she cannot carry out family duties'.[16] Yet option (b) is the one preferred by Engels, who says 'the first condition for the liberation of the wife is to bring the whole female sex back into public industry, and this in turn demands that the characteristic of the monogamous family as the economic unit of society be abolished'.[17] It is clear from this passage that Engels regards the abolition of the monogamous family as a necessary, but not a sufficient condition of married women's liberation. Moreover, it is not the abolition of the monogamous family *per se* that is called for, only its abolition as 'the economic unit of society'. The *economic* nature of monogamous marriage is that the married woman is an economically dependent, and therefore unequal, spouse. To liberate her, it is essential, to begin with, that she become economically independent. But she cannot become economically independent within the traditional monogamous structure. Therefore it has to go.

In his comments on 'proletarian marriage' Engels refers to the extent to which a change in the economic basis of marriage alters fundamental relationships within the marriage, and at the same time he hints at the fact that there is a good deal more to marriage than economics. 'Large-scale industry', he maintains, 'has taken the wife out of the home onto the labour market, and into the factory, and made her often the breadwinner of the family', so that 'no basis for any kind of male supremacy is left in the proletarian household, except, perhaps, for something of the brutality towards women that has spread since the introduction of monogamy'.[18] Here Engels adverts to domestic violence, hinting that it crosses all thresholds, including that of class.

The only *moral* basis for marriage, in Engels' opinion, is that of love, and, he declares, 'if affection definitely comes to an end or is supplanted by a new passionate love, separation is a benefit for both partners as well as for society'.[19] Engels looks forward to the day when, as he conjectures, a new generation will have grown up: 'a generation of men who never in their lives have known what it is to buy a woman's surrender with money or any other social instrument of power; a generation of women who have never known what it is to give themselves to a man from any other consideration than real love or to refuse to give themselves to their lover from fear of the economic consequences'.[20]

When I read these lines I find it hard not to recall various passages in *The Second Sex*, particularly in the section on the independent woman. It is idle, says de Beauvoir, to suppose that *by themselves* economic and social changes will bring forth the new woman, but until such changes do occur 'the new woman cannot appear'. Under the new economic regime 'erotic liberty was to be recognized by custom, but the sexual act was not to be considered a "service" to be paid for'.[21] Marriage was to be 'based on a free agreement that the contracting parties could break at will'. Engels found it difficult to conjecture about the way in which sexual relations would be ordered following 'the impending overthrow of capitalist production'. De Beauvoir had the advantage of seeing a self-styled socialist state come into being during her lifetime, one which 'promised' the many changes in women's existence that both she and Engels dearly wished for. That the Soviet Union had difficulty keeping its promises to women seems to have come as no surprise to de Beauvoir by the time she sat down to compose *The Second Sex*. She wrote, as it happens in a rebuke to Engels, 'We know how often and how radically Soviet Russia has had to change its policy on the family according to the varying relations between the immediate needs of production and those of re-production.'[22] Still and all, there is multiple irony in the fact that Simone de Beauvoir, one of Engels' most trenchant critics, should have expected so much from the first society to have attempted to put his principles into practice.

My claim is not that Simone de Beauvoir enjoyed the advantage of historical hindsight over Engels, but that in every other respect their views on the woman question were identical. Engels concludes with a paean to relationships premissed on mutuality and love. So, too, does de Beauvoir, but she insists that there will always remain a core of irreducible difference between the two sexed individualities. As she puts it, 'woman's eroticism, and therefore her sexual world, have a special form of their own and therefore cannot fail to engender a sensuality, a sensitivity, of a special nature'.[23] But this does not make her a difference feminist: she does not seek equality for different sexed subjectivities. To be more precise, she does not, as does Irigaray in *je, tu, nous*, seek equality *through difference*; she merely wants an acknowledgement that equals can be different. As she puts it herself, 'those who make much of "equality in difference" could not with good grace refuse to grant me the possible existence of differences in equality'.[24]

The difference between existentialist and difference feminism may, in any event, have been exaggerated. In *je, tu, nous*, as we know, Luce Irigaray refers, with both poignancy and bitterness, to *The Second Sex* and its author. While she has read *The Second Sex*, she confides, 'I was never close to Simone de Beauvoir'.[25] In part, there was the age difference between them; in part, she was hurt by de Beauvoir's refusal to respond to her work *Speculum. De l'autre femme*, a copy of which she had sent to de Beauvoir 'with an inscription to her as if to an older sister'. Another reason, she says, is that she was trained as a psychoanalyst, whereas 'Simone de Beauvoir and Jean-Paul Sartre were always wary of psychoanalysis.'[26]

Irigaray calls for the development of 'a culture of the sexual', one premissed on sexual difference, 'with each sex being respected'. This emphasis on sexual difference, as opposed to human similarity, seems to create an unbridgeable gap between difference and existentialist feminism. In particular, it is difficult to see how difference feminism can accommodate de Beauvoir's longing for an androgynous world in which 'If the little girl were brought up from the first with the same demands and rewards, the same severity and the same freedom, as her brothers, taking part in the same studies, the same games, promised the same future, surrounded with women and men who seemed to her undoubted equals, the meaning of the castration complex and of the Oedipus complex would be profoundly modified.'[27] The elimination of sexual difference cannot be reconciled with its recognition. But, in truth, de Beauvoir is less preoccupied with the elimination of sexual difference than with an insistence that girls not be forced to grow up in a masculinized world that relentlessly thrusts stereotypical roles upon them. Moreover, de Beauvoir herself repeatedly emphasizes sexual difference. The 'independent woman', as she sees her, 'refuses to confine herself to her role as female because she will not escape mutilation; but it would also be a mutilation to repudiate her sex. Man is a human being with sexuality; woman is a complete individual, equal to the male, only if she too is a human being with sexuality. To renounce her femininity is to renounce a part of her humanity.'[28] I cannot see that these words clash with Irigaray's plea, in her very recent work *I Love to You*, for the 'need to realize History...as the salvation of humanity comprised of men and women. That is our task. In accomplishing it, we are working for History's development by bringing about more justice, truth, and humanity in the world...We are all of us, men and women alike, sexed. Our principal task is to make the transition from nature to culture as sexed beings, to become women and men while remaining faithful to our gender.'[29] In Simone de Beauvoir's words, while not repudiating our sex.

Notes

PREFACE

1. De Beauvoir is not included in any of the following anthologies, or studies, of existentialist prose: R. Jolivet, *Les Doctrines Existentialistes de Kierkegaard à J.-P. Sartre*, which treats of Kierkegaard, Nietzsche, Heidegger, Sartre, Jaspers and Marcel; W. Barrett, *Irrational Man: A Study in Existential Philosophy*, which treats of Kierkegaard, Nietzsche, Heidegger and Sartre; W. Kaufmann, *Existentialism from Dostoevsky to Sartre*, which includes material from Kierkegaard, Nietzsche, Rilke, Kafka, Jaspers, Heidegger, Sartre and Camus. Neither the Bibliography nor the Index (of names) to J. Macquarrie's *Existentialism* contains a single reference to de Beauvoir. Her monograph *Pour une morale de l'ambiguïté* is given two pages of (worthwhile) discussion in C. Smith, *Contemporary French Philosophy*, a book containing 255 pp. of text. De Beauvoir merits no mention in A. Dondeyne's *Foi Chrétienne et Pensée Contemporaine*, which discusses, *inter alia*, J.-P. Sartre, M. Merleau-Ponty, A. Camus, Hegel, Marx, Kant, Kierkegaard, Heidegger, Husserl, M. de Biran, Marcel, Bergson, Madinier, L. Lavelle and A. de Waelhens. Finally, the Index to the recently published *The Cambridge Companion to Sartre* cites a single reference to de Beauvoir.
2. *Force of Circumstance*, p. 75.
3. Ibid., p. 76.
4. Ibid.
5. *Simone de Beauvoir, A Biography*, p. 321.
6. See M. Warnock, 'Simone: Heart of the matter', *The Observer*, 2 June 1990.
7. *Feminism and Philosophy*, p. 48.
8. *The Man of Reason*, p. 96.
9. *Force of Circumstance*, p. 202.
10. *Saint-Germain-des-Prés*, p. 157.
11. *Simone de Beauvoir*, p. 309.
12. *Feminist Thought*, p. 195.
13. Ibid.
14. *Simone de Beauvoir, A Feminist Mandarin*, pp. 56, 57.
15. *Feminism and Philosophy*, p. 59.
16. *New Left Review*, March–April 1986, p. 115.
17. Quoted in Tong, *Feminist Thought*, p. 195.
18. Ibid.
19. *The Sunday Times*, 7 June 1990.
20. Ibid.

1 EARLY PHILOSOPHICAL WRITING

1. *Pyrrhus et Cinéas*, Gallimard, 1944; *Pour une morale de l'ambiguïté*, Gallimard, 1947. An English translation of the second of these two

works was published in 1948. 'Selections' from *Pyrrhus and Cineas* were published, in English, in *The Partisan Review*, Vol. 3, No. 3, 1946. For the purposes of this chapter I have made my own translations of *Pyrrhus et Cinéas*. Page numbers refer to the French edition.

2. Grenier's chief claim to fame was his influence on Camus. He taught Philosophy at the *Grande Lycée* in Algiers when Camus was completing his secondary education there. The Camus–Grenier relationship has been discussed by biographers, critics and reviewers: see P. McCarthy, *Camus: A Critical Study of his Life and Work*, p. 32, and C. C. O'Brien, 'The Angel of the Absurd', *TLS*, 24 October 1982.

3. *The Prime of Life*, pp. 547, 548.

4. Ibid., p. 548.

5. Ibid., pp. 548, 549.

6. 'Aucun lien n'est donné d'abord', *Pour une morale de l'ambiguïté*, suivi de *Pyrrhus et Cinéas*, p. 243.

7. Ibid., p. 236.

8. Ibid., p. 253.

9. Ibid., p. 256.

10. Ibid., p. 258.

11. Ibid., p. 265.

12. Ibid., p. 267.

13. Ibid., p. 268.

14. Ibid., p. 269.

15. De Beauvoir strikes an intriguingly feminist note at this point also: ' "Hey", Missus", says the worldly, gourmet priest, as he sits down to table, "Would God have made all these lovely things if he hadn't wanted us to eat them?" But he scrupulously neglects to mention that God also created woman.' Ibid., p. 270.

16. Ibid., p. 272.

17. Ibid., p. 274.

18. Ibid., p. 275.

19. Ibid., pp. 275, 276.

20. Ibid., p. 278.

21. Ibid.

22. Ibid.

23. Ibid., p. 280.

24. Ibid., pp. 282, 283.

25. 'S'il réfuse de choisir, il s'anéantit', ibid., p. 295.

26. Ibid., pp. 296, 297.

27. Ibid., p. 298.

28. Ibid., p. 300.

29. This definition focusses on existentialism as an ethics and an anthropology, rather than as an ontology and a phenomenology.

30. *Existentialism and Humanism*, p. 28.

31. Ibid., p. 55.

32. *Pyrrhus and Cineas*, p. 300.

33. *Existentialism and Humanism*, p. 26.

34. Ibid., p. 28.

35. See ibid., p. 36.

36. Ibid., p. 56.
37. See ibid., p. 34.
38. *The Plague*, pp. 106, 107.
39. See *Existentialism and Humanism*, p. 33.
40. Ibid., pp. 33, 34.
41. See ibid., p. 49.
42. *Jean-Paul Sartre*, p. 23.
43. *Intimacy*, pp. 64, 65.
44. I have discussed these matters extensively in a paper entitled 'Existentialists Arguing about Death', which I read to the TCD Philosophy Colloquium in 1991.
45. *Being and Time*, p. 302.
46. Ibid., p. 303.
47. 'Thus death escaped man at the same time that it rounded him off with the non-human absolute', *Being and Nothingness*, p. 532.
48. Ibid.
49. Ibid., p. 533.
50. Ibid.
51. Ibid.
52. See ibid., p. 539.
53. Ibid., pp. 539, 540.
54. *A Very Easy Death*, p. 92.
55. Ibid.
56. *Force of Circumstance*, p. 674.
57. *Being and Time*, p. 289.
58. *Force of Circumstance*, pp. 604, 605.
59. *Simone de Beauvoir, A Feminist Mandarin*, pp. 33, 34.
60. *The Prime of Life*, p. 572.

2. *THE BLOOD OF OTHERS*: THE FICTIONAL PRIMER ON EXISTENTIALISM

1. *Force of Circumstance*, p. 44.
2. Quoted in D. Bair, *Simone de Beauvoir, A Biography*, p. 306.
3. Ibid., p. 305.
4. *Force of Circumstance*, p. 45.
5. *The Blood of Others*, p. 13.
6. Ibid., p. 14.
7. Ibid., p. 60.
8. Ibid., p. 72.
9. Ibid., p. 120.
10. Ibid., p. 122.
11. Ibid., p. 156.
12. Ibid., p. 183.
13. Ibid., p. 185.
14. Ibid., p. 189.
15. Ibid.

16. Ibid., p. 190.
17. Ibid.
18. Ibid.
19. Ibid.
20. Ibid., p. 224.
21. *The Novelist as Philosopher*, p. 172.
22. Cranston uses the French title *Le Sang des Autres* throughout his commentary.
23. *The Novelist as Philosopher*, p. 173.
24. Ibid.
25. Ibid., pp. 173, 174.
26. Ibid., p. 174.
27. *Simone de Beauvoir, A Feminist Mandarin*, p. 46.
28. Ibid., p. 47.
29. Ibid.
30. Ibid., p. 79.
31. Ibid.
32. Ibid., p. 80.
33. Ibid., p. 92.
34. Ibid., p. 93.
35. Ibid., p. 96.
36. *Simone de Beauvoir, A Study of her Writings*, p. 164.
37. Ibid.
38. Ibid., p. 165.
39. Ibid.
40. Ibid., p. 167.
41. *The Novels of Simone de Beauvoir*, p. 44.
42. Ibid., p. 47.
43. Ibid., p. 46.
44. Ibid., p. 45.
45. Ibid.
46. Ibid., p. 51.
47. Ibid., pp. 51, 52.
48. Ibid., p. 52.
49. Ibid.
50. Ibid., p. 54.
51. Ibid.
52. Ibid.
53. Ibid.
54. Ibid., p. 55.
55. Ibid., p. 57.
56. Ibid.
57. Ibid., p. 58.
58. Ibid., p. 59.
59. *The Blood of Others*, p. 240.
60. He may have confused 'freedom' understood as the absence of constraints, with 'freedom' understood as the absence of determinism.
61. De Beauvoir espouses a 'positive' or 'exercise' concept of freedom whereby freedom consists, not in the absence of external constraints,

but in the exercise of control over the course of one's own life. But, of course, this does not require her to hold that there are no external constraints against which the agent has to battle, and against which s/he may sometimes be powerless. For a lucid treatment of the distinction between 'positive' and 'negative' liberty, see C. Taylor, 'What's Wrong with Negative Liberty?', in A. Ryan (ed.), *The Idea of Freedom*, OUP, 1979, pp. 175–93.

62. A claim that Merleau-Ponty convincingly defends in his postwar essay 'The War Has Taken Place'. See Chapter 6.
63. See *The Blood of Others*, pp. 154, 155.
64. Evans, p. 79.
65. A point made in a review of *La Peste* in *Club*, February 1955. Camus' reply, 'Letter to Roland Barthes on *La Peste*', was also published in *Club*. It is reprinted in the collection *Lyrical and Critical*, pp. 253–5.
66. *Force of Circumstance*, p. 138.
67. *Neither Victims Nor Executioners*, p. 31.
68. I first came across this distinction in M. Ignatieff, 'Back to reality on the home front', *The Observer*, 3 March 1991.
69. For more on the existentialist theory of history, see A. Dobson, *Jean-Paul Sartre and the Politics of Reason*, CUP, 1993.

3 THE ETHICS OF AMBIGUITY: AN EXISTENTIALIST ETHICS

1. *Pour une morale de l'ambiguïté*, Gallimard, 1947. For the purposes of this chapter I propose to use the English language edition, *The Ethics of Ambiguity*, trans. B. Frechtman, The Philosophical Library, 1948.
2. *The Ethics of Ambiguity*, p. 9.
3. Ibid., p. 7.
4. Ibid., p. 9.
5. Ibid., p. 10.
6. Ibid.
7. Ibid., p. 11.
8. Here existentialism is taken to be synonymous with Sartrean existentialism.
9. *The Ethics of Ambiguity*, p. 12.
10. Ibid., p. 13.
11. De Beauvoir actually says 'any foreign absolute', but it is clear from her discussion that it is moral absolutes she has in mind.
12. *The Ethics of Ambiguity*, p. 13.
13. Ibid., pp. 14, 15.
14. Ibid., p. 16.
15. Ibid.
16. Ibid., p. 19.
17. Ibid., pp. 17, 18.
18. Ibid., p. 18.
19. Ibid.

20. Ibid., pp. 18, 19.
21. Ibid., pp. 19, 20.
22. Ibid., p. 20.
23. Ibid., pp. 20, 21.
24. Ibid., p. 21.
25. Ibid., p. 24.
26. Ibid.
27. Ibid., p. 25.
28. Ibid., p. 29.
29. Ibid.
30. Ibid., pp. 30, 31.
31. Ibid., p. 31.
32. Ibid.

4   A CHARACTER ETHICS

1. Character ethics is the systematic study of the virtues and vices, and the kinds of persons in whom these same virtues and vices are found.
2. *The Ethics of Ambiguity*, p. 35.
3. Ibid.
4. Ibid.
5. Ibid., p. 36.
6. Ibid., p. 37.
7. Ibid.
8. Ibid., p. 38.
9. Ibid.
10. Ibid.
11. Ibid.
12. Ibid., p. 39.
13. Ibid.
14. Ibid., p. 40.
15. Ibid., p. 41.
16. Ibid.
17. Ibid.
18. *Le sous-homme*. The term is unfortunate, because of its Nazi associations. But de Beauvoir assigns her own distinctive meaning to it.
19. *The Ethics of Ambiguity*, p. 42.
20. Ibid., p. 43.
21. Ibid.
22. Ibid., p. 44.
23. Ibid.
24. Ibid.
25. Ibid., p. 45.
26. Ibid., pp. 46, 47.
27. Ibid., p. 48.
28. Ibid.
29. Ibid.

30. Ibid., p. 49.
31. Ibid.
32. Ibid., pp. 49, 50.
33. Ibid., p. 51.
34. Ibid., p. 52.
35. Ibid.
36. She is referring to Sartre's biographical study of Baudelaire, published in 1947 under the title *Baudelaire*.
37. *The Ethics of Ambiguity*, p. 55.
38. Ibid., p. 57.
39. Ibid., p. 58.
40. Ibid., p. 59.
41. Ibid.
42. Ibid., p. 61.
43. Ibid.
44. Ibid., p. 64.
45. Ibid.
46. Ibid., p. 65.
47. Ibid., p. 66.
48. Ibid., p. 67.
49. Ibid., p. 69.
50. Ibid., p. 71.
51. Ibid., p. 72.
52. Ibid., p. 73.

5 ETHICS FOR VIOLENCE

1. *The Ethics of Ambiguity*, p. 75.
2. Ibid.
3. Ibid., pp. 80, 81.
4. Ibid., pp. 88, 89.
5. Ibid., p. 91.
6. Ibid., p. 98.
7. Ibid., p. 99.
8. Ibid., p. 103.
9. Ibid., p. 107.
10. Ibid.
11. Ibid.
12. Ibid., p. 109.
13. Ibid., p. 111.
14. Ibid., p. 112.
15. Ibid., p. 114.
16. Ibid.
17. 'the future is the definite direction of a particular transcendence', ibid., p. 116.
18. Ibid.
19. Ibid.

20. Ibid., p. 117.
21. Ibid., p. 119.
22. Ibid., p. 129.
23. Ibid., p. 131.
24. Ibid.
25. Ibid.
26. Ibid., p. 134.
27. Ibid., p. 135.
28. Ibid.
29. Ibid., p. 138.
30. Ibid., p. 142.
31. Ibid.
32. Ibid.
33. Ibid., p. 143.
34. Ibid., p. 147.
35. Ibid., p. 149.
36. Ibid., p. 150: 'We can merely ask that such decisions be not taken hastily and lightly, and that, all things considered, the evil that one inflicts be lesser than that which is being forestalled.'
37. Ibid., p. 153.
38. Ibid., p. 156.

6 OTHER DEFENCES OF EXISTENTIALISM: DE BEAUVOIR AND MERLEAU-PONTY

1. As de Beauvoir herself says, apropos the many attacks made on existentialism, 'some defence had to be made', *Force of Circumstance*, p. 76.
2. *Sense and Non-Sense*, p. 71.
3. Ibid., p. 72.
4. Ibid., p. 39.
5. Ibid.
6. Ibid.
7. Ibid.
8. Ibid., p. 40.
9. Ibid.
10. Ibid.
11. Ibid., p. 43.
12. Ibid.
13. Ibid., p. 45.
14. Ibid., p. 146.
15. Ibid.
16. Ibid.
17. Ibid.
18. Ibid., p. 147.
19. Ibid.
20. Ibid., p. 96.
21. Ibid., p. 95.

Notes 205

22. Ibid., p. 94.
23. Ibid.
24. *The Ethics of Ambiguity*, p. 134.
25. I owe this distinction to M. Ignatieff, 'Back to reality on the home front', *The Observer*, 3 March 1991.
26. *The Ethics of Ambiguity*, p. 149.
27. *Sense and Non-Sense*, p. 95.
28. Ibid., p. 96.
29. But this sympathy would not last: see S. Kruks, *The Political Philosophy of Merleau-Ponty*, pp. 101–18.

7 OTHER DEFENCES OF EXISTENTIALISM: DE BEAUVOIR AND SARTRE

1. *Les Carnets de la Drôle de Guerre: Novembre 1939–Mars 1940*. Gallimard, 1983. *War Diaries: Notebooks from a Phoney War, November 1939–March 1940*. Trans. Quentin Hoare, Verso, 1984.
2. Quoted in *War Diaries*, pp. viii, ix.
3. Ibid., p. ix.
4. Ibid.
5. Ibid., p. 107.
6. Ibid.
7. Ibid.
8. Ibid., p. 109.
9. Ibid.
10. Ibid., p. 110.
11. *L'Existentialisme et la sagesse des nations*, p. 13.
12. *Existentialism and Humanism*, p. 56.
13. Ibid.
14. *Being and Nothingness*, p. 38.
15. Ibid.
16. Ibid.
17. Ibid., pp. 625, 626.
18. Ibid., p. 626.
19. Ibid.
20. Ibid., p. 627.
21. *Existentialism and Humanism*, p. 28.
22. Ibid.
23. Ibid., p. 29.
24. Ibid.
25. Ibid., p. 30.
26. Ibid., pp. 30, 31.
27. On the basis that (i) if there is no God, then no one is *made* by God according to a divine plan, and (ii) if there is no God, we are not all made according to the *same* design or specification.
28. 'In other words... nothing will be changed if God does not exist; we shall re-discover the same norms of honesty, progress and humanity,

and we shall have disposed of God as an out-of-date hypothesis which will die away quietly of itself', *Existentialism and Humanism*, p. 33.
29. Ibid., pp. 33, 34.
30. Why this should be so is discussed at length by Alasdair MacIntyre in his *After Virtue*, especially in Chapter 5, 'Why the Enlightenment Project Had to Fail', pp. 49–59.
31. *Existentialism and Humanism*, p. 34.
32. Ibid., pp. 35, 36.
33. Ibid., pp. 36, 37.
34. Ibid., p. 38.
35. Ibid., p. 40.
36. *The Ethics of Ambiguity*, p. 108.
37. Ibid.
38. Ibid., p. 134.
39. *Existentialism and Humanism*, p. 34.
40. *The Ethics of Ambiguity*, p. 135.
41. Ibid.
42. Robert Brasillach, editor of *Je suis partout*, was sentenced to death for collaboration and anti-Semitism. Simone de Beauvoir refused to sign a petition seeking clemency on his behalf. She explains, and defends, her position at length in her essay 'An Eye for an Eye' (*'Oeuil pour oeuil'*).
43. *The Ethics of Ambiguity*, p. 149.
44. *Notebooks for an Ethics*, p. xix.
45. See *Being and Nothingness*, p. 628.
46. *Notebooks for an Ethics*, p. xxiv.
47. Ibid., p. 3.
48. Ibid.
49. Ibid., p. 7.
50. Ibid., p. 8.
51. Ibid., p. 13.
52. Ibid., p. 12.
53. Ibid., p. 17.
54. Ibid., p. 103.
55. Ibid.
56. Ibid., p. 104.
57. Ibid.
58. Ibid.
59. Ibid., p. 511.
60. Ibid., p. 512.
61. Ibid., p. 172.
62. Ibid.
63. Ibid.
64. Ibid.
65. Ibid., p. vii.
66. Ibid., pp. vii, viii.
67. Ibid., p. viii.
68. Ibid.
69. Ibid., p. ix.

8 DE BEAUVOIR'S *ETHICS*: A CRITICAL APPRAISAL

1. 'I was in error when I thought I could define a morality independent of a social context', *Force of Circumstance*, p. 76. I myself suspect that the *real* reason de Beauvoir reacted so harshly to this work in her later writings and interviews is that it showed how distanced she was, *philosophically*, from Sartre at the time she wrote it.
2. *L'Existentialisme et la sagesse des nations*, p. 109.
3. *Sense and Non-Sense*, p. 125.
4. Ibid., p. 126.
5. Ibid., p. 129.
6. *Karl Marx*, p. 64.
7. Ibid., p. 111.
8. Ibid.
9. Ibid., pp. 111, 112.
10. *Simone de Beauvoir: A Critical View*, p. 17.

THE HISTORICAL BACKGROUND TO *THE SECOND SEX*

1. *La Force des Choses*, Gallimard, 1963. First published in English, in 1965, under the title *Force of Circumstance*. In this chapter I shall quote from the 1987 Penguin edition.
2. *Force of Circumstance*, p. 11.
3. De Beauvoir's verdict seems harsh, but, in fact, Aragon's novel met with little response from the reading public. See Webster and Powell, *Saint-Germain-des-Prés*, p. 84.
4. *Force of Circumstance*, p. 21.
5. Ibid., p. 22.
6. *Simone de Beauvoir, A Biography*, p. 299.
7. *Force of Circumstance*, p. 31.
8. Ibid., p. 34.
9. Ibid.
10. See Francis and Gontier, *Simone de Beauvoir*, p. 215.
11. *Le Sang des Autres*.
12. *L'Invitée*.
13. *Force of Circumstance*, p. 45.
14. 'Sartre had refused Gabriel Marcel to apply this adjective to him: "My philosophy is a philosophy of existence; I don't even know what Existentialism is"', ibid., pp. 45, 46.
15. *Who Shall Die?* 'On October 13', reports Bair, '*Le Soir* welcomed the "young *Agregée* of Philosophy who is staging her First Play" with an interview in which Beauvoir talked about what happens when food is used as a weapon and various groups of people are arbitrarily selected to die of starvation. She said her aim in writing the play was "to prove that the struggle for freedom requires the unity of end with means"', *Simone de Beauvoir, A Biography*, p. 310. But the

play was neither a critical nor a box-office success: see *Force of Circumstance*, p. 59.

16. In the postwar period Paris quickly regained its ascendancy in the world of fashion. As Georgina Howell reports, 'February 2 [1947] and to the women present at the first collection of Christian Dior, the war and its drab aftermath seems to be over at last. Dior, formerly a designer at Lucien Lelong, opens in pristine premises at 30 Avenue Montaigne, and with his New Look reinstates Paris as the authoritative leader of world fashion. At the end of the show, Englishwomen can be seen tugging their skimpy skirts down over their knees, feeling suddenly uncomfortable in their square-shouldered "man-tailored" wartime suits', *In 'Vogue'*, p. 198. For a more detailed account of the fashion changes introduced by the New Look, see J. Mulvagh, *Costume Jewellery in 'Vogue'*, p. 88.

17. *Force of Circumstance*, p. 47.
18. Ibid.
19. *Tous les hommes sont mortels.*
20. *Force of Circumstance*, p. 71.
21. *Pour une morale de l'ambiguïté.*
22. *Force of Circumstance*, p. 76.
23. Ibid., p. 132.
24. She had had an affair, in 1945, with the director Michel Vitold, but I do not count this a major relationship.
25. They met in Chicago in February 1947, and became lovers almost at once. Algren, she told Deirdre Bair, '"turned (her) life upside down"... with him, she remembered, she had her "first complete orgasm" and she learned "how truly passionate love could be between men and women"', *Simone de Beauvoir, A Biography*, p. 333. For further information on the Algren–de Beauvoir relationship, see Francis and Gontier, *Simone de Beauvoir*, pp. 231–50; D. Bair, *Simone de Beauvoir, A Biography*, pp. 327–78; and B. Drew, *Nelson Algren: A Life on the Wild Side.*
26. *Force of Circumstance*, p. 135.
27. *America Day by Day.*
28. 'The Party intellectuals attacked him unmercifully because they were afraid that he would steal their clientele; that his position was so close to theirs only made them consider him as more dangerous than ever. "You are preventing people from coming to us", Garaudy told him. And Elsa Triolet: "You are a philosopher and therefore anti-Communist." ' *Force of Circumstance*, p. 140.
29. Ibid., p. 145.
30. Ibid.
31. *The Sunday Independent*, 10 February 1991.
32. *Force of Circumstance*, p. 177.
33. Jacques-Laurent Bost.
34. 'One evening in my room, Sartre, Bost and I spent several hours trying out words. I suggested: *The Other Sex?* No. Bost changed it to *The Second Sex* and when we thought it over that was exactly right.' *Force of Circumstance*, p. 178.

35. Ibid., p. 195.
36. Ibid., p. 196.
37. Ibid., p. 197.
38. Ibid.
39. *Saint-Germain-des-Prés*, pp. 155, 156.
40. *Force of Circumstance*, p. 200.
41. Ibid., p. 201.
42. Ibid.
43. Ibid.
44. Ibid., p. 202.
45. Webster and Powell, op. cit., p. 157.

10 THE PHILOSOPHICAL FOUNDATIONS OF *THE SECOND SEX*

1. *The Ethics of Ambiguity*, p. 83.
2. Ibid., p. 91.
3. See G. W. F. Hegel, *The Phenomenology of Mind*, pp. 229–40. There Hegel says such things as 'The relation of both self-consciousnesses is in this way so constituted that they prove themselves and each other through a life-and-death struggle.' *Phenomenology of Mind*, p. 232.
4. See *Being and Nothingness*, p. 509.
5. 'Others are the other, that is, the self which is *not myself*... The Other is the one who is not me and the one who I am not.' Ibid., p. 230.
6. Ibid., p. 523. This is because to the other I am 'Jew or Aryan, handsome or ugly, one-armed, etc.', ibid.
7. Someone who apprehends me as 'the-Other-as-object', ibid., p. 524.
8. 'It is this alienating process of making an object of my situation which is the constant and specific limit of my situation', ibid., p. 525.
9. 'Shame is by nature *recognition*. I recognize that I am as *the Other* sees me...', ibid., p. 222.
10. 'Thus suddenly an object has appeared which has stolen the world from me...This green turns towards the other a face which escapes me. I apprehend the relation of the green to the Other as an objective relation, but I can not apprehend the green as it appears to the Other.' Ibid., p. 255.
11. 'He belongs to my distances, the man is there, twenty paces from me, he is turning his back on me', ibid.
12. 'every concrete apprehension of a consciousness of my consciousness becomes a proof that I am conscious of that consciousness', ibid., p. 279.
13. See *The Second Sex*, p. 17.
14. 'But if the Other is not to regain the status of being the One, he must be submissive enough to accept this alien point of view', ibid., p. 18.
15. 'Throughout history they have always been subordinated to men, and hence their dependency is not the result of a historical event or a social change – it was not something that *occurred*. The reason why otherness in this case seems to be an absolute is in part that it lacks the contingent or incidental nature of historical facts', ibid.

16. 'They propose to stabilize her as object and to doom her to immanence.' Ibid., p. 29.
17. '...her transcendence is to be overshadowed and for ever transcended by another ego (*conscience*) which is essential and sovereign', ibid.
18. '...what circumstances limit woman's liberty and how can they be overcome?', ibid.
19. Ibid., pp. 94, 95.
20. Ibid., p. 95.
21. This argument can be found in Genevieve Lloyd's *The Man of Reason*. See Chapter 17.
22. For a most incisive discussion of recent debates in this area of philosophy, see D. Miller, 'Only human', *The Times Literary Supplement*, 22 May 1987.
23. Especially pp. 13–69.
24. *The Second Sex*, p. 29.
25. Ibid., p. 66.
26. Ibid.
27. See R. Tong, *Feminist Thought*, pp. 212, 213.
28. 'For, the body being the instrument of our grasp upon the world, the world is bound to seem a very different thing when apprehended in one manner or another.' *The Second Sex*, p. 65.
29. Ibid., p. 66.
30. Ibid., p. 67.
31. Ibid., p. 8.
32. *The Ethics of Ambiguity*, p. 83.
33. See her extended footnote on Lévinas, ibid., p. 16.

11 *THE SECOND SEX:* WOMAN AS THE OTHER

1. *The Second Sex*, p. 17.
2. Ibid.
3. See ibid., pp. 15, 16.
4. Ibid., p. 16.
5. Ibid., p. 23.
6. Ibid.
7. *The Second Sex* is broadly divided into two sections: Book I, entitled 'Facts and Myths', and Book II, called 'Woman's Life Today'.
8. *The Second Sex*, p. 29.
9. Ibid.
10. Ibid., p. 52.
11. Ibid.
12. Ibid., pp. 52, 53.
13. Ibid., p. 53.
14. Ibid., p. 54.
15. Ibid.
16. Ibid., p. 62.
17. Ibid.

18. Ibid., p. 63.
19. Ibid., p. 65.
20. Ibid., p. 66.
21. Ibid., pp. 70, 71.
22. Ibid., p. 71.
23. Ibid., p. 72.
24. Ibid.
25. Ibid., p. 73.
26. Ibid.
27. Ibid., pp. 80, 81.
28. Ibid., p. 84.
29. Ibid., p. 85.
30. Ibid.
31. Ibid.
32. Ibid.
33. Ibid.
34. Ibid.
35. Ibid., p. 86.
36. Ibid.
37. Ibid., p. 89.
38. Ibid.
39. Ibid.
40. Ibid., p. 90.

12 EXISTENTIALISM AND THE ORIGINS OF MALE SUPREMACY

1. *The Second Sex*, p. 91.
2. Ibid., p. 93.
3. Ibid., p. 94.
4. Ibid., pp. 94, 95.
5. Ibid., p. 95.
6. Ibid., pp. 95, 96.
7. Ibid., p. 96.
8. Ibid.
9. See ibid., pp. 93–159.
10. Ibid., pp. 159, 160.
11. Ibid., p. 161.
12. Ibid., p. 162.
13. Ibid., pp. 162, 163.
14. Ibid., p. 164.
15. Ibid., p. 165.
16. Ibid., pp. 166, 167.
17. Ibid., p. 168.
18. Ibid.

13 THE MARRIED WOMAN

Maurice Cranston, for example, writes: 'Unmarried, and uninterested in motherhood, living, in fact, to all intents and purposes just like a man, Simone de Beauvoir is not ideally qualified by experience to write the kind of book she hoped to write', *The Novelist as Philosopher*, p. 181.
2. See Bair, pp. 155, 156.
3. It was ' "the most bourgeois of institutions" ', Bair, p. 156; ' "Marriage was impossible. I had no dowry" ', ibid., and 'Marriage doubles one's domestic responsibilities, and indeed, all one's social chores', *The Prime of Life*, p. 77.
4. Bair, p. 339.
5. She quotes from the *Kinsey Report*, and also from Colette, Michaux, Stekel, Genet and Rilke.
6. *The Second Sex*, p. 463.
7. Ibid., p. 469.
8. Ibid., p. 470.
9. Ibid., p. 446.
10. Ibid., p. 447.
11. Ibid.
12. Ibid.
13. Ibid., pp. 448, 449.
14. Ibid., p. 449.
15. Ibid., p. 450.
16. Ibid.
17. Ibid., p. 451.
18. Ibid., p. 453.
19. Ibid., p. 454.
20. Ibid., p. 455.
21. Ibid., p. 458.
22. Ibid., p. 463.
23. Ibid.
24. Ibid., p. 464.
25. Ibid., p. 465.
26. Ibid., p. 469.
27. Ibid.
28. Ibid.
29. Ibid.
30. Ibid., p. 471.
31. Ibid., p. 472.
32. Ibid.
33. Ibid.
34. Ibid., p. 474.
35. Ibid.
36. Ibid.
37. Ibid.
38. Ibid., pp. 479, 480.
39. Ibid., p. 480.

40. Ibid., p. 484.
41. Ibid., pp. 484, 485.
42. Ibid., pp. 486, 487.
43. Ibid., p. 487.
44. Ibid.
45. Ibid., p. 490.
46. Ibid.
47. Ibid., p. 491.
48. Ibid., p. 493.
49. Ibid., p. 494.
50. Ibid., p. 496.
51. Ibid.

14 THE MOTHER

1. *Simone de Beauvoir, A Biography*, p. 170.
2. *The Second Sex*, p. 502.
3. Ibid., p. 509.
4. Ibid., p. 510.
5. Ibid., p. 512.
6. Ibid., p. 513.
7. Ibid., p. 514.
8. Ibid.
9. Ibid., p. 518.
10. Ibid.
11. Ibid., p. 520.
12. Ibid.
13. Ibid., p. 521.
14. Ibid., p. 522.
15. Ibid.
16. Ibid., pp. 522, 523.
17. Ibid., p. 523.
18. Ibid., p. 524.
19. Ibid., p. 525.
20. Ibid., p. 526.
21. Ibid.
22. Ibid.
23. Ibid., p. 527.
24. Ibid., pp. 528, 529.
25. Ibid., p. 529.
26. Ibid.
27. Ibid., p. 530.
28. Ibid., p. 531.
29. Ibid., pp. 531, 532.
30. Ibid., p. 534.
31. Ibid., p. 536.
32. Ibid., pp. 535, 536.

33. Ibid., p. 538.
34. Ibid., p. 539.
35. Ibid.
36. Ibid.

15   THE INDEPENDENT WOMAN

1. *The Second Sex*, p. 295.
2. Ibid.
3. Ibid., p. 691.
4. Ibid., pp. 691, 692.
5. Ibid., p. 692.
6. Ibid., p. 693.
7. Ibid.
8. Ibid., pp. 693, 694.
9. Ibid., p. 694.
10. Ibid., p. 696.
11. Ibid., p. 697.
12. Ibid., p. 698.
13. Ibid.
14. Ibid.
15. Ibid.
16. Ibid.
17. Ibid., p. 701.
18. Ibid., p. 703.
19. Ibid., p. 725.
20. Ibid.
21. Ibid., p. 726.
22. Ibid.
23. Ibid., pp. 726, 727.
24. Ibid., pp. 727, 728.
25. Ibid., p. 728.
26. Ibid., pp. 727, 728.
27. Ibid., p. 734.
28. Ibid., p. 735.
29. Ibid., p. 740.

16   RESPONSES TO *THE SECOND SEX*: 1962–79

1. *The Novelist as Philosopher*, p. 180.
2. Ibid., p. 187.
3. Ibid.
4. Ibid.
5. Ibid.
6. Ibid., p. 180.
7. Ibid.

8. Ibid., p. 181.
9. *Simone de Beauvoir*, p. 94.
10. Ibid., p. 95.
11. Ibid.
12. Ibid., p. 96.
13. Ibid., p. 97.
14. Ibid.
15. Ibid., pp. 97, 98.
16. Ibid., p. 91.
17. Ibid.
18. Ibid., p. 105.
19. Ibid.
20. Ibid., pp. 105, 106.
21. Ibid., pp. 106, 107.
22. *Simone de Beauvoir on Woman*, p. 208.
23. 'Even if Simone de Beauvoir's intentions were to defend woman's character and qualities the actual reading of *The Second Sex* seems to confirm the opposite view. That is, she castigates all the misogynist platitudes of Aristotle, St. Paul, Balzac, Michelet, Luther *et al.*, but she herself almost seems to illustrate their opinions.' Ibid., pp. 39, 40.
24. Ibid., p. 40.
25. Ibid., pp. 38, 39.
26. 'In *The Second Sex* Simone de Beauvoir's scorn for her own sex outweighs her compassion, which she nevertheless wants to express.' Ibid., p. 40.
27. Ibid.
28. Ibid., p. 39.
29. Ibid.
30. Ibid., p. 220.
31. Ibid., p. 221.
32. *Simone de Beauvoir*, pp. 118, 119.
33. Ibid., p. 114.
34. Ibid.
35. Ibid., pp. 132, 133.

17 RESPONSES TO *THE SECOND SEX*: 1981–85

1. Genevieve Lloyd maintains that 'She argues, from an explicitly anti-feminist perspective, that many feminists share dubious assumptions about rationality and human nature with philosophical rationalists', *The Man of Reason*, p. 125.
2. In a footnote, McMillan writes that 'This view of moral practices and their justification follows the conception of D. Z. Phillips and H. O. Mounce in *Moral Practices*', *Women, Reason and Nature*, p. 18; while on p. 26 she advises her readers as follows: 'For further elucidation of the relation between guilt, repentance, punishment and expiation that I

am assuming, see Peter Winch, 'Ethical Reward and Punishment', ch. 11 in *Ethics and Action*'. See also O. O'Neill's review of McMillan's book in *The London Review*, 15 September 1983.

3.   *Simone de Beauvoir and the Limits of Commitment*, p. 137.
4.   Ibid.
5.   Ibid.
6.   Ibid., pp. 144, 145.
7.   Ibid., p. 146.
8.   Ibid.
9.   Ibid., p. 147.
10. 'Her only criticism of the content, as opposed to the aesthetic value, was expressed in 1963 in *La Force des Choses*. She had come to realise, looking at the problem now in a more Marxist light, that the relegation of woman to the role of *l'autre* had an economic basis ("the facts of supply and demand") rather than an ethical one (a "struggle of consciences").' Ibid., p. 149.
11. Ibid.
12. Ibid.
13. Ibid., p. 150.
14. Ibid., p. 151.
15. *Public Man, Private Woman*, p. 210.
16. Ibid.
17. Ibid., p. 306.
18. Ibid.
19. Ibid.
20. Ibid., pp. 306, 307.
21. Ibid., p. 307.
22. Ibid.
23. Ibid.
24. Ibid.
25. Ibid., p. 308.
26. *Women, Reason and Nature*, p. 115.
27. Ibid.
28. Ibid.
29. Ibid., p. 117.
30. Ibid., p. 118.
31. Ibid., p. 121.
32. Ibid., p. 122.
33. Ibid.
34. Ibid., p. 125.
35. Ibid., p. 126.
36. Ibid., p. 127.
37. Ibid., p. 128.
38. Ibid., p. 129.
39. Ibid., pp. 130, 131.
40. Ibid., p. 133.
41. Ibid.
42. Ibid., p. 134.
43. *Simone de Beauvoir, A Study of Her Writings*, p. 104.

44. Ibid., p. 105.
45. Ibid.
46. Ibid.
47. Ibid., p. 106.
48. Ibid.
49. Ibid.
50. Ibid.
51. Ibid., p. 111.
52. *The Man of Reason*, p. 96.
53. Ibid.
54. Ibid., pp. 98, 99.
55. Ibid., p. 99.
56. Ibid., p. 100.
57. Ibid.
58. Ibid., p. 101.
59. Ibid.
60. *Simone de Beauvoir, A Feminist Mandarin*, p. x.
61. Ibid., pp. x, xi.
62. Ibid., p. 57.
63. Ibid., p. 58.
64. Ibid., p. 63.
65. Ibid.
66. Ibid.
67. Ibid.
68. Ibid., p. 65.
69. Ibid., p. 67.
70. Ibid.
71. Ibid.
72. Ibid., p. 68.
73. Ibid.
74. Ibid., p. 69.
75. Ibid.
76. Ibid., p. 70.

18 RESPONSES TO *THE SECOND SEX*: 1986–94

1. *Simone de Beauvoir, A Re-Reading*, p. 52.
2. Ibid.
3. Ibid., pp. 52, 53.
4. Ibid., p. 53.
5. Ibid., pp. 60, 61.
6. Ibid., p. 73.
7. Ibid., pp. 76, 77.
8. Ibid., p. 90.
9. Ibid., p. 95.
10. Ibid., p. 97.
11. *New Left Review*, March–April 1986, p. 116.

12. Ibid., p. 117.
13. Ibid., pp. 117, 118.
14. Ibid., p. 121.
15. Ibid., p. 122.
16. Ibid.
17. Ibid., p. 124.
18. *Feminism and Philosophy*, p. 2.
19. Ibid., p. 48.
20. Ibid., p. 49.
21. Ibid., p. 58.
22. *Hipparchia's Choice*, p. 86.
23. Ibid.
24. Ibid., p. 89.
25. Ibid., p. 90.
26. Ibid., p. 93.
27. Ibid.
28. Ibid.
29. Ibid.
30. Ibid.
31. Ibid., p. 106.
32. *Simone de Beauvoir: The Making of an Intellectual Woman*, p. 213.
33. Ibid., p. 211.
34. Ibid., p. 151.
35. Ibid.
36. Ibid., p. 153.
37. Ibid.
38. Ibid., p. 154.
39. Ibid., p. 155.
40. Ibid.
41. Ibid.
42. Ibid., p. 162.
43. Ibid., p. 163.
44. Ibid., pp. 163, 164.
45. Ibid., p. 168.
46. Ibid.

19 SIMONE DE BEAUVOIR'S EXISTENTIALIST FEMINISM: A DEFENCE

1. *The Second Sex*, p. 89.
2. Ibid., p. 691.
3. As de Beauvoir does not quote from Sartre at this juncture, I shall not pursue this aspect of the McMillan criticism any further.
4. *The Second Sex*, p. 60.
5. Ibid., p. 61.
6. Ibid.
7. Ibid., p. 65.
8. Ibid.

9. *Feminism and Equality*, p. 148.
10. Neither do I agree with her view of housework as a kind of Sisyphean torture. Keeping house for oneself is neither laborious nor time-consuming; it is having to keep house for others, whose squalid habits and indifference to one's efforts constantly undo the work done, that transform a reasonably rewarding activity into a Sisyphean nightmare.
11. *The Second Sex*, p. 52.
12. I owe this distinction to Katharine Whitehorn, the columnist with *The Observer*.
13. Carmel Leydon, Evening B.A. student, UCG, 1992.
14. *Intercourse*, p. 203.
15. For example, Stoltenberg says that 'Somewhere inside all of us, we know that our bodies harbour deep resemblances, that we are wired inside to respond in a profound harmony to the resonances of eroticism inside the body of someone near to us...The nerve networks and interlock of capillaries throughout our pelvises electrify and engorge as if plugged in together and pumping as one. That's what we feel when we feel one another's feelings. That's what can happen during sex that is mutual, equal, reciprocal, profoundly communing.' *Refusing to Be a Man*, p. 41.
16. *The Origin of the Family*, pp. 104, 105.
17. Ibid., p. 105.
18. Ibid., p. 103.
19. Ibid., p. 114.
20. Ibid.
21. *The Second Sex*, p. 733.
22. Ibid., p. 89.
23. Ibid., p. 740.
24. Ibid.
25. *je, tu, nous*, p. 10.
26. Ibid., p. 11.
27. *The Second Sex*, p. 735.
28. Ibid., pp. 691, 692.
29. *I Love to You*, pp. 29, 30.

Bibliography

G. Annan, 'Serious Lady', review of S. de Beauvoir, *All Said and Done*, in *The Listener*, 6 June 1974.

K. Ansell-Pearson, 'Igniting a fuse to explore the canon', review of J.A. Winders, *Gender, Theory and the Canon*, in *The Times Higher Education Supplement*, 24 January 1992.

R. Arditti et al. (eds), *Test-Tube Women*. Pandora, 1984.

C. Ascher, *Simone de Beauvoir: A Life of Freedom*. Harvester Press, 1982.

D. Bair, *Simone de Beauvoir, A Biography*. Summit Books, 1990. Cape, 1990.

W. Barrett, *Irrational Man*. Doubleday, 1958. Anchor, 1962.

M. Beard, 'Genitalia and other Othernesses', review of T. Laqueur, *Making Sex: Body and Gender from the Greeks to Freud*, in *The Times Literary Supplement*, 5 September 1991.

S. de Beauvoir, *L'Invitée*. Gallimard, 1943. (*She Came to Stay*. Penguin, Secker & Warburg, 1966.)

——, *Pyrrhus et Cinéas*. Gallimard, 1944. 'Pyrrhus and Cineas Selections', *Partisan Review*, Vol. 3, No. 3, 1946, pp. 430–37.

——, *Le Sang des Autres*. Gallimard, 1945. (*The Blood of Others*. Secker and Warburg and Lindsay Drummond, 1948.)

——, *Pour une morale de l'ambiguïté*. Gallimard, 1947. (*The Ethics of Ambiguity*. The Philosophical Library, 1948.)

——, *L'Existentialisme et la sagesse des nations*. Nagel, 1948.

——, *Le Deuxième Sexe*. Gallimard, 1949. (*The Second Sex*. Jonathan Cape, 1953. Penguin Books, 1972.)

——, *Les Mandarins*. Gallimard, 1954. (*The Mandarins*. Collins, 1957.)

——, *Mémoires d'une jeune fille rangée*. Gallimard, 1958. (*Memoirs of a dutiful daughter*. A. Deutsch, Weidenfeld and Nicolson, 1959. Penguin Books, 1963.)

——, *La Force de l'Âge*. Gallimard, 1960. (*The Prime of Life*. A. Deutsch, Weidenfeld and Nicolson, 1962. Penguin Books, 1965.)

——, *La Force des choses*. Gallimard, 1963. (*Force of Circumstance*. A. Deutsch, Weidenfeld and Nicolson, 1965. Penguin Books, 1968.)

——, *Une Mort très douce*. Gallimard, 1964. (*A Very Easy Death*. A. Deutsch, Weidenfeld and Nicolson, 1966. Penguin Books, 1969.)

——, *Les Belles Images*. Gallimard, 1966. (*Les Belles Images*. Collins, 1968. Fontana, 1969.)

——, *La Vieillesse*. Gallimard, 1970. (*Old Age*. Penguin Books, 1977.)

——, *Tout Compte Fait*. Gallimard, 1972. (*All Said and Done*. A. Deutsch, Weidenfeld and Nicolson, G. P. Putman, 1974.)

——, *Quand prime le spirituel*. Gallimard, 1979. (*When Things of the Spirit Come First*. A. Deutsch, Weidenfeld and Nicolson, 1982.)

——, *La Cérémonie des adieux*. Gallimard, 1981. (*Adieux, A Farewell to Sartre*. A. Deutsch, Weidenfeld and Nicolson, 1984. Penguin Books, 1985.)

——, *Lettres à Sartre*. Gallimard, 1990. (*Letters to Sartre*. Vintage, 1992.)

A. Beevor and A. Cooper, *Paris After the Liberation*. Hamish Hamilton, 1994.

H.J. Blackham, *Six Existentialist Thinkers*. Harper and Row, 1959.

A. Camus, *L'Étranger*. Gallimard, 1942. (*The Outsider*. Trans. J. Laredo. Hamish Hamilton, 1982. Penguin Books, 1983.)

——, *Le Mythe de Sisyphe*. Gallimard, 1942. (*The Myth of Sisyphus*. Hamish Hamilton, 1955.)

——, *Le Malentendu et Caligula*. Gallimard, 1944. (*Caligula and Cross Purpose*. Hamish Hamilton, 1948. Penguin Books, 1962.)

——, *La Peste*. Gallimard, 1947. (*The Plague*. Hamish Hamilton, 1948. Penguin Books, 1962.)

——, *Carnets 1935–1942*. Gallimard, 1962. (*Carnets 1942–1951*. Gallimard, 1964.)

——, *Selected Essays and Notebooks*. Hamish Hamilton, 1963. Penguin Books, 1970.

——, *Lyrical and Critical*. Hamish Hamilton, 1967.

——, *La Mort Heureuse*. Gallimard, 1971. (*A Happy Death*. Hamish Hamilton, 1972. Penguin Books, 1982.)

——, *Écrits de Jeunesse d'Albert Camus*. Gallimard, 1973. (*Youthful Writings*. Hamish Hamilton, 1977. Penguin Books, 1980.)

——, *Le Premier Homme*. Gallimard, 1994. (*The First Man*. Hamish Hamilton, 1995.)

E. Canestier et H. Mathieu, 'L'Amour Interrompu: entretien avec Hélène de Beauvoir', *Marie Claire*, Août, 1986, pp. 62–8.

H. Carpenter, 'Secondary sexual character', review of D. Bair, *Simone de Beauvoir*, in *The Sunday Times*, 17 June 1990.

——, 'Downhill all the way', review of B. Drew, *Nelson Algren*, in *The Sunday Times*, 20 January 1991.

P. Caws, 'Oracular Lives: Sartre and the Twentieth Century', *Revue Internationale de Philosophie*, Nos 152–3, 1985, pp. 172–83.

J. Charvet, *Feminism*. Dent, 1982.

R. Clare, 'Can Marriage damage your health?' *The Irish Times*, 21 April 1993.

G.A. Cohen, *Karl Marx's Theory of History: A Defence*. Oxford University Press, 1978.

——, *History, Labour and Freedom*. Clarendon Press, 1988.

A. Cohen-Solal, *Sartre: A Life*. Heinemann, 1987.

——, 'Sartre: The Lovers' Contract', *The Observer*, 11 October 1987.

R.D. Cottrell, *Simone de Beauvoir*. Frederick Ungar, 1975.

M. Cranston, 'Simone de Beauvoir', in J. Cruickshank (ed.), *The Novelist As Philosopher*, pp. 166–82.

——, 'A Second Voltaire?', *The Sunday Times*, 20 April 1980.

J. Cruickshank (ed.), *The Novelist As Philosopher: Studies in French Fiction, 1935–1960*. Oxford University Press, 1962.

——, 'Camus', in *The Novelist as Philosopher*, pp. 206–29.

J. Dewey, 'Means and Ends', *New International*, August 1938. Reprinted in L. Trotsky, *Their Morals and Ours*, 1973.

A. Dondeyne, *Foi Chrétienne et Pensée Contemporaine*. Publications Universitaires de Louvain, 1951.

C. Doyle, 'The female heart', *The Observer*, 13 April 1986.

B. Drew, *Nelson Algren: A Life on the Wild Side*. Bloomsbury, 1991.

A. Dworkin, *Right-Wing Women: The Politics of Domesticated Females.* The Women's Press, 1983.

——, *Intercourse.* Secker and Warburg, 1987. Arrow Books, 1988.

J.B. Elshtain, *Public Man, Private Woman.* Princeton University Press, 1981.

——, 'Against Androgyny', *Telos* 47, Spring 1981. Reprinted in A. Phillips (ed.), *Feminism and Equality.* Blackwell, 1987, pp. 139–59.

J. Elster, *Making Sense of Marx.* Cambridge University Press, 1985.

F. Engels, *The Origin of the Family, Private Property and the State.* First published 1884. Lawrence and Wishart, 1972. Penguin Books, 1985.

M. Evans, *Simone de Beauvoir, A Feminist Mandarin.* Tavistock, 1985.

E. Fallaize, *The Novels of Simone de Beauvoir.* Routledge, 1988.

S. Firestone, *The Dialectic of Sex.* Jonathan Cape, 1971. The Women's Press, 1979.

G. Fitzgerald, 'Radical shifts in society's structure', *The Irish Times,* 21 December 1991.

C. Francis and F. Gontier, *Les Écrits de Simone de Beauvoir.* Gallimard, 1979.

——, *Simone de Beauvoir.* Sidgwick and Jackson, 1987.

E. Frazer et al. (eds), *Ethics: A Feminist Reader.* Blackwell, 1992.

B. Friedan, *The Feminine Mystique.* V. Gollancz, 1963. Penguin Books, 1965.

——, *The Fountain of Age.* Jonathan Cape, 1993. Vintage, 1994.

M. Gatens, *Feminism and Philosophy.* Polity Press, 1991.

R.T. de George (ed.), *Ethics and Society.* Macmillan, 1968.

L. Goldstein, 'Mill, Marx and Women's Liberation', *Journal of the History of Philosophy,* Vol. XVII, 1980, pp. 319–34.

S.J. Gould, 'The Birth of the Two-Sex World', review of T. Laqueur, *Making Sex,* in *The New York Review,* 13 June 1991, pp. 11–17.

J. Harris, 'Nature's Chastity', in *The London Review,* 15 September 1983.

R. Hayman, *Writing Against: A Biography of Sartre.* Weidenfeld and Nicolson, 1986.

——, 'Kissing and telling Beaver', review of J.-P. Sartre, *Lettres au Castor et à quelques autres,* in *The Observer,* 13 November 1983.

G.W.F. Hegel, *The Phenomenology of Mind.* George Allen and Unwin, 1910, 1966.

M. Heidegger, *Being and Time.* Blackwell, 1962.

S. Hite, *Women as Revolutionary Agents of Change: The Hite Reports 1972–1993.* Bloomsbury, 1993.

G. Howell, *In 'Vogue'.* Penguin Books, 1978.

C. Howells (ed.), *The Cambridge Companion to Sartre.* Cambridge University Press, 1992.

L. Hughes-Hallett, 'Menage à trois, quatre, cinq...', review of Simone de Beauvoir, *Letters to Sartre,* in *The Sunday Times,* 8 December 1991.

M. Ignatieff, 'Back to reality on the home front', *The Observer,* 3 March 1991.

L. Irigaray, *je, tu, nous.* Routledge, 1993.

——, *I Love to You.* Routledge, 1996.

A.M. Jagger, 'Feminist Ethics: Some Issues for the Nineties', in W.H. Shaw (ed.), *Social and Personal Ethics,* Wadsworth, 1993.

F. Jeanson, *Simone de Beauvoir ou l'entreprise de vivre.* Éditions du Seuil, 1966.

D. Johnson, 'La Grande Sartreuse', review of A. Whitmarsh, *Simone de Beauvoir and the Limits of Commitment*, and O. Todd, *Un Fils Rebelle*, in *The London Review*, 15 October 1981.

R. Jolivet, *Les Doctrines Existentialistes de Kierkegaard à J.-P. Sartre*. Éditions de Fontenelle, 1948.

W. Kaufmann, *Existentialism from Dostoevsky to Sartre*. Meridian, 1969.

T. Keefe, *Simone de Beauvoir: A Study of Her Writings*. Harrap, 1983.

S. Kruks, *The Political Philosophy of Merleau-Ponty*. Harvester Press, 1981.

T. Laqueur, *Making Sex: Body and Gender from the Greeks to Freud*. Harvard University Press, 1990.

M. Le Doeuff, *Hipparchia's Choice: An Essay Concerning Women, Philosophy, etc.* Blackwell, 1991.

J. Leighton, *Simone de Beauvoir on Woman*. Associated University Presses, 1975.

D. Leitch, 'Sartre: the legacy of a passionate man', *The Sunday Times*, 20 April 1980.

G. Lloyd, *The Man of Reason: Male and Female in Western Philosophy*. Routledge, 2nd edition, 1993.

H. Lottman, *Albert Camus: A Biography*. Picador, 1981.

P. McCarthy, *Camus: A Critical Study of his Life and Work*. Hamish Hamilton, 1982.

A. MacIntyre, 'Existentialism', in D.J. O'Connor (ed.), *A Critical History of Western Philosophy*. The Free Press, 1964, pp. 509–29.

——, *After Virtue*. University of Notre Dame Press, 1981.

C. McMillan, *Women, Reason and Nature*. Blackwell, 1982.

J. Macquarrie, *Existentialism*. Pelican, 1973.

M. Maher, 'Asking all the right questions', review of *The Hite Reports*, in *The Irish Times*, 13 March 1993.

E. Mahon, 'Women's Rights and Catholicism in Ireland', *New Left Review*, No. 166, November–December 1986, pp. 53–77.

——, *Motherhood, Work and Equal Opportunity*. Government Stationery Office, July 1991.

J. Mahon, 'Responsibility, Moral Judgement and Moral Obligation', *Journal of Moral Education*, Vol. 1, No. 3, 1972, pp. 195–201.

——, 'Consciousness and the Marxist Tradition', *Philosophical Studies*, Vol. XXVII, 1980, pp. 143–58.

——, *An Introduction to Practical Ethics*. Turoe Press, 1984.

——, 'Divorce California-style and its implications for the Irish debate', *In Dublin*, 12 June 1986, pp. 23–7.

——, 'Poetry, Biography and Truth', *Krino*, No. 4, Autumn 1987, pp. 35–41.

——, 'Ethics and Drug Testing in Human Beings', in J.D.G. Evans (ed.), *Moral Philosophy and Contemporary Problems*. Cambridge University Press, 1988, pp. 199–211.

——, 'Change from genetic to social motherhood', *The Irish Medical Times*, 24 February 1989.

——, 'Marx as a social historian', *History of European Ideas*, Vol. 12, No. 6, 1990, pp. 749–66.

——, 'Existentialism, Feminism and Simone de Beauvoir', Critical Notice of D. Bair, *Simone de Beauvoir* in *History of European Ideas*, Vol. 17, No. 5, 1993, pp. 651–8.

——, 'The Legacy of Jean-Paul Sartre', Critical Notice of C. Howells (ed.), *The Cambridge Companion to Sartre*, in *HEI*, Vol. 21, No. 3, 1995, pp. 401–10.

——, 'The Making of Sartre's Theory of History', Critical Notice of A. Dobson, *Jean-Paul Sartre and the Politics of Reason*, in *HEI*, Vol. 21, No. 3, 1995, pp. 411–20.

——, Review of A. Caplan, *Moral Matters: Ethical Issues in Medicine and the Life Sciences*, in *Journal of Medical Ethics*, Vol. 22, No. 1, 1996, pp. 61, 62.

H. Marcuse, 'Ethics and Revolution', in R.T. de George (ed.), *Ethics and Society*, pp. 133–47.

M. Merleau-Ponty, *Sens et Non-Sens*. Nagel, 1948. (*Sense and Non-Sense*. Northwestern University Press, 1964.)

J.S. Mill, *On Liberty, The Subjection of Women, and Chapters on Socialism*. S. Collini (ed.), Cambridge University Press, 1989.

D. Miller, 'Only human', *The Times Literary Supplement*, 22 May 1987.

K. Millett, *Sexual Politics*. Simon and Schuster, 1969. Doubleday, 1972.

J. Mitchell and A. Oakley (eds), *What is Feminism?* Blackwell, 1986.

T. Moi (ed.), *French Feminist Thought: A Reader*. Blackwell, 1987.

T. Moi, *Simone de Beauvoir: The Making of an Intellectual Woman*. Blackwell, 1994.

S. Moller Okin, *Justice, Gender and the Family*. Basic Books, 1989.

A. Montefiore, 'The work done by foreign philosophers', *The Listener*, 4 March 1971.

C. Murphy, 'The agonising choice of home or career', *The Irish Times*, 8 February 1988.

M. Murphy, 'A Life of subordination to Sartre', *The Irish Times*, 9 June 1990.

T. Murtagh, ' "The kind of woman I've always liked" – Jean-Paul Sartre', *The Sunday Tribune*, 20 April 1986.

M. Nussbaum, 'Justice for Women', review of S. Moller Okin, *Justice, Gender and the Family*, in *The New York Review*, 8 October, 1992, pp. 43–8.

C.C. O'Brien, *Camus*. Fontana, 1970.

——, 'The Angel of the Absurd', review of P. McCarthy, *Camus: A Critical Study of his Life and Work*, in *The Times Literary Supplement*, 7 May 1982.

U. O'Connor, 'Nelson in exile', review of B. Drew, *Nelson Algren*, in *The Sunday Independent*, 10 February 1991.

J. Okely, *Simone de Beauvoir, A Re-Reading*. Virago, 1986.

O. O'Neill, 'The Androgynous Claim', review of J. Charvet, *Feminism*, and C. McMillan, *Women, Reason and Nature*, in *The London Review*, 15 September 1983.

Y. Patterson, *Simone de Beauvoir and the Demystification of Motherhood*. UMI Research Press, 1991.

A. Phillips (ed.), *Feminism and Equality*. Blackwell, 1987.

A. Phillips, *Engendering Democracy*. Polity Press, 1991.

A. Rich, *Of Woman Born: Motherhood as Experience and Institution*. Norton, 1976.

L. Sage, 'Last Testament', review of S. de Beauvoir, *Adieux: A Farewell to Sartre*, in *The Observer*, 17 June 1984.

——, 'Woman's whole existence', review of S. Hite, *Women and Love: The New Hite Report*, in *The Observer*, 28 February 1988.

——, 'Dear Jean Letters', review of S. de Beauvoir, *Letters to Sartre*, in *The Sunday Times*, 29 December 1991.

J.-P. Sartre, *La Nausée*. Gallimard, 1938.

——, *Nausea*. Penguin Books, 1965.

——, *Le Mur*. Gallimard, 1939.

——, *Intimacy*. Neville Spearman, 1949. Panther Books, 1960. Also published under the title *The Wall and Other Stories*. New Directions, 1948.

——, *L'Être et le Néant*. Gallimard, 1943. (*Being and Nothingness*. Methuen, 1957.)

——, *L'Existentialisme est un humanisme*. Nagel, 1946. (*Existentialism and Humanism*. Methuen, 1948, 1957.)

——, *Literary and Philosophical Essays*. Hutchinson, 1955.

——, *Critique de la raison dialectique, précedé de questions de méthode, I*. Gallimard, 1960.

——, *Critique of Dialectical Reason*. New Left Books, 1976.

——, *Search for a method*. A. Knopf Inc., 1963. Vintage Books, 1968.

——, *Les Mots*. Gallimard, 1963. (*Words*. Hamish Hamilton, 1964. Penguin Books, 1967.)

——, *Between Existentialism and Marxism*. New Left Books, 1974.

——, *Life/Situations*. Pantheon Books, 1977.

——, *Lettres au Castor*. Gallimard, 1983.

——, '"Where I got it wrong on despair": interview with B. Levy', *The Observer*, 20 April 1980.

——, *Les Carnets de la Drôle de Guerre: Novembre 1939–Mars 1940*. Gallimard, 1983.

——, *War Diaries: Notebooks from a Phoney War: November 1939–March 1940*. Verso, 1984.

——, *Witness to My Life: The Letters of Jean-Paul Sartre to Simone de Beauvoir, 1926–1939*. Hamish Hamilton, 1992.

——, *Cahiers pour une morale*. Gallimard, 1988. (*Notebooks for an Ethics*. University of Chicago Press, 1992.)

A. Sington, 'Fidelity and Feminism', *The Irish Times*, 17 April 1986.

R. Smyth, 'Simone de Beauvoir', *The Observer*, 20 April 1986.

——, 'La vie en prose', *The Observer*, 17 December 1989.

K. Soper, 'The Qualities of Simone de Beauvoir', *New Left Review*, No. 156, March–April 1986, pp. 114–28.

G. Steiner, *Heidegger*. Fontana, 1978.

——, 'In France "an entire intellectual era is coming to a close"', *The Sunday Times*, 11 June 1981.

G. Steinem, *Outrageous Acts and Everyday Rebellions*. Jonathan Cape, 1984. Fontana, 1984.

J. Stoltenberg, *Refusing to Be a Man*. Fontana, 1990.

C. Taylor, 'What's Wrong with Negative Liberty?', in A. Ryan (ed.), *The Idea of Freedom*. Oxford University Press, 1979, pp. 175–93.

P. Thody, *Jean-Paul Sartre*. Hamish Hamilton, 1960.

C. Tomalin, 'Out of Bondage', review of C. Francis and F. Gontier, *Simone de Beauvoir*, in *The Observer*, 26 July 1987.

R. Tong, *Feminist Thought*. Unwin Hyman, 1989.

J. Trebilcot, 'Two Forms of Androgynism', in Vetterling-Braggin et al. (eds), *Feminism and Philosophy*, pp. 70–78.

N. Tuana, *The Less Noble Sex*. Indiana University Press, 1993.

M. Vetterling-Braggin et al. (eds), *Feminism and Philosophy*. Littlefield, Adam and Co., 1977. Helix, 1985.

M. Warnock, 'Simone: Heart of the Matter', review of D. Bair, *Simone de Beauvoir*, in *The Observer*, 3 June 1990.

P. Webster and N. Powell, *Saint-Germain-des-Prés*. Constable, 1984.

J. Weightman, 'Jean-Paul Sartre', in J. Cruickshank (ed.), *The Novelist as Philosopher*, pp. 102–27.

——, 'In the state of grace', *The Observer*, 3 January 1982.

——, 'Manic genius', review of J.-P. Sartre, *War Diaries*, in *The Observer*, 18 November 1984.

A. Whitmarsh, *Simone de Beauvoir and the Limits of Commitment*. Cambridge University Press, 1981.

R. Winegarten, *Simone de Beauvoir: A Critical View*. Berg, 1988.

A. Wood, *Karl Marx*. Routledge and Kegan Paul, 1981.

Index

227